0802852

TURNING POINTS—ACTUAL AND ALTERNATE HISTORIES

America in Revolt during the 1960s and 1970s

Other titles in ABC-CLIO's

TURNING POINTS—ACTUAL AND ALTERNATE HISTORIES

series

Books in the Turning Points—Actual and Alternate Histories series ask the question, What would have happened if . . . ? In a unique editorial format, each book examines a specific period in American history, presents the real, or actual, history, and then offers an alternate history—speculations from historical experts on what might have happened had the course of history turned.

If a particular event had turned out differently, history from that turning point forward could be affected. Important outcomes frequently hinge on an individual decision, an accidental encounter, a turn in the weather, the spread of a disease, or a missed piece of information. Such events stimulate our imagination, accentuating the role of luck, chance, and individual decision or character at particular moments in time. The examination of such key turning points is one of the reasons the study of history is so fascinating.

For the student, examining alternate histories springing from turning points and exploring, What would have happened if . . . ? gives insight into many of the questions at the heart of our civilization today.

America in Revolt during the 1960s and 1970s

Rodney P. Carlisle and J. Geoffrey Golson, *Editors*

A B C ✺ C L I O

Santa Barbara, California
Denver, Colorado
Oxford, England

Library of Congress Cataloging-in-Publication Data
America in revolt during the 1960s and 1970s / Rodney P. Carlisle and J. Geoffrey Golson, editors.
    p.cm. — (Turning points—actual and alternate histories)
    Includes bibliographical references and index.
    ISBN 978-1-85109-883-5 (hard copy : alk. paper) —
    ISBN 978-1-85109-884-2 (ebook)
1. United States—History—1961–1969. 2. United States—History—1969–.
3. United States—Politics and government—1945–1989. 4. Social problems—United States—History—20th century. 5. Social movements—United States—History—20th century. 6. United States—Social conditions—1960–1980.
7. Nineteen sixties. 8. Nineteen seventies. 9. Imaginary histories. I. Carlisle, Rodney P. II. Golson, J. Geoffrey.

  E839.A48 2008
  973.922—dc22   2007016502

12 11 10 09 08 1 2 3 4 5 6 7 8 9 10

Production Editor: Kristine Swift
Editorial Assistant: Sara Springer
Production Manager: Don Schmidt
Media Production Coordinator: Ellen Brenna Dougherty
Media Resources Manager: Caroline Price
File Manager: Paula Gerard
Text design: Devenish Design

This book is also available on the World Wide Web as an ebook. Visit http://www.abc-clio.com for details.

ABC-CLIO, Inc.
130 Cremona Drive, P.O. Box 1911
Santa Barbara, California 93116-1911

This book is printed on acid-free paper ∞

Manufactured in the United States of America

Contents

1   Civil Rights 1

TURNING POINT

The Civil Rights Act of 1964 was a milestone in the quest for equality in the United States. What if the act had not passed?

2   John F. Kennedy 21

TURNING POINT

What if Lee Harvey Oswald had missed on November 22, 1963, and President Kennedy had survived?

3   War on Poverty 43

TURNING POINT

President Johnson's War on Poverty was largely sidelined by politics and the Vietnam War. What if the War on Poverty had been won?

Contributors

Chapter 1 • Civil Rights
John H. Barnhill
Independent Scholar

Chapter 2 • John F. Kennedy
David Treviño
Donna Klein Jewish Academy

Chapter 3 • War on Poverty
J. Brooks Flippen
Southeastern Oklahoma State University

Chapter 4 • The Vietnam War
Bill Kte'pi
Independent Scholar

Chapter 5 • Martin Luther King, Jr.
Glenn Robert Gray
California State University, Fresno

Chapter 6 • The Tet Offensive
Chino Fernandez
Quezon City, Philippines

Chapter 7 • Kent State
Marcella Bush Trevino
Barry University

Chapter 8 • March on Washington
Elizabeth A. Kramer
Independent Scholar

Chapter 9 • Women's Rights
Heather A. Beasley
University of Colorado at Boulder

Chapter 10 • Counterculture
Kimberly Wilmot Voss
Southern Illinois University, Edwardsville

Chapter 11 • Free Speech Movement
Luca Prono
Independent Scholar

Chapter 12 • Richard M. Nixon
Marcella Bush Trevino
Barry University

Introduction

I . . . regard the chief utility of all historical and sociological investigations to be to admonish us of the alternative possibilities of history.

—Oscar Jaszi, *The Dissolution of the Habsburg Monarchy*

There is nothing new about counterfactual inference. Historians have been doing it for at least two thousand years.

—Philip Tetlock and Aaron Belkin, *Counterfactual Thought Experiments in World Politics*

The question, What would have happened if . . . ? is asked all the time as historians, students, and readers of history examine past events. If some event had turned out differently, the whole course of history from that particular turning point forward could have been affected, we are often reminded. Important outcomes frequently hinge on an individual decision, an accidental encounter, a missed piece of information. Such events stimulate our imagination, accentuating the role of luck, chance, and individual decision or character at particular moments in time. The examination of such key hinge points is one of the reasons that the study of history is so fascinating.

"Alternate history" has become a fictional genre, similar to science fiction, in that it proposes other worlds, spun off from the one we live in, derived from some key hinge point in the past. Harry Turtledove, among others, has produced novels along these lines. Turtledove has written a widely sold sequence of books that follow an alternate past from "counterfactual" Confederate victory at the battle of Antietam, resulting in the rise of the Confederate States of America as a separate nation, with consequences well into the twentieth century.

Alternate or counterfactual history is more than a form of imaginative speculation or engaging entertainment, however. Historians are able to highlight the significance of an event they examine by pointing to the consequences of the event. When many significant consequences flow from a single event, the alternate history question is implicit—the consequences would have been different, and a strange and different history would have flowed from that time forward if the specific event in question had turned out differently. Those events that would have made the most dramatic or drastic alternate set of consequences are clearly among the most important; thus key battles in wars are often studied in great detail, but not only for their own sake. The importance of such battles as Gettysburg and Antietam is not simply military. Instead, those battles and others are significant because such deep consequences flowed from their outcomes. The same could be said of General Erich Ludendorff's offensive in 1918—had it been successful, the Allies might have been defeated in World War I, and the map of Europe and the rest of the twentieth century would have been very different from the way they actually turned out. Similarly, if for some reason, the nuclear weapons used at Hiroshima and Nagasaki in 1945 had failed, the outcome of World War II could have been very different, perhaps with a greater role for the Soviet Union in the dissolution of the Japanese Empire. Others have argued that had the bombs not been used, Japan would have been defeated quite promptly even without them.

Every key event raises similar issues. What might the world have been like if Christopher Columbus and his sailors had failed to return from their voyage in 1492? What if Hernán Cortés and Francisco Pizarro had been soundly defeated in their attempts to defeat the Aztecs and the Inca Empire? What if John Wilkes Booth had failed in his assassination attempt against Abraham Lincoln? What sort of world would we live in if any of the other famous victims of assassination had survived, such as John F. Kennedy, Martin Luther King, Jr., or Malcolm X?

For the student, examining alternate histories springing from multiple turning points and exploring What would have happened if . . . , gives insight into many of the questions at the heart of history. What was the role of specific individuals, and how did their exercise of free will and choice at a moment in time affect later events? On the other hand, to what extent are the actions of individuals irrelevant to the larger outcomes? That is, in any particular period of history, were certain underlying forces at work that would have led to the same result, no matter what the individual did? Do underlying structures, and deeper causes, such as economic conditions, technological progress, climate, natural resources, and diseases, force events into a mold that individuals have always been powerless to alter?

The classic contest of free will and determinism is constantly at work in history, and an examination of pivotal turning points is key to understanding the balance between deep determining forces and the role of individuals. Frequently, it seems, no matter what individuals tried to do to affect the course of events, the events flowed onward in their same course; in other cases, however, a single small mistake or different personal decision seems to have affected events and altered the course of history. Close study of specific events and how they might have otherwise turned out can illuminate this challenging and recurrent issue.

Of course, when reviewing What would have happened if . . . , it is important to realize exactly what in fact really did happen. So in every chapter presented in this series, we are careful to explain first what actually happened, before turning to a possible alternative set of events that could have happened, and the consequences through later history that might have flowed from an alternate development at a particular turning point. By looking at a wide variety of such alternatives, we see how much of history is contingent, and we gain greater insight into its specific events and developments.

Alternate histories would have flowed had there been different outcomes of a great variety of events, many of them far less famous than the outstanding battles, and the lives and deaths of explorers, conquerors, statesmen, and political leaders. Seemingly obscure or little-recognized events in the past, such as legislative decisions, court cases, small military engagements, and even the lives of obscure minor officials, preachers, writers, and private citizens, frequently played a crucial part in shaping the flow of events. It is clear that if any of the great leaders of the world had died as infants, the events in which they participated would have been altered; but we tend to forget that millions of minor players and less famous people take actions in their daily lives in events such as battles, elections, legislative and judicial decisions, sermons, speeches, and published statements that have sometimes altered the course of history.

Alternate histories are known as "counterfactuals," that is, events that did not in fact happen. Some counterfactuals are more plausible than others. A few historians have argued that all counterfactuals are absurd and should not be studied or considered. However, any historical work that goes beyond simply presenting a narrative or chronological list of what happened, and begins to explore causes through the use of such terms as "influenced," "precipitated," or "led to," is in fact implying some counterfactual sequences. A historian, in describing one event as having consequences, is by implication suggesting the counterfactual that if the event had not occurred, the consequences would have been different.

If history is to be more than a chronicle or simple listing of what happened and is to present "lessons" about statecraft, society, technology development, diplomacy, the flow of ideas, military affairs, and economic policy, it must explore how causes led to consequences. Only by the study of such relationships can future leaders, military officers, businesspeople and bankers, legislators and judges, and perhaps most important, voters in democratic nations gain any knowledge of how to conduct their affairs. To derive the lessons of history, one has to ask what the important causes were, the important hinge events that made a difference. And once that question is asked, counterfactuals are implied. Thus the defenders of the approach suggest that counterfactual reasoning is a prerequisite to learning lessons from history. Even many historians who resolutely avoid talking about "what might have been" are implying that what in fact happened was important because the alternative, counterfactual event did *not* happen.

Two scholars who have studied counterfactuals in depth, Philip E. Tetlock and Aaron Belkin, in an edited collection of articles, *Counterfactual Thought Experiments in World Politics* (Princeton University Press, 1996), have concluded that counterfactual reasoning can serve several quite different purposes in the study of history. They define these types of counterfactual work:

1. Case-study counterfactuals that "highlight moments of indeterminacy" in history by showing how things might have turned out differently at such hinge points because of individual free choices. These studies tend to focus on the uniqueness of specific events.

2. "Nomothetic" counterfactuals that focus on underlying deterministic laws or processes, examining key events to show how likely or unlikely it was for events to have turned out differently. The purpose of this type of study is to test how powerful an underlying law or process is by imagining alternative situations or decisions.

3. A combination of types one and two above, blending the test of theory or underlying law approach with the unique event approach.

4. "Mental stimulation" counterfactuals that highlight underlying assumptions most people have by showing how causes that most people believe are inconsequential could have major effects, and other causes that most people believe are very important might have little or no effect in changing the course of history.

The reader will recognize aspects of each of these different models in the accounts that follow. Moreover, the reader can find the contrasts between actual history and alternate history quite puzzling and thought provoking, as they are intended to be. As readers study the cases, they may want to keep asking questions such as these:

What was the key hinge point on which the author focused?

Is the altered key event a plausible change—something that could easily have happened?

Was the change "minimal" in the sense that only one or a few turning point events had to turn out differently than they in fact did?

Did the alternate outcome seem to develop in a realistic way; that is, does the alternate sequence of events seem to be one that would be likely once the precipitating change took place?

How plausible is the alternate long-term outcome or consequence that the author suggested?

Was the changed key event a matter of an individual person's choice, a matter of accident, or a change in some broader social or technological development?

Does the counterfactual story help us make judgments about the actual quality of leadership displayed in fact at the time? That is, did key actors in real history act more or less wisely in fact than they did in the counterfactual account?

Does the outcome of the episode suggest that despite the role of chance and individual choice, certain powerful forces shaped history in similar directions, in both the factual and counterfactual account?

Does the account make me think differently about what was important in history?

Does the counterfactual story challenge any assumptions I had before I read it?

Remember, however, that what really happened is the object of historical study. We examine the counterfactual, alternate histories to get a better understanding of the forces and people that were at work in what really did occur. These counterfactual stories will make you think about history in ways that you have never encountered before; but when you have explored them, you should be able to go back to the real events with fresh questions in mind.

Introduction to the America in Revolt Volume

In this volume of the series, we see how counterfactual and alternative history can shed light on the very recent past in the United States. Many dramatic events of the 1960s and 1970s left an imprint on following decades, still felt in the early twenty-first century. It was a period of "revolt" in several ways. By contrast to the era of World War II and the 1950s, the 1960s and 1970s were characterized by organized protest against conditions and policies. While only sometimes taking a violent turn with gunfire or riots, the revolt was more often in the form of nonviolent demonstration, boycott, marches, and political action. Nevertheless, it was an era of revolt in that fundamental changes were demanded, and some achieved. Out of the period of turbulence, some positive social change appeared to result. Advocates and historians debate, however, whether the changes were superficial or deep-seated, whether America emerged from the decades of crisis with progress or with a continuation and a worsening of underlying problems of racism, sexism, and poverty. By examining alternatives, we can think through such issues, gaining some insight into whether progress resulted or whether the turbulent times simply allowed a temporary venting of anger.

A combination of events pushed the nation into recognizing and addressing questions of racial injustice, with legislation and administrative changes embodying recognition of civil rights. At first focused on discrimination against African Americans, the movement soon spread to address issues confronting other ethnic groups, women, the elderly, and the disabled. Even as reforms were implemented, advocacy organizations emerged, representing all such groups and using tactics ranging from voting campaigns and boycotts to nonviolent protest and demonstration. In the mid-1960s, the U.S. government, under the leadership of Lyndon Johnson, implemented a War on Poverty, which had some limited success. Despite gains, however, the goals set by the civil rights movement and the War on Poverty remain on the nation's agenda.

From the mid-1960s through 1973, the United States was deeply involved in the war in Vietnam. As more and more Americans came to question whether that war was a just war and whether American troops should be dying to preserve a corrupt anti-communist regime, protests mounted and the United States gradually withdrew its troops and eventually signed a truce. Within two years, by 1975, the North Vietnamese were able to invade and overthrow the regime Americans had left in charge in the south.

During this era of revolt, the United States suffered through several assassinations of key leaders, some of them linked to the reform movements, including President John F. Kennedy, his brother Robert Kennedy, and African American spokesmen and leaders Martin Luther King, Jr., and Malcolm X. Other killings, of black youths and civil rights activists, together with attempted assassinations of other leaders, shocked the nation and sometimes galvanized activists around the causes of the martyrs.

When Richard Nixon ran for reelection to the presidency in 1972, a group funded by his reelection campaign burglarized the offices of the Democratic National Committee in the Watergate building in Washington. Officials of Nixon's administration and Nixon himself worked to cover up the linkage between the burglars and his own campaign, and Nixon became a coconspirator in a criminal activity. His resignation in the face of the threat of impeachment was the first resignation of an American president in history.

Deeper insights into all of these developments and events can be gained by considering how they might have turned out differently under slightly different conditions. If the civil rights movement had faltered, or if the War on Poverty had been more of a success, how would conditions in America have been different in the 1990s and in the early twenty-first century? If the United States and South Vietnam had clearly won the Vietnam War, or if the United States had withdrawn more promptly, how would that have affected the course of the Cold War? If any of the assassinations had not occurred, how would these men's careers have developed—leaders such as John Kennedy and Martin Luther King, Jr.? On the other hand, what would have happened if certain key leaders who actually lived out their lives had themselves been killed? If Richard Nixon had chosen to face full impeachment in the Senate, rather than resigning, what would have happened?

Through the chapters that follow, we gain deeper insight into the underlying developments of the period. Each of the chapters asks how things might have turned out differently. In some cases, the turning point in history depended on the action of a few individuals. In other cases, the turning point came with a broader set of circumstances, such as the outcome of legislation or a change in political will. If things had gone a little differently at some of these turning points, we realize, the history not only of the United States but of many other countries might very well have been different. More important, by looking at the alternatives, we can learn more about actual history and the long-term impact of specific events.

In actual history, the United States of America went through a period of political and social turbulence, leading to many reforms, but leaving deep social issues unresolved. Furthermore, the experience of the Vietnam War set the stage for later periods in which Americans closely examined the foreign policy and military policy of their presidents, no longer taking on trust the assurances emanating from the White House regarding correctness of policy. The American public appeared far less willing to support the use of American military power overseas in defense of democracy, simply on the word of the administration that such a course was advised. If the seeds of distrust and skepticism had not been sown with the assassinations, with Watergate, and with the tragic Vietnam War, how would the United States have responded to the domestic and international issues of the early twenty-first century? The answer to those questions suggests how crucial to life in the present were the events of the past.

WARNING!

You are probably used to reading a book of history to find out what happened. We offer this book with a major warning. In this volume, the reader will see what actually happened, and that part of history is always designated ACTUAL HISTORY.

However, the last part of each chapter presents a history that never happened, and that is presented as the ALTERNATE HISTORY.

To be sure it is clear that the ALTERNATE HISTORY is an account of what would have happened differently if a TURNING POINT had turned out differently than it really did, the ALTERNATE HISTORY is always presented against a gray background, like these lines. The ALTERNATE HISTORY is what might have happened, what could have happened, and perhaps what would have happened if the TURNING POINT had gone a little differently. Think about this alternate history and why it would have been different. But don't think that it represents the way things actually happened!

Each chapter is also accompanied by informative sidebars and a few discussion questions that take off from the ACTUAL HISTORY and the ALTERNATE HISTORY that allow readers to think through and argue the different sides of the issues that are raised here.

We also want to warn readers that some may be surprised to discover that history, when viewed in this light, suddenly becomes so fascinating that they may never want to stop learning about it!

Rodney Carlisle

The Civil Rights Act of 1964 was a milestone in the quest for equality in the United States. What if the act had not passed?

INTRODUCTION

The United States entered World War II as a segregated society, with discrimination prevalent in all areas of life, including the federal government. It quickly became apparent that there was more than a touch of hypocrisy in waging a war against the Nazi regime, with its racist ideology, while practicing racial segregation at home. The war saw steps toward equal employment in federal defense industries and the inclusion of blacks in the military, albeit in segregated units and limited functions.

During and after the war, President Harry Truman had to deal with immediate issues—the ending of the world war, the beginning of the Cold War, and the dilemma over what to do with the atomic bomb. He had no history of involvement with civil rights, even declining to support President Franklin D. Roosevelt's Fair Employment Practices Commission (FEPC) in a 1945 case involving discrimination in a Washington, D.C., transportation company. Truman failed to get Congress to fund the FEPC. Yet in 1946 he established a special commission on civil rights and loaded it with liberals who would issue a strong report in October 1947. *To Secure These Rights* called for abolition of the poll tax, federal intervention to overturn segregation, voting rights for African Americans, a permanent FEPC, a federal anti-lynching law, an end to discrimination in interstate travel, the desegregation of the armed forces, a civil rights section in the Department of Justice, federal financial support for civil rights lawsuits in federal courts, and the establishment of a U.S. civil rights commission.

Truman called for legislative enactment of the commission's recommendations in his State of the Union speeches of 1947 and 1948. Congress failed to act, and in the election year of 1948 Truman, by executive order, desegregated the armed forces and established fair employment in the civil service. The military was slow to react, but desegregated frontline units fought in the Korean War, even if the officer corps remained overwhelmingly white. A powerless and underfunded Federal Employment Board came into being in 1948 as the minority representative in federal employment. Truman's

President Harry Truman desegregated the U.S. armed forces in 1948. (Library of Congress)

1951 Committee on Government Contract Compliance tried to force government contractors to abide by fair employment practices but lacked enforcement powers. Truman's 1949 inaugural was desegregated.

Despite Truman's efforts, the law of the land remained "separate but equal," yet pressure for equality of rights was growing. Court challenges in the 1930s and 1940s in Missouri, Oklahoma, Texas, and elsewhere generated belated efforts to equalize resources, particularly in higher education, and to begin the end of segregation.

The U.S. Supreme Court ruled on May 17, 1954, in *Brown v. Board of Education,* that the old *Plessy* doctrine of separate but equal was unconstitutional. The *Plessy v. Ferguson* case ruled that as long as equal facilities were provided to both blacks and whites, as in railroad cars, there was no denial of equal rights. Separation by itself, the court had ruled, was not an injustice. This doctrine of "separate but equal" had been applied to all sorts of facilities throughout the South. Although separate schools had been built for African Americans, it was common knowledge that the facilities were not at all equal in budget, qualifications of teachers, or quality of education, nor in such basics as structural repair, plumbing, and space.

In response, white southern extremists pushed moderates out of the picture and used all sorts of legal—and not so legal—methods to thwart the will of the court. Harking back to antebellum slavery advocates and Reconstruction night riders, segregationists used the Ku Klux Klan (KKK), White Citizens Councils, white womanhood and white manhood, and the Bible in the battle against black rights.

When the Supreme Court failed to specify a timetable for ending segregation, leaving it with a fuzzy "with all deliberate speed," southern segregationists took the opportunity to implement massive resistance. In the consolidated case involving several segregated school districts, known as *Brown v. Topeka,* in 1954, the Supreme Court ruled that in education, separation was inherently unequal. However, the court ruled that the system should be changed with all deliberate speed, but did not set a timetable for ending segregation.

Many southern congressmen and senators signed the Southern Manifesto, attempting to revive the old nullification/interposition doctrines. Under the interposition doctrine, states held that they had a right to interpose their authority between the operation of the federal government and the citizens of the state. While the doctrine had been attempted before, it had never been sustained in the federal courts. Other Southerners organized locally as White Citizens Councils and, more covertly, Ku Klux Klan. Opposition intensified.

Before 1955, civil rights had been largely a battle in the courts, but the times were changing. A brutal murder in 1955 galvanized black public opinion. Emmett Till, a Chicago teen visiting Money, Mississippi, was murdered, allegedly for whistling at a white woman. When his mother had an open casket funeral to display Till's injuries and *Jet* magazine published a photo of his battered corpse, Till's murder became a cause celebre. The rapid trial and acquittal of his murderers by a white jury further aroused public opinion.

That same year, civil rights veteran Rosa Parks became the "mother of the Civil Rights Movement" when she refused to give a white man her seat on a Montgomery, Alabama, bus on December 1, 1955. Her conviction for disorderly conduct and violation of the city segregation ordinance led to the Montgomery bus boycott, which, unlike earlier boycott efforts that fizzled quickly, lasted 381 days before the absence of ridership forced the city to rescind its ordinance in 1956. The Montgomery boycott showed the way for subsequent successful local boycotts and brought to prominence a young minister, Martin Luther King, Jr.

The NAACP (National Association for the Advancement of Colored People) in the South had only limited success in protesting discrimination and registering voters. Harassment by

Martin Luther King, Jr., first came to prominence during the 1955–1956 Montgomery, Alabama, bus boycott. (Library of Congress)

local authorities was a major problem, as was lack of coordination of the black efforts. Alabama effectively killed the NAACP within its borders in 1956 by ordering the group to turn over membership lists and enjoining NAACP activity within the state for failure to comply. *Brown*, the murder of Till, the bus boycott in Montgomery, and the ineffectiveness of the mainstream legal-oriented civil rights efforts (the *Brown* case) triggered a direct action campaign that included the sit-in and freedom ride movements and other uses of mass mobilization for nonviolent civil disobedience and resistance. Direct action dominated the movement for a decade until 1965.

King and other church leaders with similar boycott experience joined forces in the Southern Christian Leadership Conference (SCLC) in 1957. The SCLC was less structured than the NAACP, providing training, funds, and other assistance for local efforts as needed. It was a conduit for northern funds to southern grassroots campaigns and was nonviolent above all. And it was flexible—for example, taking over the Citizenship Schools of South Carolina's Sea Islands in 1957 and spreading them to several states in the South.

Desegregation hit Little Rock, Arkansas, in 1957 as an NAACP-stimulated action. Arkansas had a moderate governor, and the cities of Hoxie and Fayetteville had already desegregated without excessive resistance (although Hoxie did require litigation), so the NAACP thought Little Rock would be an easy victory. Instead, Governor Orval Faubus pandered to the conservatives in his party and precipitated a crisis by calling out the

A rally in 1959 protesting the admission of African Americans to Little Rock Central High School in Arkansas. (Library of Congress)

National Guard to prevent the admission of nine black students who had sued for the right to attend Little Rock Central High School. After President Dwight Eisenhower deployed the 101st Airborne Division and federalized the National Guard and after the governor shut down the school system, Little Rock finally desegregated in 1960.

In 1960 in Greensboro, North Carolina, African American college students decided to have lunch at stores that refused to desegregate. Neatly dressed and quiet, they sat on every other stool, with white sympathizers between them. What they got were arrests, sometimes quite physical. As with the boycott, the sit-in idea was not new. The Congress of Racial Equality had used it in the Midwest in the 1940s. This time, the effort drew national attention. The idea spread quickly, and by the end of 1960 there were sit-ins in every southern and border state as well as Ohio, Illinois, and Nevada. Sit-ins moved from lunch counters to libraries, parks, museums—all public places. The leaders of the sit-in movement established the Student Nonviolent Coordinating Committee (SNCC) in 1960.

Federal inactivity became harder to justify. In the presidential campaign of 1960, John F. Kennedy of Massachusetts, who opposed the weak 1957 Civil Rights Act, called for a stronger civil rights law. At that time 57 percent of African American housing was substandard, life expectancy was seven years less than that of whites, infant mortality was double that of whites, and African Americans had severe difficulties in getting mortgages. Property values actually dropped if an African American family moved into a nonghetto neighborhood. In office, Kennedy talked passionately about civil rights and he recognized that the civil rights crisis was a Cold War black eye, but his focus was on the Cuban missile crisis, Vietnam, and other foreign issues. The polls discouraged him—one reported civil rights as dead last among issues worrying Americans. Also, Kennedy's razor-thin 500,000 1960 vote margin gave him little in the way of a mandate.

After winning more than 70 percent of the black vote in 1960, Kennedy spent the first two years of his administration without acting on his promise for new civil rights legislation.

SNCC expanded its efforts in 1961, attempting to force Deep South compliance with federal law, desegregating interstate bus terminals by sending integrated groups of blacks and whites, known as "freedom riders" to ride on interstate buses. A bus was firebombed by die-hard segregationists in Anniston, Alabama. In Birmingham, Alabama, the KKK, with encouragement from police commissioner Eugene "Bull" Connor, severely beat the riders. Again, in Montgomery, beatings were vicious. Like the demonstrators at the sit-ins, the riders refused bail to overcrowd local facilities. In Mississippi, riders did hard labor at Jackson or went to the notorious Parchman penitentiary. The movement persisted, and the media continued to broadcast the struggle.

In 1962 Robert Moses of the Mississippi SNCC united the state's civil rights organizations into the Council of Federated Organizations (COFO). Mississippi was the most dangerous of all the states, but COFO began door-to-door voter education while trying to bring in northern students as voter registration volunteers.

While COFO was pressing the grass roots in 1962, James Meredith sued for the right to attend the University of Mississippi and won. His attempts to enter on September 20, 25, and 26, 1962, were blocked by Governor Ross Barnett, who, with his lieutenant governor, was found in contempt of court. Meredith entered the campus accompanied by a force of U.S. marshals on September 30, 1962. That evening a white riot began, and rioters shot and wounded twenty-eight marshals, killed a journalist, and injured 160 others. Kennedy sent in the army, and the riot ended. Meredith began school on October 1.

The SCLC and other mainstream organizations came under criticism for inactivity during the freedom rides. In November 1961, King and the SCLC attempted to desegregate Albany, Georgia. Local authorities avoided the violent confrontation that had brought publicity to the Alabama desegregation efforts—and they made sure they had ample jail space. The local police chief refused King the opportunity to sit in jail, and the movement failed in 1962. Needing a success, King went to Birmingham, Alabama, in 1963, where he was jailed. He wrote his April 16, 1963, "Letter from Birmingham Jail" and smuggled it out for press release. With King in jail, supporters pressured the Kennedy administration. Still the movement struggled until the SCLC began using students in its mass demonstrations and Police Commissioner Connor loosed police dogs and fire hoses on them. Television captured it all. The administration intervened, Birmingham desegregated, and King had his victory. Critics within the movement felt that King had settled for too

Flanked by U.S. marshals, James Meredith (center) is escorted to the University of Mississippi on October 1, 1962. (Library of Congress)

little and on the other side of the spectrum, segregationists bombed the SCLC headquarters.

In June 1963, George Wallace, governor of Alabama, failed to stop the desegregation of the state university after Kennedy made sure there was a large enough force to keep the peace. However, events continued to outpace restraint. Medgar Evers, an African American civil rights activist from Mississippi, was murdered on June 12, only hours after Kennedy had given a speech the night before on television in support of civil rights. A week later, on June 19, Kennedy sent the civil rights bill to Congress. While the bill languished, the Civil Rights March on Washington took place on August 28, 1963, and King gave his "I Have a Dream" speech.

The march was a success; civil rights leaders met with Kennedy, but the bill lacked the votes to pass. Segregationists bombed the Sixteenth Street Baptist Church in Birmingham, Alabama, in September, murdering four black girls. During the 1964 Mississippi Freedom Summer, racists killed three civil rights workers. The Federal Bureau of Investigation inquiry that discovered their bodies also revealed the bodies of other black Mississippians who had disappeared in previous years. The public outrage that built over the six weeks that it took to discover the bodies provided a backdrop for President Lyndon Johnson to bring forth the Civil Rights Act of 1964.

TURNING POINT

On June 11, 1963, Kennedy spoke on television. He wanted Congress to enact his long-delayed Civil Rights Act of 1963. But Congress failed to act, and the bill languished on November 22, 1963, when Kennedy made his fateful trip to Dallas, Texas, where he was assassinated. Replacing Kennedy was Johnson, who had not signed the Southern Manifesto but who had diluted the Civil Rights Act of 1957. His friend and mentor, Senator Richard B. Russell, led a group of eighteen southern Democratic senators who began filibustering the Civil Rights bill.

But Johnson had ambitions. In the spring of 1964 he had indicated that his programs would far surpass the Kennedy legacy. Convention has it that the Civil Rights Act became law because the public mood demanded that "Kennedy's bill" become law in the form that he wanted it. Congress seemed to think otherwise. On March 9, 1964, the Senate began a filibuster that would exceed fifty-seven days. Johnson did play the sympathy card—do it for the memory of the late president, do it for patriotism. Johnson played to the people over the heads of Congress. He also promised Southerners that he was not giving blacks any easy ride at the expense of whites. And the polls were promising in January 1964; 68 percent wanted a meaningful civil rights law.

Johnson had a sympathetic public after the assassination and the violence of the civil rights resisters. Awareness of poverty was more prevalent, and the Cold War was in a semi-thaw so that public and official attention could turn to domestic problems.

He also had Russell and an adamant group of southern filibusterers set against any civil rights law. He could depend on at most forty-seven votes from Senate Democrats. Without the Republicans, in the face of a largely united southern wing of his party, Johnson was no more able than Kennedy to bring about civil rights reform. The Republican leader, Everett Dirksen of Illinois, opposed cloture because he regarded the filibuster as the one tool the minority had to prevent the tyranny of the majority. Dirksen controlled nearly two dozen Republican votes that Johnson and Majority Whip Hubert Humphrey needed to invoke cloture. Using all his political skills and capital, and compromising, however grudgingly, Johnson used majority whip Humphrey to split the Republicans from the southern Democrats.

Dirksen and Humphrey developed a compromise bill despite Johnson's desire for a bill unchanged from the one Kennedy had endorsed. With the compromise, Dirksen delivered the votes, and Russell lost the battle. Johnson had a real civil rights law, not the watered-down version he had steered through Congress seven years earlier.

On June 10, 1964, Senator Robert Byrd of West Virginia concluded a speech that had begun over fourteen hours before. Russell followed with a short speech. Then majority leader Mike Mansfield introduced cloture. The cloture vote was 71 to 29, with forty-one Democrats and twenty-seven Republicans in favor, twenty-three Democrats and six Republicans opposed. After 534 hours, 1 minute, and 51 seconds, the longest filibuster in history was broken. Never before had the Senate broken a civil rights filibuster.

KEY CONCEPT   Filibuster and Cloture

Everett Dirksen opposed the invocation of cloture—the formal procedure to end a filibuster. He wanted to preserve minority power in the Senate, a power that had a lot of tradition behind it. The word *filibuster* is from the Dutch word for pirate. In the nineteenth century filibusters were people who engaged in unauthorized foreign affairs, such as invading Latin American countries. The first use in the modern context came in the 1850s when critics used it in reference to those who were attempting to talk a bill to death, to keep the Senate floor in order to block a vote.

The tactic was available to both houses in the early Congresses. When the House of Representatives grew with an increase of the population, changes in rules limited debate. The Senate, smaller, retained the right of unlimited debate. Thorough discussion was more important than timely decision making. That did not mean that the rule went unchallenged. As early as 1841 Senator Henry Clay tried to establish a rule that allowed a majority to close debate. He failed. In 1917, however, at the request of President Woodrow Wilson, the Senate adopted Rule 22. This rule authorized cloture, the ending of debate, on a vote of two-thirds of the Senate. The first use of cloture came in 1919 to end a filibuster against the Treaty of Versailles.

Still, two-thirds was a hard majority to attain. Until amended in 1975 to require only three-fifths rather than two-thirds, the filibuster remained a highly effective method of blocking legislation that the minority opposed. For five decades the Senate lived with the filibuster, overturning it only once in the 1920s. Huey Long was an expert on the filibuster in the 1930s, reciting Shakespeare and reading recipes to a bemused Senate and an amused gallery. The record holder was Strom Thurmond, who filibustered against the Civil Rights Act of 1957 for twenty-four hours and eighteen minutes.

The filibuster came into play particularly when Southerners wanted to block anti-lynching laws and other legislation they deemed inimical to their interests and their institutions. The use of cloture to end the fifty-seven-day filibuster in 1964 was extraordinary.

The turning point, the end of the filibuster, was a year in the making. On June 15, 1964, Russell told Mansfield and Humphrey in private that he would not attempt to continue the filibuster. The bill went to the floor, where an amendment was inserted to expand coverage to women as well as blacks. The sponsor thought the amendment would cause revulsion in the senators and lead to the bill's defeat. Instead, the bill passed 73 to 27. Having defeated Russell and the Senate diehards, the victors would find that their victory was less than complete.

ACTUAL HISTORY

The Civil Rights Act of 1964 was the most important civil rights law since Reconstruction. Earlier civil rights actions, particularly the Fourteenth Amendment, applied only to states, not individuals. Supreme Court rulings since 1964 had expanded the amendment to include individual discrimination. The Civil Rights Act of 1964 rested on the commerce clause of the Constitution. It prohibited discrimination based on race, color, religion, or national origin in public establishments including hotels, motels, trailer parks, gas stations, bars and taverns, restaurants, and places of entertainment. It also made discrimination in schools and colleges more difficult. Title VI prohibited discrimination in federally funded programs, and Title VII outlawed discrimination in employment where the employer is engaged in interstate commerce. Discrimination could result in loss of funds.

A weak voting rights section provided that standards for voting eligibility must be uniform, a sixth-grade education equaled literacy, and the attorney general could intervene where he found a pattern of resistance to the law. Segregation in housing, education, and employment was now illegal. At a stroke, the South's Jim Crow laws were history. The power of the government to enforce the laws was initially weak, but over time modifications made that stronger, and the government instituted affirmative action.

The Civil Rights Act of 1964 displeased Southerners, but it displeased many blacks even more. In the northeast, African Americans rioted because the law was insufficient. In the South the Mississippi Freedom Democratic Party demanded that it be seated in place of the white Mississippi delegation to the 1964 Democratic convention. Johnson was dismayed. Even so, after the dust settled, the act proved to be a moral corrective to an immoral situation, and the law of 1964 produced forty years of progress.

Now that the government had the means of enforcing the 1954 desegregation ruling, change began. In 1964 only two southern states (Texas and Tennessee) had more than 2 percent of black students in integrated schools. Within a year, the number of integrated black students in the entire South was 6 percent.

The weakness of the voting rights section meant that the Voting Rights Act of 1965 was necessary. The corrective legislation failed to address the problem of black militancy. In 1965, thirty-four people were killed in riots in Watts, the black Los Angeles slum. In 1966, riots occurred in virtually every major American city. Black radicals moved beyond the civil rights organizations and began practicing SNCC leader Stokely Carmichael's "black power." SNCC expelled its white members in 1967.

In 1967, integration proceeded apace, with about 22 percent of black students in the seventeen southern and border states integrated. Still, the National Advisory Commission on Civil Disorders (Kerner Commission) in 1968 reported that the nation was moving toward separate and unequal divisions. Then King was assassinated in the summer of 1968, provoking rioting in 125 cities.

In 1970 President Richard Nixon said that he would deemphasize desegregation and let the courts handle it. Even so, he did not turn back the clock on the real accomplishments of the previous half dozen years. In 1964, 51 percent of black college and university students were in historically black colleges and universities. By 1971 the percentage was down to 34 percent. Even though the South had had tax-exempt private segregated schools since the early 1960s, by the fall of 1972, 44 percent of the South's black students were in predominantly white schools. In the North only 30 percent were integrated.

In the early 1970s integration moved north, with school busing the tool of choice (busing black children to white schools and vice versa). The

President Lyndon Johnson signs the Civil Rights Act of 1964, which barred discrimination in property rights. (Library of Congress)

Supreme Court initially supported busing, but in the 1974 *Miliken v. Bradley* case, a more conservative court backed away, allowing Detroit's predominantly white suburbs to exclude themselves from the city's desegregation plan. Nevertheless, by the mid-1970s only about 12 percent of America's black students were still in completely segregated schools. The tide had turned, and by the late 1990s about a third of black students were in schools that were 90 percent nonwhite. From the mid-1980s through the 1990s, though, public school segregation increased due to court decisions limiting or reversing desegregation, decreased federal support for desegregation, and persisting de facto segregation in housing.

Affirmative action was part of the civil rights legacy. It tried to compensate for segregation and other past discrimination by setting aside jobs for affected groups, including African Americans. Set-asides too often became quotas, leading to a backlash and charges of reverse discrimination in the late 1970s. The 1980s saw the federal involvement in affirmative action fade considerably, and a 1989 Supreme Court decision made it easier to bring reverse discrimination cases. The Civil Rights Act of 1991 reaffirmed the government's commitment to affirmative action, but a 1995 Supreme Court case added limits to the use of race-based government contracts. States, led by California, began banning such preferences in the late 1990s.

On the positive side, blacks and other minorities increasingly won elective office. In 1966 Edward Brooke of Massachusetts became the first black senator since Reconstruction. Carl Stokes won the mayoralty of Cleveland, becoming the first black mayor of a major American city. New York, Los Angeles, Chicago, and other major cities have since elected minority mayors. And Jesse Jackson ran for the Democratic presidential nomination in 1984 and 1988. In 1989 Douglas Wilder won the governorship of Virginia, becoming the first elected black governor of any state. And Colin Powell was the first black head of the Joint Chiefs of Staff and later, secretary of state. He declined to run for the 1996 Republican presidential nomination.

The act of 1964 vitalized other minorities to demand equal rights. For instance, Mexican Americans became Chicanos/Chicanas. As early as 1929 Mexican Americans, tired of generations of discrimination, banded together into the League of United Latin American Citizens (LULAC). And after World War II, returning Mexican American veterans formed the American G.I. Forum. These organizations sought inclusion of Mexican Americans in the middle-class American way of life. As late as 1958 the Mexican American Political Association worked for political access within the system. In the 1960s, young Mexican Americans began noticing and participating in the black civil rights movement. Among them was Reies Lopez Tijerina who sought the return of ancestral lands in New Mexico before joining the civil rights movement and co-sponsoring the Poor People's March on Washington in 1967.

In 1969 Rodolfo "Corky" Gonzalez proclaimed Aztlan as the true Chicano heritage; he wanted a Chicano society set apart from the dominant white one. Mostly, though, the Chicano movement sought access—equal employment opportunity, voter registration. The political party, La Raza Unida, had its electoral successes mostly in the small towns of south Texas, but by the 1980s it was influential at the state level.

Native Americans were also exploited and denied access. The American Indian Movement (AIM) came into being in 1968 under the leadership of Dennis Banks, Russell Means, and others who objected to the mistreatment of Native Americans both off and on the reservation. AIM protests in the early 1970s could be violent, but the organization's activism helped to bring about cultural revitalization, reduce police harassment, and provide employment programs on and off the reservations. AIM also opposed the use of caricatures as sports mascots. Its leaders have entered the "establishment"—managing government programs, running for state political office, and administering schools.

The women's movement progressed after the act of 1964 too. Women had been slowly making progress since getting the vote in the 1920s. Franklin Roosevelt appointed Frances Perkins secretary of labor in the 1930s, but women still faced legal challenges. In 1961 Esther Peterson, director of the Women's Bureau of the Department of Labor, convinced Kennedy to establish the Commission on the Status of Women, chaired by Eleanor Roosevelt. The commission's report of 1963 documented discrimination against women in all areas of life. State and local commissions found comparable discrimination. Betty Friedan published *The Feminine Mystique* in 1963, inspiring women to demand more than a stultifying life as a homemaker. When sex became a category of prohibited discrimination in the 1964 act, the Equal Employment Opportunity Commission (EEOC) was empowered to hear sex discrimination cases. It received 50,000 complaints in its first five years.

When feminists discerned that the EEOC was hesitant to pursue these complaints, they united in 1966 as the National Organization for Women,

Betty Friedan, author of *The Feminine Mystique*, which galvanized the women's movement. (Library of Congress)

followed quickly by other women's rights organizations—black, Hispanic, Asian American, lesbian, welfare recipients, businesswomen, and politicians. On college campuses women, dissatisfied with their secondary roles in the anti-war and civil rights movements, began to break away and form their own organizations. Together they were the Women's Rights Movement, working at the grass roots to establish battered women's shelters, rape crisis centers, child care centers, women's clinics, and the like. The Education Codes of 1972 provided equal access to higher education and professional schools. Women gained equality in sports but more importantly as lawyers, engineers, doctors, architects, airline pilots, and members of other professions.

Women sought an equal rights amendment in the 1970s, but the tide had turned. Still, they were no longer segregated in the help wanted ads, and they had the right to credit cards in their own names, to bank loans without a male co-signer, to equal access in virtually all occupations in the military services, no longer segregated as Women Accepted for Volunteer Emergency Service (WAVE), Women's Army Corps (WAC), and Women in the Air Force (WAF). Control over their bodies came with the *Roe v. Wade* Supreme Court decision, but they remain discriminated against in many religions, and pay parity is still an elusive goal.

For disabled Americans, the act of 1964 was a model for legislation that came only in 1990, but there was slow, incremental progress in the intervening twenty-six years. They benefited from Medicare and Medicaid and vocational rehabilitation laws of 1965. Johnson set up a committee on mental retardation that year. The Architectural Barriers Act of 1968 gave access to federal buildings. It was the first-ever disabilities rights legislation. Rights organizations sprang up in the 1960s and 1970s, and additional laws eased access to mass transportation. The first legal advocacy organization was the National Center for Law and the Handicapped, established in South Bend, Indiana. Handicap parking stickers appeared for the first time in Washington, D.C., in 1973.

The Rehabilitation Act of 1973, passed over presidential veto, prohibited discrimination against the disabled. When Nixon vetoed the act, organizations protesting the veto included the Disabled in Action, Paralyzed Veterans of America, and the National Paraplegia Foundation. Lawsuits brought under the 1973 law established the case law that would be the basis for the Americans with Disabilities Act of 1990. During the 1980s disabled rights activists were strong enough to compel the Ronald Reagan administration to abandon attempts to roll back gains of the 1970s, and access broadened. Finally, on June 26, 1990, George H. W. Bush signed the Americans with Disabilities Act that gave the disabled full legal citizenship for the first time.

IN CONTEXT   Cold War

For the black activists and civil rights organizations, civil rights were a moral and political issue. For the foreign policy establishment, it was a matter of national security. Early in the Cold War, the civil rights issue became an embarrassment to the United States, which was trying to woo the third world to democracy instead of communism. International publicity of American repression was a major black eye to the United States and a godsend for Soviet propagandists. Thus, the Truman administration determined that since it was impossible to hide the sordid story they would incorporate it into a story of redemption, a lesson in the power of democracy to correct injustice. Eisenhower amplified the Truman message, tightened it, and redirected it from the Soviet bloc to the third world.

For this master narrative to work, reality had at least to approximate it. Thus, the justice department began filing amicus curiae briefs in the civil rights cases leading up to the *Brown* decision, and national security was part of their rationale. Then, during the eleven months prior to the election of Kennedy, seventeen African nations won their independence. The struggle for their hearts and minds required Kennedy, as a matter of foreign policy to switch from indifference to civil rights, which characterized the first two years of his administration, to a more activist role after Bull Connor provoked international condemnation with his ruthless riot control. Johnson culminated this approach by successfully winning the Civil Rights Act of 1964. Having moved from being part of the problem to being part of the solution, the federal government could claim victory in both the propaganda battle and the struggle for civil rights. Thus, it could safely turn its attention to more pressing issues. The effort to win black allegiance shifted to the struggle to prevent the falling of a domino in Southeast Asia.

Because the underlying motive was propaganda rather than commitment to justice, the federal involvement in civil rights produced tokenism. A decade after *Brown* won international acclaim, only a handful of southern schools were desegregated. In addition, the commitment to civil rights did not apply when American blacks presented an image abroad that clashed with the American myth. Such individuals as Josephine Baker, Malcolm X, and W. E. B. Du Bois had their freedom of movement and speech circumscribed by the U.S. State Department during the Cold War.

The Civil Rights Act of 1964 also helped to change the face of American immigration. The Immigration Act of 1965 eliminated discriminatory quotas set in the 1920s. It shifted immigrant places of origin from Europe to Asia, Africa, the Middle East, and Latin America. Korean and Filipina nurses, Indian and Pakistani doctors, African and Asian engineers and computer scientists were among the millions of new immigrants who came under occupational or family reunification provisions of the law. Korean and Arab entrepreneurs immigrated in large numbers. Also, millions of Cuban and Asian and African refugees swelled America's population.

Politics changed markedly after 1964. Nixon implemented the southern strategy, emphasizing states' rights as a means of attracting southern voters to the Republican Party. The southern strategy has in recent years incorporated cultural themes that appeal strongly to Southerners but also attract conservative voters throughout the United States.

The southern states returned to the Union during and after Reconstruction with increased seats in the House of Representatives and votes in the electoral college because blacks were citizens rather than three-fifths of a person as previously defined by the U.S. Constitution. The withdrawal of federal troops under the Compromise of 1877 ended the Republican Party's power in the South. For generations, the Democratic

Party dominated, especially after Jim Crow laws disenfranchised black voters. Without the black vote, the Republican Party was uncompetitive, and the "solid South" was solidly Democratic until the middle of the twentieth century, when civil rights began weakening the Democrats' dominance.

The first crack in the solid South came in 1948 when the States Rights Democratic Party, the Dixiecrats, bolted the Democratic Party after a pro–civil rights speech by Senator Hubert Humphrey of Minnesota. The candidacy of Strom Thurmond was a failure, and most southern states remained faithful to the Democrats. The party reunified. Dixiecrat principles revived in 1964 with the candidacy of Barry Goldwater of Arizona. The Republican Party's northeastern wing—exemplified by New York governor Nelson Rockefeller—was quite liberal on civil rights at the time, and a higher percentage of Republicans than Democrats supported the Civil Rights Act of 1964. Goldwater's victory began the slow demise of Republican liberalism.

Although not a segregationist, Goldwater opposed the Civil Rights Act of 1964 as an intrusion into the rights of both states and individuals by an overly activist federal government. Although not overtly racist, Goldwater's position had undertones that could be read as covertly supporting the racist position, and it did draw southern voters, many of whom were overtly racist; some were violent against even civil rights sympathizers, and many public officials showed deference to white supremacists. The electoral result shows that the message, whether given or not, was received. Goldwater won his home state, Arizona, and five Deep South states: South Carolina, Georgia, Alabama, Mississippi, and Louisiana.

In 1968 Nixon thought he had an opportunity to widen the crack, to get some of those southern voters the Republicans had never had before. America was wracked by turmoil—Martin Luther King, Jr., was assassinated, as was Robert Kennedy. Blacks rioted in the aftermath of King's death. The civil rights movement became more radical and fractured as the student groups such as SNCC repudiated the SCLC and the old organizations. The Vietnam War and the hippies and the drug subculture appalled conservative "hard hats." Nixon advisors Harry Dent and Strom Thurmond (who had moved to the Republican Party in 1964) advised Nixon to run on states' rights and law and order; liberals called it pandering to the racists. In 1968 every former Confederate state except Texas voted either for Nixon or for the independent George Wallace. Nixon took the states' rights South and the law-and-order states elsewhere in this realigning election.

Public opinion was moving to accept civil rights, so the southern strategists talked less of states' rights and more of federalism. The Republicans became protectors of the people against the states during the culture wars of the 1980s. In 1980 Reagan supported states' rights in a speech at Philadelphia, Mississippi, where the three civil rights workers had been murdered in 1964. Reagan also praised Jefferson Davis at Stone Mountain, Georgia, site of the founding of the Klan. Although Reagan got an unsolicited endorsement from a noted Klan leader, he also got backing from civil rights leaders Hosea Williams and Ralph Abernathy.

ANOTHER VIEW   Economics and Political Parties

The civil rights movement of the mid-twentieth century was insignificant to southern political history in comparison to the economic changes of the time. When Lyndon Johnson said that he had lost the South for the Democrats for a generation, he was right that the South was lost, but he was wrong that he—and the Civil Rights Act of 1964—had been the cause. If anyone lost the South for the Democrats, it was Franklin Roosevelt. By defining the South as the nation's number one economic problem and funneling federal funds southward through the New Deal and World War II, Roosevelt established the foundation for what would become—during the Cold War when federal funds continued to flow freely to defense contractors such as Brown and Root and Halliburton (companies tied closely to both the Bushes and Johnson)—the sunbelt/gunbelt.

Prior to the massive federal transfer payments, the South could be viewed as having two classes: rich and poor. And it had one dominant party: Democrats. Prosperity changed all that. It brought the South a white middle class, which repaid its Democratic benefactors by turning on them as the party of welfare and moral decay. Even as they were benefiting economically from the Democratic policies, the upwardly mobile Southerners joined the Republican Party that better reflected their moral and economic values. Blacks did not really have any place in the newly conservative Republican Party, so they switched to the Democratic Party that more naturally reflected their interests.

ALTERNATE HISTORY

The act of 1964 would not have passed because Johnson would have gotten into one of his famous snits and refused to let Humphrey broker a deal with Dirksen. He was on record as being determined to pass the law exactly as John Kennedy wanted it. When Dirksen leaked to the press that he would demand modifications in return for supporting cloture, that embarrassed, then enraged Johnson, who never tolerated those who stole his show. He would have forced Humphrey to break off the deal. That failure would have allowed the filibuster to run until finally Johnson would have approved the withdrawal of the bill because the filibuster would have kept him from developing a legislative record to run on in the fall election against Nelson Rockefeller. He would have felt confident that with a united Democratic Party he could handle the upstart left-winger. Even if Rockefeller had strong Cold War credentials, the Republicans would have been split, with a strong anti-civil rights fringe able to push Arizona's Barry Goldwater into a viable candidacy that would have forced Rockefeller to take the Arizonan as his running mate to heal the split brought about by the bitter nomination fight.

Johnson would have had his fill of civil rights. He would have cared more about perpetuating and expanding the New Deal that had formed him politically. He would have selected Richard Russell as a ticket-balancing Southerner who was in accord with the New Deal and had a civil rights record sure to hold the South for the Democrats. Then Johnson would have run in a low-key campaign against radicalism and communism, ratcheting up his rhetorical defense of South

Vietnam by alluding to Eisenhower's domino theory. He would have sent Russell to the South and West to neutralize Goldwater's extreme conservative positions and would have taken for himself the task of attacking Rockefeller's extreme liberal ones. He would have worn the mantle of Kennedy moderation in a campaign against the Republicans' alliance of the radical fringes. In a tight contest that fall, the Johnson-Russell ticket would have edged Rockefeller-Goldwater, and the political realignment threatened by the civil rights movement would have ended and attention would have turned from civil rights to war.

The loss of White House support would have killed the civil rights movement, but not overnight. The SCLC would have continued to march in Alabama and Mississippi. And southern resisters would have continued to attack marchers, bomb black churches, and kill civil rights workers. The federal government would have reverted to its Eisenhower administration approach of limited intervention, which in effect would have become nonintervention, as the segregationists measured the administration and established just how far it could go without provoking a federal response. That would prove be quite far because Attorney General Robert Kennedy and FBI director J. Edgar Hoover would have been more concerned with controlling the anti-war movement than with the fading civil rights effort.

As the casualty counts would have risen in Vietnam and in Alabama, protesters would have lost interest in facing potential death in the civil rights movement and would have begun making public nuisances of themselves in the anti-war movement, especially on college campuses.

Because the Civil Rights Act of 1964 would not have passed, when the Voting Rights Act of 1965 came before the Senate there would have been no strong sentiment for pushing it forward in the face of another filibuster. The NAACP would have been busily trying to protect itself in Alabama and Mississippi, totally preoccupied with the court cases that its underfunded legal department would be finding increasingly burdensome. The filibuster would not even have been necessary. Merely the threat would have been sufficient to push the bill into committee in perpetuity. Without the Voting Rights Act of 1965 and without the experience of the black civil rights effort, there would have been no Chicano, women's, Indian, Americans with disabilities, Asian, or gay rights movement. Blacks and browns would have remained less than equal citizens, with lower incomes, higher death and disease rates, and lower life expectancies. White Americans would have remained structured by class, with the elites using the threat of race to keep the lower classes pacified and distracted from America's major economic disparities.

Immigration reform would have been on the agenda in 1965, but it would have failed to materialize. The supporters would have talked of the need to eliminate racial quotas because they reflected poorly on the United States in its Cold War fight for the hearts and minds of the third world. But the combined forces of the Daughters of the American Revolution, the American Legion, the KKK, and White Citizens

Councils—with the sympathy of the Black Panthers and Black Muslims—would have been sufficient to table the bill. Without the act of 1965, there would have been no huge influx of skilled Asian and African workers and no rush of family immigrants.

The war in Vietnam would have taken surplus workers, creating a need for illegal immigrants to continue to cross the Rio Grande or to sneak in from Europe on student visas and disappear into the immigrant underground. But the volume would have been relatively low. The low-paying jobs would have remained in the hands of blacks in the East and South and in the hands of Mexicans in the West. Non-union white men would have retained their control of construction, fishing, and other relatively well-paid manual labor. The United States would have been a white-black society, and the draft would have ensured that distinctions in government treatment of the two were in favor of the whites. The problem would have been manageable—or at least it would have been ignorable. The Vietnam War would have been going poorly.

In the election of 1968, Robert Kennedy, who would have ruthlessly smeared Russell as a warmongering racist to win the Democratic nomination, would have faced Republican Rockefeller, who would have prevailed over Reagan by linking him to Goldwater's "lunatic" conservatism.

The South would have remained solidly Democratic, and the Republicans would have become the party of liberalism. There would have been no southern strategy, with all that entailed for the Republican morality play. But there would have been the war, and Kennedy would have had to run on his brother's legacy. Rockefeller would have prevailed, and the way would have been open for a revival of the civil rights movement. But first Rockefeller would have had to end the war, which he was reluctant to do because his Cold War credentials were as impeccable as Johnson's, and he would have had no desire to be the first American president to lose a war. He would have announced that he had a plan to end the war, but would have failed to make much headway during his first administration. Working with a Democratic Congress, he would have managed to enact some small anti-poverty programs. And in the midterm elections of 1970 he would have received a slight liberal margin, as the two parties polarized between their conservative and liberal wings.

Through the 1970s the black migration from the South would have continued, leading to periodic outbreaks of violence between newly arrived blacks and second- or third-generation ethnics squeezed by inflation and competition from illegal immigrants.

The student protests would have continued in the background, but the student protests would have lacked the catalysts of actual history, and they would have faded once the FBI exposed its alleged communist underpinnings. With overwhelming popular support, the Selective Service System would have begun revoking draft deferments and drafting student protesters into the infantry. A mass exodus of white males to Canada and Europe from universities would have forced college administrators to look back to the days of World War II and open their doors to women and minorities wthout the quotas or absolute bans.

Junior colleges and prestigious universities alike would have become hotbeds of new ethnic radicalism—home to small but noisy and potentially influential groups of Chicanos and Asian Americans and Native Americans. Women would have begun forming campus organizations of their own too, as would the disabled and gays/lesbians. But none of these groups would have had the clout or experience to do more than develop self-awareness because they would have had no experience with influencing government and would have lacked strong leadership and unified goals. They would not have been civil rights organizations at all. Women generally would have dropped out as they married and moved to the suburbs. Ethnic minorities would have slowly accepted their second-class status and barely would have made a noticeable protest when the war's end allowed the return of white males and the reestablishment of the higher education system as a white male preserve.

The civil rights movement would have remained under the thumb of the NAACP. Even though it was weak, it would have been a grass-roots organization and would have not really required that much money, especially as the courts turned hostile to its efforts, at least on the national level. Besides, it would have been the only civil rights organization—other than the Urban League—remaining in the game, especially after the obscure, failed SCLC under Martin Luther King, Jr., would have turned anti-war, losing what little northern sympathy remained for the cause.

Because the draft of white students would have generated the exodus to Canada and local draft boards would have continued to discriminate in favor of whites, blacks would have continued to die disproportionately in Vietnam.

Southern college sports would have remained mediocre and all white.

In the backwater that was the American South, businesses that had relocated during and after World War II would have begun backing away from governments led by men such as George Wallace and Lester Maddox. Lacking the agitation of civil rights to act righteously against, the new southern populists would have begun instituting realistic property taxes and repealing right-to-work laws and building infrastructures for their white populations. The South would have become inhospitable to business but an integral part of the American defense establishment and the education-military complex. And tight controls on the energy sector would have forced the major companies to abandon southern oil and gas. They would have explored in the Middle East and elsewhere around the world as early as the 1960s. With the assistance of the CIA they would have had limited success in getting secure supplies of Nigerian and Venezuelan oil as well as a toehold in the Middle East. Energy prices would have been higher, of course, and American oil would have remained in the ground as the companies would have awaited the day when environmental controls would be lifted.

Without the immigration that followed 1965, the United States would have remained black-white-brown. There would have been no influx of Vietnamese or Haitians or Cubans or Chinese—not even a large migration from Bosnia and Armenia and Greece and Italy. Immigration would have died as an issue, and the United States might never have noticed that it quickly lost its initial leadership in personal computers to India and Pakistan, that its aging population would have included a lot of old and obsolete doctors, that its businesses would have become staid, and that entrepeneurship would have become just another myth from the Horatio Alger days. Yet life would have been good as the United States declined to second-rate status.

Martin Luther King, Jr., would have returned to the ministry and probably would have become the subject of a less-than-well-received made-for-television movie. He would have aged gracefully though and would have become a respected leader of Atlanta's segregated black community. He might have accepted, grudgingly, that he was living in a Jim Crow world after the NAACP, working with the Black Muslims, would have sued to reinstate segregation rather than have blacks downtrodden in a white supremacist society. After all those years, his world would still have been separate—but perhaps a lot closer to equal.

John H. Barnhill

Discussion Questions

1. If there had been no effort to establish a "Southern Strategy" for the Republicans, which political leaders might have emerged to dominate a liberal Republican party?

2. In the alternate scenario suggested here, various black nationalist groups work with segregationists. What factors would have made such an alliance likely? What factors would have made such an alliance difficult or impossible?

3. If Robert Kennedy, Malcolm X, and Martin Luther King, Jr., had never been assassinated, what types of careers might each of them have had through the 1980s and 1990s?

4. If formal and legal segregation had persisted into the 1970s and 1980s, do you think that civil rights activists would have become more or less willing to adopt radical measures to oppose those practices?

5. If there had not been a successful civil rights movement in the 1960s, how do you think that might have affected television, other mass media, and sports in the United States?

Bibliography and Further Reading

Cornell, Stephen. *The Return of the Native.* New York: Oxford University Press, 1988.

Dudziak, Mary L. *Cold War Civil Rights: Race and the Image of American Democracy.* Princeton, NJ: Princeton University Press, 2000.

Egerton, John. *Speak Now against the Day.* Chapel Hill: University of North Carolina Press, 1995.

Gardner, Michael R. *Harry Truman and Civil Rights.* Carbondale: Southern Illinois University Press, 2003.

Gutierrez, David. *Walls and Mirrors: Mexican Americans, Mexican Immigrants.* Berkeley: University of California Press, 1995.

Klarman, Michael. *From Jim Crow to Civil Rights.* New York: Oxford University Press, 2004.

Kotz, Nick. *Judgment Days: Lyndon Baines Johnson, Martin Luther King Jr., and the Laws That Changed America.* New York: Houghton Mifflin, 2005.

Longmore, Paul K., and Lauri Umansky, eds. *The New Disability History: American Perspectives.* New York: New York University Press, 2001.

Loevy, Robert D., ed. *The Civil Rights Act of 1964.* Albany: State University of New York Press, 1997.

Mann, Robert. *The Walls of Jericho: Lyndon Johnson, Hubert Humphrey, Richard Russell, and the Struggle for Civil Rights.* New York: Harvest Books, 1997.

Osgood, Kenneth. *Total Cold War: Eisenhower's Secret Propaganda Battle at Home and Abroad.* Lawrence: University Press of Kansas, 2006.

Shafer, Byron E., and Richard Johnson. *The End of Southern Exceptionalism* .Cambridge, MA: Harvard University Press, 2006.

Shesol, Jeff. *Mutual Contempt: Lyndon Johnson, Robert Kennedy, and the Feud That Defined a Decade.* New York: W. W. Norton, 1998.

U.S. Senate. "Filibuster and Cloture," www.senate.gov/artandhistory/ history/common/ briefing/Filibuster_Cloture.htm (accessed August 2006).

Webb, Clive, ed. *Massive Resistance: Southern Opposition to the Second Reconstruction.* New York: Oxford University Press, 2005.

Wilkinson, Charles. *Blood Struggle: The Rise of Modern Indian Nations.* New York: W. W. Norton, 2005.

Wolters, Raymond. *Right Turn.* New Brunswick, NJ: Transaction, 1996.

John F. Kennedy

TURNING POINT

What if Lee Harvey Oswald had missed on November 22, 1963, and President Kennedy had survived?

INTRODUCTION

John F. Kennedy (JFK) was the youngest man ever elected president of the United States. He beat Republican candidate and Vice President Richard M. Nixon in 1960 in one of the closest presidential elections in history. The Kennedy family had a long political record. Kennedy's grandfather, John F. "Honey Fitz" Fitzgerald, was mayor of Boston, and his father, Joseph P. Kennedy, was a rich businessman who was very influential within the national Democratic Party. President Franklin D. Roosevelt appointed him U.S. ambassador to Great Britain in 1937.

The Kennedy family supported Francisco Franco's fascist regime in Spain during the 1930s, and sought to appease Adolf Hitler, fearing that another world war would lead to another communist revolution. Joe Kennedy had presidential ambitions but was recalled as ambassador by Roosevelt, which ended his presidential hopes. He transferred those hopes to his sons.

JFK served in the U.S. Navy during World War II and was awarded the Purple Heart and the Navy and Marine Corps Medal. After the war his military experience helped him in politics, and he was elected to serve in Congress in 1947. Kennedy supported the policies that made the United States a world power and a deterrent to communist expansion. He became a U.S. senator in 1952 after defeating incumbent Republican senator Henry Cabot Lodge, a victory he won with the help of his father's money. Kennedy supported some of the most repressive anti-communist legislation considered in the 1950s.

Kennedy won a Pulitzer Prize in 1957 for the book *Profiles in Courage*, a work that chronicled the lives of past Senate leaders. As senator, Kennedy positioned himself for a jump toward the presidency and he realized that he needed to establish a reputation fighting national corruption. He and his brother Robert F. Kennedy (RFK), who was also in politics, chose to fight union corruption, especially the Teamsters Union led by James Hoffa, which reportedly had ties to organized crime. Corruption

A TIME FOR
GREATNESS

U. S. SENATOR
JOHN F.
KENNEDY
FOR
PRESIDENT

The cover of a brochure promoting John F. Kennedy
in the 1960 presidential election. (JFK Presidential
Library and Museum)

and the underworld ties of labor leaders were
used as issues to set up congressional hearings.
Kennedy spearheaded the round of hearings
that resulted in new federal laws regulating
trade union activity.

The 1960 presidential election was shaped
by the Cold War. Politicians and some in the
general public incorrectly alleged that the
departing Dwight Eisenhower administration
had allowed a missile gap to form between the
United States and the Soviet Union, with the
United States on the losing end. There was also
the issue of civil rights, but Kennedy did not
take an adamant stand on this before the election. He was cautious about civil rights and
chose Texas Senator Lyndon B. Johnson to be
his running mate. Johnson was a segregationist
and his selection was to appease southern
Democrats. When Kennedy won the 1960 election, he did so with a little more than 100,000
votes out of 69 million votes cast.

Kennedy set his agenda in his inauguration
speech. Some have argued that his speech was
representative of liberal activism. Others have
declared that it was a conservative, Cold War,
anti-communist speech. Historians argued that
when Kennedy declared "Ask not what your
country can do for you but what you can do for
your country," he was not asking people to go
out and fight poverty; he was saying do not
expect the federal government to hugely
expand social welfare programs. Further, when
Kennedy said, "Let every nation know . . . that
we shall pay any price, bear any burden . . . in
order to ensure the survival and success of liberty," he was not talking about the United States
defending the right of nations to self-determination but that America would intervene against
any threats to its power, as in Cuba, which had
just had a successful revolution against a U.S.-
backed dictatorship.

Kennedy was *Time* magazine's "Man of the
Year" in 1961. His greatest fear was that he might
be the president to start a nuclear war. He believed that nuclear prolifera-
tion was the single greatest problem in the 1960s. This explains his policies
throughout his short-lived presidency. Much of it centered on Fidel Castro's
Cuba and Kennedy's attempt to liberate it from a communist grip.

A covert plan was created to train an army of anti-Castro Cuban
exiles and have them invade Cuba and overthrow Castro. This plan
reached its climax on Monday, April 17, 1961, at the Bay of Pigs in Cuba.
American officials believed that the army of Cuban exiles would be met

President and Mrs. Kennedy greet leaders of the Cuban Invasion Brigade in Miami, Florida, December 29, 1962. (JFK Presidential Library and Museum)

with open arms by the Cuban populace. This would then begin a movement to oust Castro from power. The plan was months in the making, and the plot itself had its origins in the Eisenhower administration and the Central Intelligence Agency (CIA). Still, it was Kennedy who implemented it.

The CIA asked Kennedy to order air cover for the Cuban exiles as they landed on the beach, but Kennedy refused, arguing that such support would have constituted armed intervention, which he had told the American people he would not pursue with American forces. Castro's military ambushed the exiles and the uprising in the interior never occurred. It was a major political blow for Kennedy. Castro had ordered mass arrests of political dissidents in the days leading up to the invasion.

The other event that defined the Kennedy administration was the Cuban missile crisis. Soviet leader Nikita Khrushchev saw the Bay of Pigs fiasco as the opening to start arming Cuba more heavily. American spy planes picked up the presence of missiles in Cuba, and for thirteen days in October 1962 the world was on the brink of war. Kennedy demanded that the missile sites be dismantled and removed from Cuba, and he initiated a naval blockade of the island country. The United States and the Soviet Union struck a compromise, with the Americans withdrawing missiles from Turkey and the Soviets from Cuba. On Sunday, October 28, Radio Moscow announced that the missiles would be crated and returned to Moscow. There would be no nuclear war for now.

KEY CONCEPT   Containment

Containment policy, or containing communism, grew out of World War II. There were two superpowers after the war—the United States and the Soviet Union—and any dreams of postwar cooperation between these two giants quickly evaporated. The map of Europe had been redrawn, and an "Iron Curtain" had descended across Eastern Europe, as the Soviets established socialist states around its flank to protect itself from the capitalist states in Western Europe.

In 1947, Greece and Turkey appeared as the next countries to be taken over by communism and President Harry Truman asked Congress for aid to both countries. This concept became known as the Truman Doctrine—the idea that the United States must support free peoples who are resisting subjugation by armed minorities. With about $400 million worth of American advisors and military help, the Greek and Turkish governments resisted the communist threat. But instead of installing democratic governments, these countries came under the rule of oppressive, right-wing military regimes.

The philosophy of the Truman Doctrine came from state department official George F. Kennan. He outlined the concept of containment in the very influential journal *Foreign Affairs*. The term essentially meant using American power to counter Soviet pressure wherever it developed, and it shaped American foreign policy until the fall of communism in the late twentieth century. Containment also led to the creation of the North Atlantic Treaty Organization (NATO) in 1949 to defend Western Europe against a Soviet bloc attack.

Containment policy reached its height under the administration of Richard Nixon and his secretary of state, Henry Kissinger. They sought to stabilize relations with communist nations by withdrawing from Vietnam, recognizing China, and reducing the rivalry with the Soviet Union.

The brief Kennedy administration—from January 1961 to November 1963—did not last long enough to leave behind great achievements. However, the thirty-four months created a different atmosphere of youthful excitement surrounding the White House. Kennedy received credit for the creation of the Peace Corps, an international aid organization staffed by mostly young volunteers who worked for two years abroad on a subsistence salary to help underdeveloped nations. He was also credited with or blamed for having supported the abortive attempt to overthrow the Cuban dictator Fidel Castro, in an invasion by Cuban refugees that was halted at the Bay of Pigs in April 1961.

Kennedy was assassinated a little more than a year later. The president's assassin, Lee Harvey Oswald, was born in 1939 and was identified early on as withdrawn and demanding. He moved constantly during his childhood, going to many different schools; for a period he was placed in a home for disturbed boys and was given psychiatric care. By the time he was fifteen he wanted to join the Communist Party. Instead, he joined the U.S. Marines two years later, and soon thereafter, exceeded the score needed to qualify as a sharpshooter. Historians point out that Oswald suffered from a superiority complex; he was disappointed that he was not given the proper recognition for his intelligence. When he was twenty, in 1959, he went to the Soviet Union, believing that he would be given the proper respect and stature there. He had studied the Russian language beforehand and had saved some money to make the transition easier.

The Soviets did not give Oswald the respect he thought he deserved. He came back to the United States in May 1962 with his Russian wife, Marina, and their child. Oswald had a difficult time keeping a job and was a very frustrated man by this time—he was ready to unleash that anger in the form of assassination. His first target was right-wing Major General Edwin A. Walker. He planned the shooting for ten weeks, ordered a $20 rifle with a four-power (4x) scope, and waited for the opportune moment. Oswald photographed the Dallas, Texas, alley near Walker's house. When the moment came, he fired one shot as the general sat behind a window. The wooden frame on the window deflected the bullet and the assassination attempt failed.

Oswald decided to leave Dallas and look for work in New Orleans. By late 1962 and early 1963 Oswald's attention turned to Castro's Cuba. He started a chapter of the Fair Play for Cuba Committee. In the fall of 1963 he traveled to Mexico City where he expected to acquire a visa to travel to Cuba and was shocked when he was turned down. He also was turned down when he tried to get a visa to again visit the Soviet Union. Oswald, again frustrated, returned to Dallas in early October 1963.

Marina and Oswald lived separately at this time. Marina was staying with a family friend, Ruth Paine, until Oswald found a job and an apartment. Paine heard that the Texas School Book Depository was hiring, and Oswald began work there in mid-October. The following month, Dallas newspapers published the presidential motorcade route: it ran right past the School Book Depository building.

On November 22, 1963, Oswald brought his rifle to work in a brown paper parcel. He used book cartons to make a sniper's nest on the sixth floor of the building. There, the windows overlooked Dealey Plaza. At 12:30 P.M., in the space of eight seconds, Oswald fired three shots at the open car carrying President Kennedy, Texas governor John Connally, and their wives as they passed by. The third shot was the fatal shot, and Kennedy was pronounced dead at 1:00 P.M. After firing the three shots, Oswald left the School Book Depository, despite the surrounding chaos, and returned to his Dallas apartment. He picked up a pistol from his apartment and later shot and killed Dallas police officer J. D. Tippit. Oswald tried to hide in the Texas Theatre but was captured there about ninety minutes after he shot Kennedy. While in police custody, Oswald was gunned down by nightclub owner Jack Ruby. The killing of Oswald was captured live on television before millions of viewers.

There have been numerous theories about the assassination of JFK that differ from the record above. Some conspiracy theories involve questioning whether Oswald was a lone gunman—the ability to fire three shots in eight seconds seemed impossible to some. Other theories point to CIA, Cuban, or organized crime influence to retaliate against one Kennedy policy or another.

On November 29, 1963, one week after the assassination, President Lyndon B. Johnson (LBJ), to stave off all other investigations, issued Executive Order #11130, which created a blue-ribbon commission to prepare a report explaining exactly what had happened. The distinguished panel was headed by Chief Justice Earl Warren of the Supreme Court, the highest judicial officer in the country.

ANOTHER VIEW   Conspiracy Theorists

Conspiracy theorists have a long list of suspects as to who might have killed Kennedy. That list includes, but is not limited to, the CIA, Castro, anti-Castro Cubans, the Federal Bureau of Investigation (FBI), the Mafia, right-wingers, the Teamsters, Texas oil millionaires, the Secret Service, and Lyndon Johnson. Many conspiracy theorists have built their theories on highly questionable evidence.

With regard to the CIA, during the first year of the Kennedy presidency, it essentially worked under its own direction: operatives did what they wanted, including developing plans to kill foreign leaders. After the CIA's disastrous Bay of Pigs invasion, Kennedy began firing high-ranking officials and taking away the CIA's autonomy. Theorists believe the CIA killed Kennedy because he threatened its power.

Others suggest that the Mafia killed Kennedy. Attorney General Robert Kennedy set out to crush organized crime in America and some conspiracy theorists believe organized crime figures killed Kennedy in revenge for his administration's policies.

Most researchers who argue for a conspiracy believe the following: (1) The shooting of President Kennedy was beyond the capability of any one man to perform, and therefore there must have been more than one gunman. They point out that no rifleman in any of the assassination simulations has scored two hits in three shots in six to nine seconds against a moving target from a sixty-foot elevation on the first attempt, which is what Oswald allegedly did; (2) much of the evidence against Oswald was planted; (3) at least one shot was fired from in front of Kennedy's vehicle, most likely from the grassy knoll; (4) there was a large wound in the right-rear area of Kennedy's skull, indicating a shot from the front; (5) the Abraham Zapruder film seems to show reactions to more than just three shots; (6) the single-bullet theory (that one of the bullets fired can account for one of Kennedy's wounds and all of Texas governor John Connally's wounds) is impossible; (7) Oswald was being impersonated, and his impersonators left a trail of false evidence that was to be used against Oswald later; and (8) there was a large-scale cover-up of the facts about the assassination, in an attempt to lead the public to believe there was only one gunman and no conspiracy.

The Warren Commission considered itself a fact-finding committee and not a court. It was not there to prove innocence or guilt but to acquire the truth. In the investigative process, the commission did not come up with a specific motive for Oswald. They did conclude that Oswald was the only assassin and acted on his own; that he shot from the sixth floor of the School Book Depository building, which was behind Kennedy's vehicle at the moment of the shooting; that he used a Italian Mannlicher-Carcano rifle found in the building; and that he shot a Dallas police officer, Tippit, when he was being hunted by the police.

The Warren Commission found that neither the sniper nor his killer was part of any conspiracy, domestic or foreign, to assassinate President Kennedy, and that Oswald had acted alone. The commission, however, was not able to convincingly explain all the particular circumstances of Kennedy's murder. In 1979 a special committee of the U.S. House of Representatives declared that although the president had undoubtedly been slain by Oswald, acoustic analysis suggested the presence of a second gunman who had missed. It did little to destroy the theories that Oswald was part of a vast conspiracy involving CIA agents angered over Kennedy's handling of the Bay of Pigs fiasco or members of organized crime seeking revenge for Attorney General Bobby Kennedy's relentless criminal investigations.

The commission was under pressure to come up with conclusions quickly and to dispel rumors. Because of this, some historians point out that the commission did not pursue conflicting testimony, ambiguous photographs, or contradictory evidence. The commission also closed its hearings to the public. It was reported later that four of the seven commission members expressed skepticism about their conclusion.

There were witnesses in Dealey Plaza who saw things differently from what was expressed in the Warren Commission report. Some people reported that shots were fired from the grassy knoll, not the Texas School Book Depository. Witnesses also alleged that a cloud of smoke was visible in the area of the grassy knoll; that even before Kennedy's motorcade arrived, men with rifles were seen in downtown Dallas; and there were unexplained reports of witnesses encountering mysterious Secret Service men in Dealey Plaza shortly after the shooting. The entire assassination was caught on film by an amateur photographer, Abraham Zapruder; the footage is now known simply as the Zapruder film.

TURNING POINT

On November 22, 1963, Kennedy was warmly welcomed by the people of Dallas. He was to ride in a motorcade through the streets of downtown Dallas in an open convertible. In the car with him were Texas governor John Connally and his wife, as well as Mrs. Kennedy.

When the motorcade arrived in Dealey Plaza at 12:30 P.M., it took the 120-degree turn onto Elm Street, passing the School Book Depository building. Mrs. Connally heard gunshots. When she turned, looking at the president, she saw him move his hand to his throat, covering a shooting wound. The next second Governor Connally felt an ache in his back, which he recognized as a gunshot. Just seconds later he could hear the third shot. Mrs. Kennedy turned to her husband: She saw her husband hit in the head, the fatal shot.

One of the three shots that Oswald fired missed. Maybe the trigger was accidentally nudged as Oswald was bringing the Mannlicher-Carcano rifle to bear on the limousine, or Oswald hurried a shot as he saw the oak branches approaching in the scope, or the branches caused a deflection. Each succeeding shot demonstrated an increasing familiarity with the weapon. With time to recycle the bolt on his rifle, Oswald's second shot came three-and-one-half seconds after the first. The limousine was now clear of the oak's branches, and perhaps the nonreaction of the Secret Service agents (though a few had jerked their heads to their right immediately) renewed Oswald's confidence.

The second bullet struck just six inches below Kennedy's skull. It had passed through the soft tissue of Kennedy's neck without directly striking a bone, leaving the bullet 100-percent intact and undistorted. It emerged from the throat leaving a clean circular wound many mistook for an entrance wound.

Oswald's last shot was the easiest. It would later be determined that Oswald had caught the president's upper right skull by just an inch. If the

President Kennedy speaks at the Rice Hotel in Houston, Texas, on November 21, 1963. (JFK Presidential Library and Museum)

bullet had struck the intended target, the center of the rear skull, it would have likely exited through the president's face.

By the time the bullet reached Connally, its tumbling caused a slightly elongated entrance wound. The bullet traveled along Connally's right chest muscles and did not directly strike a bone; rather, pressure from the bullet caused the fifth rib to implode into the right lung. The bullet suffered distortion (an elongated twist) when it glanced off the right radius bone. Connally's right wrist would heal without pins or an artificial joint because the deflected bullet had taken no bone with it. The nearly spent bullet then nestled into the left thigh where it apparently stayed until Connally was lifted from his stretcher onto the operating table at Parkland Memorial Hospital. This was the now famous "single bullet."

Several men were arrested in and near Dealey Plaza and in the Dallas-Ft. Worth area in the aftermath of the shooting. Eventually, the Dallas Police Department released all of them. The police detectives then focused their attention on a man who was arrested in a movie theater a few miles from Dealey Plaza about ninety minutes after the assassination. This was Oswald. He was arrested on the suspicion that he had killed a policeman named J. D. Tippit about thirty-five to forty-five minutes after the assassination in a suburb of Dallas, just a few miles from Dealey Plaza.

The presidential motorcade on November 22, 1963. Texas Governor John Connally and Mrs. Connally are in front with the President and Mrs. Kennedy in the rear. (Library of Congress)

The police learned that Oswald worked in the same School Book Depository building from which many witnesses said shots were fired and in which the police found a rifle and some spent bullet shells by one of the windows facing the plaza.

But what if Oswald had missed?

ACTUAL HISTORY

Lyndon B. Johnson was president from 1963 to 1969, and like Kennedy, he presided over the ongoing Cold War and practiced containment (containing communism and checking its spread around the world). The Johnson administration's foreign policy was dominated by an escalation in military policy in Southeast Asia, namely Vietnam. Johnson also intervened in the Dominican Republic, gave military support to pro-U.S. factions in the African Congo, increased America's nuclear arsenal with the intercontinental ballistic missile (ICBM), and ordered more jet bombers and submarines. On the domestic front, the Johnson years were tumultuous with urban riots, civil rights protests, and the assassinations of

Lyndon B. Johnson takes the oath of office aboard Air Force One on November 22, 1963. (JFK Presidential Library and Museum)

Malcolm X, Martin Luther King, Jr., and Robert Kennedy. Despite the challenges, Johnson did begin the Great Society programs. Two main targets of the Great Society social agenda were the reduction of poverty and the elimination of racial injustice in the United States. New major spending programs were launched to address needs in education, medical care, urban problems, and transportation.

In the 1968 presidential election, Republican Richard Nixon defeated Democrat Hubert Humphrey. Nixon, like Johnson, had to deal with the issue of Vietnam and increasing opposition against the war at home. During Nixon's presidency, inflation increased due to the costs of the Vietnam War. Despite these challenges, Nixon was reelected in 1972 but faced scandals and crises in his second term. One crisis began with telephone wiretaps in 1969 of U.S. citizens on an "enemies list," mainly composed of those who opposed the U.S. invasion of Cambodia during the Vietnam War.

In May 1972 the headquarters of the Democratic National Committee (DNC) was burglarized to put a wiretap on the telephones. A few weeks later, the DNC was broken into again, supposedly to check on wiretaps that were not working and to photograph documents. Investigative reporting by Carl Bernstein and Bob Woodward of the *Washington Post* helped to reveal that the burglaries were the work of the Committee to Re-elect the President, or CREEP. Five burglars were arrested on June 17, 1972, during the second break-in of the Watergate Hotel headquarters. The Watergate crisis led to Nixon's political downfall as it became evident through White House tape recordings that Nixon had ordered his advisors to lie to the FBI and used the CIA to stop the investigation of the burglars. Ultimately, the trail led all the way to the presidency and the cover-up was exposed. Nixon resigned his office on August 9, 1974.

Vice President Gerald Ford assumed the presidency of the United States. Ford quickly pardoned Nixon for all crimes committed, which was an extremely unpopular move. The United States gradually withdrew from Vietnam, and shortly thereafter, South Vietnam fell to the communists. Ford faced a severe recession at home that continued throughout his administration. He was not elected in 1976, as Democrat Jimmy Carter won the election with an appeal to a fresh start in Washington, D.C.

President Carter worked hard to combat inflation and unemployment, but inflation and interest rates were at near-record highs, and efforts to reduce them caused a recession. Most of his domestic policy focused on an energy shortage, which had Americans waiting in long lines for gas and turning down heating thermostats across the country. Unlike Johnson and Nixon, Carter was an outsider to Washington politics, and his relations with Congress were often strained, leading to a perception of ineffectiveness in the Carter administration.

Carter set his own style in foreign affairs, demanding an accountability for human rights in international relations. Through the Camp David agreement of 1978, he helped bring about a peace treaty between Egypt and Israel. He obtained ratification of the Panama Canal treaties, which handed the Panama Canal over to Panama, established full diplomatic relations with the People's Republic of China, and completed negotiation of the second Strategic Arms Limitation Treaty, or SALT II, with the Soviet Union.

But the Soviet invasion of Afghanistan in 1979 suspended the ratification of the SALT II pact. In the meantime, Iranian revolutionaries seized U.S. hostages from the embassy staff in Tehran, as Iran underwent a revolution that ousted the U.S.-backed shah of Iran. The hostage crisis plagued Carter's administration during his last fourteen months in office. The hostage situation, coupled with continuing inflation at home, contributed to Carter's electoral defeat in 1980. Iran released the fifty-two American hostages the same day Carter left office and newly elected president Ronald Reagan took over.

Reagan came to the presidency determined to reduce the growth of the national government, restore the power of the states in the federal system, reduce government expenditures through massive domestic budget cuts, and expand the military and defense establishments. He also sought to lower taxes and restructure foreign policy away from détente (an easing of tensions between the Cold War powers) with the Soviet Union to a posture of peace through strength. To achieve these goals he sought to restore the dominance of the presidency over the Congress.

Reagan's first term was dominated by efforts to carry out his economic program—dubbed "Reaganomics" by the media. Reaganomics consisted in part of large budget reductions in domestic programs and big tax cuts for individuals and businesses. He was an adherent of supply-side economics, which generated growth by creating a greater supply of goods and services, thereby increasing jobs.

Soviet-U.S. relations were generally chilly during Reagan's first term. But by 1985, in his second term, a cordial meeting with Soviet leader Mikhail Gorbachev began a warming trend. In 1987 they both signed a treaty in Washington, D.C., that would drastically reduce Soviet and U.S. intermediate-range nuclear missile stockpiles. In 1988, Reagan had a friendly summit meeting in Moscow, the capital of what he had once called an evil empire.

Reagan's other long-standing foreign-policy initiative was to aid anti-communist guerrillas in Nicaragua, known as Contras, in thwarting alleged Soviet-Cuban inroads into that country and to pressure the ruling Sandinista government to hold elections and negotiate with its neighbors. Congress reversed itself several times on whether to give humanitarian or military aid to the Contras. In 1986 the administration admitted that it had been secretly selling arms to Iran, with some of the profits possibly going to the guerrillas in Nicaragua.

Vice President George H.W. Bush won the 1988 presidential election. He was a proponent of American consumer capitalism and promoted globalization of American-produced products. Yet the economic recession of 1990–1992, the loss of 2 million jobs, the need to raise taxes to pay for the Reagan deficit, and a hostile Congress controlled by the Democratic Party prevented the realization of the Bush economic doctrine.

Bush's principal focus became foreign affairs. He saw his chief task in foreign policy as overseeing an end to the Cold War and continued the cordial relationship with Gorbachev. Eventually, communism collapsed in the Soviet Union and subsequently the Cold War came to an end, leaving the United States without a clear mission in world affairs.

Bush faced new challenges abroad, and his greatest test came when Iraqi president Saddam Hussein invaded neighboring Kuwait. Vowing to free Kuwait, Bush rallied the United Nations, the American public, and Congress and sent 425,000 American troops to liberate Kuwait. Bush placed personal calls to dozens of world leaders and brought together a coalition of nations to oppose Iraq, carefully holding that coalition together throughout the war. His conduct of the Gulf War and the U.S. victory left him with the highest approval ratings of any president in the history of the Gallup polls. Still, it did not give him a second term. The economy was in bad shape; it had weakened and voters voiced their frustration in the 1992 presidential election. Bush received the lowest percentage of votes of any sitting president in eighty years and lost the election to Arkansas governor, Bill Clinton.

During his first year as president, Clinton battled Congress to secure adoption of an economic package that combined tax increases (which fell mainly on the upper class) and spending cuts (which hurt mainly impoverished Americans). By 1999, with the deficit lowered, surging tax revenues from a booming economy had generated a surplus of $124 billion. Equally important were the pace of economic growth and low inflation. Combined with historically low interest and unemployment rates, these factors positioned the American economy as the world's strongest and most robust.

Clinton's other domestic policies included passage of the North American Free Trade Agreement (NAFTA) in 1993, which made it possible for Canada, Mexico, and the United States to trade freely. In 1996, Congress passed a sweeping welfare reform bill. The legislation replaced the long-standing Aid to Families with Dependent Children (AFDC) program with a system of block grants to individual states. The welfare reform package dropped the eligibility of legal immigrants for welfare assistance during the first five years of their residency. Clinton blocked Republican attempts to bar public education to children of illegal immigrants.

The United States was the only industrialized nation in the world without a universal health care system, and Clinton felt passionately about the fact that 60 million Americans did not have adequate health insurance, but Republicans successfully blocked Clinton's health care initiatives. Many Americans worried that national health insurance was too socialistic, denying Americans the freedom to see a doctor of their choice while placing physicians in the service of a government bureaucracy.

Clinton was plagued by scandals and was impeached during his presidency. The most serious came in 1998 and involved Clinton's adulterous affair with a White House intern named Monica Lewinsky. Investigators questioned Clinton under oath about his relationship with Lewinsky, and it later became evident that he had lied during that testimony. To many people, impeachment or resignation seemed to be the only resolution.

The House adopted two articles of impeachment, charging the president with perjury in his grand jury testimony and obstructing justice in his dealings with various potential witnesses. It became clear that the Senate would not remove Clinton from office. Those voting against impeachment argued that the president's actions constituted "low" crimes, involving private matters, not "high crimes and misdemeanors," amounting to offenses against the state. Clinton was acquitted on both counts on February 12, 1999.

George W. Bush, the son of the George H. W. Bush, won the 2000 presidential election amid much controversy because Florida had to recount its votes in a narrow contest. Eventually, Florida and the election went to Bush, as he defeated Democratic vice president Al Gore. Bush laid out the agenda of his administration: lowering taxes, improving education, and upgrading the military. During his first few months in office, he set about implementing this agenda, giving special emphasis to his plan for a $1.6 trillion tax cut, which was criticized by the Democrats as mainly benefiting the rich and eliminating tax revenues that could have been used to shore up Social Security and Medicare and pay down the national debt. In May 2001, after much debate, Congress passed a tax cut of $1.35 trillion. Bush's first budget increased spending for education and the military but reduced funding for transportation, agriculture, and environmental protection. By doing the latter, he moved away from Clinton-era policies.

The first major international crisis that President Bush had to deal with was the September 11, 2001, terrorist attacks on the United States in which close to 3,000 people died. The terrorist group, al-Qaeda, which was blamed for the attacks, had bases in Afghanistan as well as a large network of terrorist cells throughout the globe. Their leader was Osama bin Laden. Bush ordered troops to invade Afghanistan and destroy al-Qaeda and its training camps, as well as the country's Taliban leadership that was harboring the terrorists.

The war in Afghanistan began on October 7, 2001, and was quickly won, though key leaders, such as al-Qaeda's Osama Bin Laden escaped. A fledgling democracy was installed in Afghanistan, but even before that country was truly pacified, the Bush administration had turned its attention to an old adversary, Iraqi strongman Saddam Hussein. Iraq had not been implicated in the attacks of September 11, but Bush said that his decision to invade the country in 2003 and seek to replace its regime with a democracy was based on several considerations that grew out of the September 11 attacks.

ALTERNATE HISTORY

What if Oswald had fired three shots from the Texas School Book Depository and had failed to hit his target? He could have, however, managed to hit Texas governor Connally in the arm. Oswald would have been surprised and disappointed that he had missed his target. Oswald would have hurriedly put away his rifle and hidden it underneath the makeshift "sniper's nest" he had so carefully constructed. After the shooting, the presidential limousine would have sped away toward Parkland Hospital just to make sure the president and the others, besides Connally, were not injured.

Oswald would have raced home fearing that the police would soon be on his trail. He would have picked up a gun from his apartment and looked for a place to hide out. But he would have soon been discovered in a theater in downtown Dallas and arrested for the attempted murder of the president. Kennedy would have been unharmed in the attempted assassination and Connally would have recovered.

Kennedy would have arrived back in Washington, D.C., on November 23 and received a hero's welcome. He would have vowed to continue working hard for the American people, which included fighting communism. Kennedy would have become very popular after the attempted assassination and would have had another "honeymoon" phase with the American public. He would have campaigned hard throughout 1963 and into the fall of 1964. But no more open limousines. The Secret Service would have seen to that. In the 1964 presidential election, Kennedy and Johnson would have won reelection by a landslide against Barry Goldwater, a conservative Republican senator from Arizona.

Understanding the debacle that was the Bay of Pigs invasion, Kennedy would have attempted to address communist aggression through diplomatic means rather than military action. He might have forced South Vietnam to negotiate with its communist neighbor to the north. By the end of 1964, the United States might have modified its policy of armed containment of communist expansion and pulled its advisors from South Vietnam, much as it did in actual history a decade later. Without U.S. support, South Vietnam would have been forced, either through diplomacy or by military means, to accept a regime dominated by the communists.

Kennedy would have been immersed in international politics. Up to 1964, his greatest international achievement would have been the successful conclusion of the Cuban missile crisis, as well as a treaty that he would have signed with the Soviet Union and Great Britain to ban all nuclear tests in the atmosphere. Still, he would have built up the country's military, economic, and scientific strength as a deterrent to war. Kennedy would have increased conventional forces and accelerated the missile and space programs. It would have been during his second term that programs such as the Peace Corps, Food for Peace, and Alliance for Progress would have helped improve the U.S. position with Latin America, Asia, and Africa.

Kennedy would have implored Congress to work hard on some type of civil rights legislation. There would have been a civil rights and a tax cut bill passed in 1964 and 1966, respectively. The civil rights bill would have outlawed job discrimination based on race, color, religion, national origin, or sex. Kennedy would have fallen short in programs dealing with medical assistance for the elderly, addressing the blight in the cities, and the state of American education. With the tax cuts, aid to third world countries, and domestic bills such as civil rights, Congress would not have allocated funds for these other programs.

Kennedy also would have poured money into the American space program, still vowing to send men to the moon by the end of the decade. The National Aeronautics and Space Administration, or NASA, would have been set up to challenge the Soviets in space. The dream of sending a man to the moon would have been realized during the presidency of his brother in 1969.

In the fall of 1967, Vice President Johnson could have announced that he would not be running for president of the United States in the upcoming presidential election. Robert F. Kennedy would then have announced his candidacy for president, and could have won in 1968, defeating Nixon by a slim margin. Both Kennedys would have seen this as an affirmation of their policy goals. JFK would not have sat idly by after his presidency: RFK would have appointed him ambassador to Great Britain (as their father had been) in 1972, and JFK would have served in that position until 1976.

After making agreements with the Soviet Union during the Cuban missile crisis not to interfere with the Castro regime, it is entirely possible that both Kennedys would have worked on improving relations with Castro. By the early 1970s, U.S.-Cuban travel controls would have been lifted. Whereas JFK might not necessarily have wanted to be viewed as a champion of civil rights, RFK would have been willing to take more risks. One of the first things RFK would have done as the new president in early 1969 would have been to sign new civil rights legislation. This last civil rights legislation of the 1960s would have barred discrimination in public places. RFK would have continued JFK's policies of preserving urban open spaces, developing mass transit, and building middle-income housing.

In an alternate history, Robert F. Kennedy would have served as president after his brother and would have pursued a vigorous civil rights program. (Library of Congress)

The domestic policies that would have failed or not been implemented during John F. Kennedy's terms would now have gained momentum during his brother's administration. A Medicare and Medicaid bill would have passed, and the administration would have declared its War on Poverty. RFK would have signed a Voting Rights Act of 1970, which essentially would have made African Americans equal with whites in the area of universal franchise. RFK would have become a good friend of civil rights leader, Dr. Martin Luther King, Jr., and would have invited King often to the White House.

In the last year of his presidency, RFK and the Soviets would have begun a series of talks aimed at limiting the nuclear arsenal of both countries; these would have been called the Strategic Arms Limitation Treaty, or SALT, talks. The 1975 SALT talks would have started in Helsinki, Finland, and would have been internationally praised. Among other things, SALT would have included agreements to limit the construction and deployment of new offensive missiles. At the same time, RFK would also have recognized the People's Republic of China and pursued a policy of détente with Vietnam.

The Democrats would have lost the White House in 1976 to California governor Ronald Reagan. The American public would have been convinced by Reagan that America had lost prestige throughout the world because of its "soft" stance against communism and third-world country threats. The Soviet Union would still have been flexing its muscles in Eastern Europe and Asia. Voters could have believed that the Kennedy brothers had not addressed the communist issue worldwide and that they had been too lax, as would have been evidenced by their handling of Cuba, Vietnam, and the advances in Soviet science and mathematics.

Reagan would have won the 1976 election against Democrat Hubert Humphrey by a landslide. It would have been a testament that Americans wanted to see a change in party leadership in the executive branch. Reagan would have served two terms, along with his vice president, George H. W. Bush, and would have been considered a highly successful president. Unlike RFK, Reagan would have pursued an aggressive foreign policy aimed at winning or gaining an advantage in the Cold War.

Reagan would have confronted Panamanian nationalists with a military show of force and refused to end American control of the Panama Canal. After the U.S. Navy had positioned itself along the coasts of Panama, the nationalists would have given in to American demands. Reagan also would have presided over talks to relieve Arab-Israeli tensions and pressured Israel and Egypt to sign a peace treaty at the presidential retreat in Maryland—Camp David.

In 1979, the Iranian pro-U.S. leader, Shah Mohammed Reza Pahlavi, would have been ousted by those who despised his repressive methods, his friendship with the West, and his attempts to modernize Iran. He would have fled to Mexico and then the United States, where he would have been admitted to a New York hospital for treatment of cancer. This would have outraged the Iranian revolutionaries (as it did in actual history). A group of pro-Islamic Revolution Iranian students would have invaded the U.S. embassy in the capital, Tehran, and would have taken hostage more than sixty American citizens, mostly embassy employees.

The United States would have warned Iran that if any of the hostages were harmed it would suffer heavy military consequences. Reagan's first move would have been to attack Iran financially. He would have frozen billions of dollars of Iranian assets in the United States and cut off all trade with Iran. Then would have come the military response. The U.S. Navy would have blockaded Iran and the entire Persian Gulf. After eight weeks a rescue mission would have been sent in to free the hostages, as U.S. soldiers would have stormed the compound. After several hours, ten soldiers would have been killed as well as five hostages in the exchange of gunfire. The rest would have been successfully flown to safety on U.S. ships waiting in the gulf. Despite the losses, the rescue mission would have been hailed as a diplomatic and military success for Reagan. His popularity would have soared.

JFK would have been writing his memoirs during this time and afterward would have become president of Harvard University in 1982. He would have remained at that post until 1995. During this time he also would have founded a newspaper and magazine that dealt with domestic affairs and international politics. The newspaper would have been highly popular in New England, and his magazine would have become known worldwide.

Reagan would have easily won reelection in 1980 over Walter Mondale of Minnesota. In his second term Reagan would have continued to cut back on many domestic social programs that would have been put in place during the administrations of both Kennedys. He would have put most of the money from these programs into defense spending, implemented tax cuts, and presided over the deregulation of industries.

Much of the alternate history of the Reagan era would have followed the course of actual history. Disregarding his predecessors' SALT talks, Reagan would have added new missiles in Europe in the early 1980s and militarily put down Marxists insurgencies in El Salvador and the Caribbean island of Grenada. In the Middle East, Reagan would have encouraged an Israeli invasion of Lebanon in 1982 to stop aggression against Israel. Reagan would have sent American marines to Beirut in hopes of pacifying and policing the chaos after Israel's military offensive. The Marines would have become targets of warring factions in Lebanon; many would have been anti-American, pro-Iranian terror groups. In the fall of 1983, a Muslim terrorist would have detonated an explosive-laden truck parked next to the Marine barracks in Beirut. The attack would have killed 241 American servicemen and Reagan would have retaliated by bombing terrorists' compounds and weapons caches. These attacks would have continued until early 1984, when Reagan would have removed the remaining marines from Lebanon.

The 1984 presidential election would have gone to Reagan's vice president, George H. W. Bush. He would have defeated Democrat Walter Mondale by a large margin. Bush would have continued Reagan's policies of reducing domestic programs; since Reagan's first term, there would have been a shift of income from the poorest groups to the richest, with the richest 1 percent improving their relative standing more than any other sector in American society. In most of Bush's second term he would have been preoccupied with foreign policy while neglecting the economy at home.

Like Reagan, Bush would have pledged to restore world respect for the United States and to reduce Soviet power and political influence. By the early 1990s, the Soviet Union would have ceased to be a threat to any nation; communism would have been either collapsing or on the decline. By the end of Bush's second term, communism would have collapsed in the Soviet Union, and the United States would have won the Cold War. The most serious problem the Bush presidency would have faced during its second term would have been Iraq's invasion of Kuwait. Bush would have formed a united bloc of countries in the United Nations to impose economic sanctions on Iraq. But before Bush could have dispatched 125,000 U.S. troops into Saudi Arabia to protect that neighboring kingdom, Iraq's Saddam Hussein would have made another move. The infamous Iraqi Republican Guard would have progressed unchecked into Saudi Arabia. The Saudi kingdom would have been rich but militarily weak and within weeks Iraq would have controlled half of Saudi Arabia.

The United Nations would have quickly given the U.S.-led coalition the authority to remove Iraq from both countries, but the United States would have had to bear the brunt of military operations. An air war would have continued for several months until early 1991 when Bush would have decided to invade Saudi Arabia and push the Iraqis back into Iraq. Five hundred U.S. troops would have died in the invasion of Saudi Arabia and Kuwait. Hussein's troops would have surrendered in droves or retreated back to Iraq.

Bush would have contemplated what to do next, and though he would have been very much influenced by Reagan policies, he would have also sought the counsel of former president John F. Kennedy. At a White House dinner in 1991 in this alternate history, JFK would have advised Bush that U.S. policy in this war should be the removal of Hussein and the creation of a more sympathetic state. In early 1991, the United States would have invaded Iraq and begun an offensive toward Baghdad. The ground war would have been over in two weeks with the capture of Hussein. However, the United States would have become bogged down in Iraq for the next year as it tried to quell the many factions that would have been waging war against one another and against the United States as well.

Because of Bush's preoccupation with foreign policy and neglect of domestic issues, the country would have spiraled into a serious recession. With Bush's failure on the home front, his vice president, Dan Quayle, would have been assured of a defeat by Arkansas governor Bill Clinton in the 1992 presidential election. Clinton would have admired JFK and would have sought him out as a close advisor. Clinton would have removed the last remaining troops from Iraq in mid-1993, and the invasion of Iraq would have been largely seen as a U.S. failure. Iran would have taken advantage of the situation and invaded Iraq, its old nemesis. The Clinton administration would not have stood idly by. The U.S. Persian Gulf task force would have repeatedly sent jets to bomb Iranian positions in Iraq and by 1994, most Iranian positions would have been knocked out, but not before Iranian missiles had been launched into Israel from Iraq. Israel would have responded with its own missile attack on supposed Iranian armaments facilities.

The Middle East crisis would have diverted the Clinton administration's attention from atrocities that were being committed elsewhere in the world, such as in Somalia and the Balkans. But by 1996, Clinton would have committed troops to the Balkans and to Somalia to stop the violence between ethnic groups. It would have been an extremely unpopular move, especially within the Democratic Party, and after a disastrous military campaign in Somalia, Clinton would have lost the 1996 presidential election to Senator Bob Dole of Kansas.

It would have been clear that U.S. forces had been stretched to their limit, yet it would still have taken some time for Dole to bring back troops from Somalia and the Balkans; by 1998, most U.S. troops would have been out. Moreover, the United States would have been attacked by the terrorist group al-Qaeda in the fall of 1998. A series of bombs would have exploded beneath the World Trade Center in New York City, killing some 300 people. A few months later, three planes would have been hijacked and crashed in New York City, Washington, D.C., and Chicago. The Dole administration would have begun an aggressive antiterrorist campaign by invading the regions where most of the terrorists and terror cells were located. U.S. troops would have been sent into Afghanistan, Pakistan, and Saudi Arabia to search for and destroy terror cells. At the same time, Iran would have still been attacking Iraq.

There would have been no clear-cut leader for the Democrats to challenge Dole in the 2000 presidential election. Dole's reelection would have been an affirmation that the American public agreed with a worldwide war on terror. But by 2004, the American public would have wanted a president who would end the war on terror and not risk the lives of any more American men and women. The public would have turned against the Republican Party and toward the Democrats and Independents: They would have elected Democrat and former U.S. senator and vice president Al Gore. By late 2005, Gore would have removed most U.S. troops from Afghanistan, Pakistan, and Saudi Arabia. Still, he would have vowed to continue the war from the air and sea if necessary to capture or kill terrorists. He also would have urged world governments to join the fight in ridding the world of terrorists and oppressors of freedom and liberty. He would have told the country that it would be a long sporadic war, but that the end result would bring victory for the United States.

As for former President John F. Kennedy, he would have died in 2000, at age eighty-three. He would have been hailed as one of the most important chief executives of the second half of the twentieth century. He would have helped the United States win the Cold War and would have advised his successors on what course of action he thought they should take on international and domestic issues. JFK would have been buried at the Kennedy family compound in Hyannisport, Massachusetts.

David Treviño

Discussion Questions

1. Considering the strong anti-communist stands taken by John Kennedy, do you agree that his policies regarding Vietnam would have been less militaristic than those taken in actual history by Lyndon Johnson?

2. If Kennedy had not been assassinated in 1963, do you think his reputation in history would be stronger or less strong than it is in actual history?

3. In actual history, the Civil Rights Acts of 1964 and 1965 were passed under the leadership of Lyndon Johnson, who was an expert in leading legislation through Congress. Do you believe John Kennedy or Robert Kennedy would have had as much success as Johnson did in fact?

4. Since John Kennedy was strongly anti-communist and was not a particularly strong advocate of civil rights, why do you think his reputation as a strong liberal has developed?

5. In the alternate history suggested here, Robert Kennedy became president after John Kennedy. In fact, he did run in 1968 and was assassinated. Their younger brother, Ted Kennedy, has been senator from Massachusetts since being first elected in 1962. Do you think it is a good or bad tendency in the United States for multiple members of particular families (like the Kennedys and the Bushes) to run for high political office?

Bibliography and Further Reading

Bruns, Roger. Introduction by Douglas Brinkley. *Almost History: Close Calls, Plan B's, and Twists of Fate in America's Past.* New York: Hyperion, 2000.

Cowley, Robert, ed. *What Ifs? of American History.* New York: Berkley Books, 2003.

Dallek, Robert. *An Unfinished Life: John F. Kennedy, 1917–1963.* Boston: Little, Brown, 2003.

Dallek, Robert, and Terry Golway. *Let Every Nation Know: John F. Kennedy in His Own Words.* Naperville, IL: Sourcebooks MediaFusion, 2006.

Freedman, Lawrence. *Kennedy's Wars: Berlin, Cuba, Laos, and Vietnam.* New York: Oxford University Press, 2000.

Giglio, James N. *The Presidency of John F. Kennedy.* Lawrence: University Press of Kansas, 1991.

Lamb, Brian. *Booknotes: On American Character.* New York: Public Affairs, 2004.

Lowe, Jacques, and Wilfrid Sheed. *The Kennedy Legacy: A Generation Later.* New York: Viking Penguin, 1988.

Rubin, Gretchen. *Forty Ways to Look at JFK.* New York: Ballantine Books, 2005.

Russo, Gus. *Live by the Sword: The Secret War against Castro and the Death of JFK.* Baltimore: Bancroft Press, 1998.

Unger, Irwin. *These United States: The Questions of Our Past.* Upper Saddle River, NJ: Prentice Hall, 1999.

TURNING POINT

President Johnson's War on Poverty was largely sidelined by politics and the Vietnam War. What if the War on Poverty had been won?

INTRODUCTION

Campaigning for the presidency of the United States in late 1928, Herbert Hoover declared that the poorhouse is vanishing from among us. With the 1920s economy apparently booming, America was nearer to the final triumph over poverty than ever before in the history of any land. Although this claim was well crafted and helped make Hoover's campaign successful, the confident Republican could not have been more wrong. Less than a year later, the infamous Wall Street stock market crash of October 1929 began the worst economic downturn in American history. By 1933, national unemployment stood at 25 percent with rates much higher in many industrial cities. For African Americans, competing with whites for scarce jobs, unemployment rates surpassed 50 percent. Those fortunate enough to have employment found their wages and hours slashed. Although the federal government still did not formally classify poverty, the poor became ubiquitous in the Great Depression. Thousands stood in breadlines and lived in shanties sarcastically dubbed Hoovervilles. The hard times seemed never to end.

When the New York Democrat Franklin Delano Roosevelt (FDR) replaced Hoover early in 1933, he moved quickly to address the issue. Roosevelt's New Deal policies included a great number and variety of programs designed to help the poor. Accepting in part the arguments of the Harvard economist John Maynard Keynes that government intervention had a key role to play in revitalizing the national economy, FDR laid the groundwork for the modern welfare state. In addition to banking and stock market reforms, FDR created the Federal Emergency Relief Administration to coordinate direct aid to the poor, including food and medicine. New work programs included the Public Works Administration, whose projects included the construction of roads, housing, and schools, and the Civilian Conservation Corps, which harnessed the power of young men in military-style camps to aid in soil conservation. Unable to find work in the private sector, these beneficiaries now had a paycheck to sustain them.

KEY CONCEPT   Keynsian Economics

Until the Great Depression, the majority of economists assumed that the law of markets—simply put, the balance between supply and demand—could provide for full employment, provide for jobs for the overwhelming majority of workers. In 1936, however, the British economist John Maynard Keynes challenged this classical paradigm with a revolutionary theory. Deficit spending on public works and other projects would augment purchasing power and produce jobs, he maintained. In a broader sense, government intervention had a key role to play in the economy and would help meet the demands of the working-class movement. Franklin Roosevelt wrestled with Keynesian economics, but not until World War II and the immediate reconstruction did it truly gain a foothold in American economic policy. After several decades of relative success, however, any consensus among economists dissolved amid the economic turmoil of the 1970s. Today debate continues among economists on the merits of Keynes's concepts.

Their spending, in turn, further stimulated the economy. Expanding upon the government as employer of last resort, FDR later created the Works Progress Administration (WPA).

The WPA employed not only construction workers but also artists, writers, and teachers. To aid industrial workers, the New Deal strictly regulated wages and prices while working to encourage collective bargaining and empower unions. In a similar fashion, it battled deflation in the farm economy through strict regulation. The government began to ensure mortgages to fight foreclosures and combat homelessness, and it launched one of the first regional development agencies in American history, the Tennessee Valley Authority (TVA). The TVA's hydroelectric dams provided cheap electricity to Appalachia, a particularly depressed area of the country. Perhaps most important, the New Deal created Social Security, a program that provided federal pensions for the elderly and compensation for the unemployed and disabled. It also included the Aid to Dependent Children program.

Revolutionary in its scope, Roosevelt's New Deal eased the national crisis by raising employment. Speaking directly to the public in radio broadcasts dubbed fireside chats, FDR rebuilt confidence in the economy, stimulating consumption. However, the New Deal hardly eradicated poverty or ended the Great Depression. In fact, a recession in 1937—the Roosevelt Recession—still saw one in five Americans unemployed. Poverty persisted throughout the 1930s as the national economy slowly fought to recover.

President Franklin Roosevelt's New Deal policies helped alleviate Depression-era poverty. (Library of Congress)

It was not the New Deal that finally brought prosperity but World War II. Suddenly, as men rushed off the war, unemployment was no longer a problem; finding workers was. With the nation mobilized in a war economy, all debate over federal deficits and all doubts about Keynesian economics evaporated. Women were forced into industrial jobs and African Americans continued their migration from the rural South to the urban North where they found factory work plentiful. Although inflation was a problem with the Consumer Price Index advancing over 23 percent between 1941 and 1945, weekly earnings of those in manufacturing increased 70 percent. Farmers experienced prosperity not known since 1919 with net farm income increasing over 300 percent. Racial and labor strife persisted, but there was no doubt that the Great Depression had ended. New Deal relief and work programs to combat poverty were no longer necessary and withered on the vine.

Fears that depression would return at the conclusion of the hostilities proved baseless. Pent-up consumer demand, new technologies, the needs of a devastated Europe, and continued government spending through the G.I. Bill of Rights, which provided aid to returning veterans, kept the economy growing. The new postwar baby boom helped fuel a growth in consumerism and a new suburbia. Economist John Kenneth Galbraith seemed to capture the nation's mood in his 1958 book, *The Affluent Society.* "[Capitalism] works," Galbraith wrote, "and in the years since World War II, quite brilliantly." To much of America, poverty was simply invisible. At a quick glance, the nation seemed like that portrayed in a popular television comedy of the time, *Father Knows Best*, which promoted middle-class values and contentment. American society was placid, homogenous, and above all, prosperous.

The reality was something different. Although not in the desperate straits of the Great Depression, a subclass of poor continued to exist. The problem of poverty within the world's richest nation was something of a paradox. While new technologies heralded progress, the emerging industries and streamlined production led to the displacement of certain workers, lost in the new economy. In the automobile industry, for example, automation displaced large numbers of low-skill workers. In the agricultural economy, it was the mechanical cotton-picking machine. Increasing specialization, requiring more education than ever, frequently meant less opportunity for those without access to good schools. In addition, prosperity varied from region to region. Growth was significant in the West and South—the Sunbelt—while the older economies of the large midwestern and northeastern cities continued to struggle. Many got rich, but others did not. Pockets of poverty remained in many cities and rural landscapes.

Race, of course, played a role. African Americans and the growing number of Hispanics were disproportionately poor. The Jim Crow South not only meant disenfranchisement of African Americans, a block to full voting rights, but segregation in public and private facilities. Relegated to the back seats, the hardest jobs, and the poorest living conditions, blacks found equal opportunity only a theory. American blacks had fought valiantly during the war, and their labor had helped sustain the miracle of wartime production. Under the wartime leadership of A. Philip Randolph, one of the first great modern civil rights leaders, they had pressured FDR into concessions, most notably the creation of the Fair Employment

Practices Commission. Now expectations ran high and they demanded more. Hispanics suffered from the Bracero program, which allowed large numbers of Mexicans to enter the United States in search of work. This policy kept agricultural wages low among native-born workers. Combined with discriminatory bank lending practices and so-called neighborhood improvement associations, which encouraged segregated housing, poverty remained real to many Americans. Among the population, minorities still had the lowest life expectancies and levels of education but the highest rates of infant mortality and crime. It was a problem activists thought ripe to address.

As African Americans and others prepared for the future, the Democrats found themselves defending the New Deal welfare state. On the other end of the political spectrum, many in a resurgent Republican Party sought a complete retreat in government activism, a return to economic freedom and limited government. The result was for much of the next two decades a policy of moderation, far from dismantling FDR's economic safety net but also not attacking inequity. Roosevelt's successor, Harry S. Truman, tried to reinvigorate liberalism with his Fair Deal policies but found new Republican strength constricting. His proposal for a full employment bill faced emasculation at the hands of Congress, as did his plans for a system of national health insurance and federal funding for public schools. Truman was able to sign bills to build public housing, raise the minimum wage, and expand Social Security, but he could not sustain his veto of the Taft-Hartley Act, a bill designed to weaken unions that its opponents dubbed a slave labor bill. He could also not challenge the southern conservatives in his own party over civil rights, for doing so might provoke a revolt that could disrupt his entire economic program. While he did what he could without congressional consent, including notable achievements such as desegregating the military and appointing the first black federal jurist, Jim Crow remained the law of the land throughout much of the South.

Truman's successor, the wartime commander Dwight Eisenhower, did not share Truman's liberalism and deliberately guided a more conservative fiscal policy. Stocking his cabinet with executives from the business community, "Ike," as many called him, exhibited a growing concern over federal deficits. His early budgets dramatically reduced spending and offered no new anti-poverty programs. He ended wage and price controls and reduced farm price subsidies. At the same time Eisenhower was hardly doctrinaire, fashioning himself a moderate. His policies became known as dynamic conservatism, an oxymoron that he described as conservative when it came to money and liberal when it came to human beings. His fiscal policies grew more flexible as the years passed, and in 1956, he authorized the construction of the interstate highway system, which provided its own boom to the economy. In addition, he allowed an expansion of Social Security and the minimum wage while supporting an increase in spending for public health.

Eisenhower was a popular president but could not completely avoid the growing rumblings emanating from the forgotten underclass, people mired in the pockets of poverty that remained in many ethnic and urban cities. While most Americans enjoyed the bounty of consumerism, the unemployment rate slowly climbed to almost 7 percent by early 1961.

Emboldened by an activist Supreme Court of Roosevelt appointees and the seminal case *Brown v. Board of Education of Topeka, Kansas,* which ruled segregation in public schools unconstitutional, the modern civil rights movement was born. Following in the shoes of Randolph, the young Baptist preacher Dr. Martin Luther King, Jr., organized nonviolent protests. King's goal was clear: economic and legal justice, and true equality in the marketplace and courthouse. While today Americans celebrate his efforts with a national holiday, at the time his movement often met with violence. The new medium of television captured it all, projecting into the homes of the affluent American suburbanites the uncomfortable reality they liked to ignore: poverty persisted and unless true equal opportunity emerged, the future could get ugly.

The new president in 1961, the young John F. Kennedy (JFK), saw himself as the bearer of the Roosevelt liberal tradition, although he addressed fiscal and monetary stimuli more than structural inequities in confronting the problems of poverty. Facing the same conservative constraints as had Truman, however, Kennedy at first moved cautiously. Tax cuts and the expansion of international trade through lower tariffs created jobs, the administration argued. Pegging wage and price guidelines to the growth in productivity, Kennedy counted few major legislative victories on behalf of the poor. Proposals to expand federal aid to education fell below expectations, and Congress blocked more ambitious plans to create a department of urban affairs and to provide health insurance for the aged, the latter still championed by former President Truman. Kennedy did achieve new housing legislation and, like his predecessors, increases in Social Security and the minimum wage. His record was, in short, moderate.

By the end of 1963, Kennedy had begun to look to a second term. With his idealistic brother Robert, eight years his junior, urging him on, JFK planned a more aggressive program to combat poverty and address civil rights after his reelection. A new task force, led by advisor Walter Heller, was already working on proposals. The task was daunting. What were respective federal and state responsibilities, and which agencies should take charge? What exactly was the poverty line? Should the second term bring a renewed push for old proposals or a completely fresh agenda? Heller and his colleagues were wrestling with such questions when Kennedy left to campaign in Dallas, Texas.

What happened next shocked the nation and forever changed the politics of poverty. When the assassin Lee Harvey Oswald's bullet felled President Kennedy on November 22, 1963, Vice President Lyndon Baines Johnson (LBJ) of Texas succeeded him. With him came a new momentum for a rebirth of liberalism. The days of moderation were over, with the future uncertain.

TURNING POINT

At first glance, Johnson was an unlikely candidate to lead the battle against poverty. Different from the young, idealistic Kennedy, Johnson was a consummate politician selected as Kennedy's vice president to appease southern conservatives. His record in the Senate demonstrated his political skill but did not distinguish him as a champion of the disadvantaged. He supported the Taft-Hartley Act, for example, and opposed antilynching legislation. Senator Johnson was, according to one columnist, riding in the first class coach of arch Republicanism. He was the master compromiser, a man who built consensus by avoiding conflict. It did not bode well for liberalism.

Appearances, however, were deceiving. For one, unlike Kennedy, LBJ had grown up among the hard-scrabble poor of Texas, the son of a farmer and minor politician known more for his raucous language than his high culture. Johnson's first job was teaching poor Hispanic children, exposing him to the illiteracy and disease that plagued their community. He matured politically during the New Deal, serving as head of Texas's National Youth Administration. In Congress, he ingratiated himself with FDR, pledging fidelity but still not alienating conservatives, an early sign of his political mastery. His skill in persuasion and compromise led him to the Senate and ultimately to the vice presidency. Suddenly thrust into the Oval Office after Kennedy's death, Johnson believed himself emancipated from his southern conservative base. More important, he quickly recognized that assassination had made Kennedy a martyr and his

President Lyndon Johnson shakes the hand of a resident of Appalachia during his Poverty Tour of the country. (LBJ Library)

IN CONTEXT　　What Constitutes Poverty?

Poverty is, in many respects, an artificial construct. Clearly it is grounded in one's material circumstances—the absence of food, shelter, or clothing. It also involves the culture of those struggling to meet these bare necessities. As a political term, however, its definition can vary. In America the definition of poverty is constantly changed according to such factors as inflation, the sizes of families, and marital status. What exactly constitutes the absolute minimum one needs to survive is debatable. Today and in recent years, conservatives tend to perceive less poverty and to diminish its significance within the grander scheme of economic prosperity. Where it does exist, they tend to perceive individual failings as a root cause. Liberals, on the other hand, tend to emphasize poverty to a greater extent and to argue that its causes are more systemic in the society. This debate, of course, takes place in one of the richest nations on the Earth. What officially constitutes poverty in the United States may be perceived as adequate in poorer nations. Because of different cultures and obvious disparities in the cost of living, a family of four surviving on $13,000 may be considered at the poverty level in America but middle class in many African or Asian nations. Simply put, the poor in many rich nations may be the rich in many poor nations.

programs popular. If Kennedy had planned a new assault on civil rights and poverty, then he, Johnson, should take up the banner. It was his chance for consensus, great achievement, and popularity. Michael Harrington's best seller *The Other America* also impressed him. Loaded with statistics and theories of social pathology, this book argued that over 40 million were in a culture of poverty and to most Americans socially invisible.

Anxious to get started, Johnson immediately called for passage of the two major bills Kennedy had proposed just before his death—a package of tax cuts to stimulate the economy and major civil rights legislation to outlaw discrimination. Speaking in his first State of the Union message only weeks after Kennedy's assassination in Dallas, Johnson referenced Kennedy numerous times. Many Americans live on the outskirts of hope, he declared, some because of their poverty and some because of their color, and all too many because of both. Promising specific proposals, Johnson concluded by declaring an unconditional "war on poverty."

Behind the scenes, Johnson appointed R. Sargent Shriver to take over from Heller a larger task force of 137 experts. Eventually settling on a poverty line of $3,100 for a family of four and $1,500 for a single individual, they concluded that roughly 40 million Americans, over 20 percent of the nation, languished to some degree in poverty. Over 70 percent were white, although half of black citizens and single women with children were poor, as were a third of the elderly.

The first strike came in August 1964, when Congress passed the Economic Opportunity Act of 1964. The centerpiece of Johnson's War on Poverty, the law created the U.S. Office of Economic Opportunity (OEO) to oversee an amazing slate of programs to encourage employment and education. Overseeing the OEO was Shriver. The Head Start program provided free nursery schools for disadvantaged children. The Jobs Corps and the Neighborhood Youth Corps provided jobs and vocational training for young people while the Upward Bound program trained low-income students in the skills they needed for college. Modeled after

Kennedy's Peace Corps, Volunteers in Service to America (VISTA) promoted community service among young people in both poor urban and rural areas. The Community Action Programs (CAPs) encouraged citizens in such communities to become involved and gave them a say in the way federal money was spent. In many communities, these programs involved elected representatives of the poor, together with representatives of local nonprofit organizations and charities. Depending on the mix of representatives, some CAPs became quite radical in their demands, acting independently to challenge other local, established authorities and governments.

Speaking at Ann Arbor, Michigan, Johnson gave a name to his plan: the Great Society. The promise of the Great Society appealed to voters, still reeling in the wake of Kennedy's assassination. In addition, the Republican candidate, Arizona senator Barry Goldwater, scared many voters with his call for dismantling Social Security. He appeared on the fringe, dangerously conservative. The result was a landslide victory for Johnson in the 1964 election. Winning 61 percent of the popular vote and with Democrats gaining in Congress, Johnson demanded further action quickly. Landslide Lyndon, Johnson told his staff, would soon be Lame Duck Lyndon. The Great Society had only begun.

In the next two years, Johnson flooded Congress with proposals, ultimately signing over 400 bills. His first major success, the Elementary and Secondary Education Act, authorized $1 billion to teach impoverished children. The Higher Education Act followed, providing for scholarships to post-secondary education. These bills essentially ended debate over whether the federal government should support education, traditionally the sole responsibility of states. To combat homelessness, Johnson signed the Housing and Urban Development Act, which provided for the construction of 240,000 housing units and $3 billion for urban renewal. Funds for rent subsidies for low-income families came next, as did the creation of the Department of Housing and Urban Development to handle all the money. Johnson selected the first black cabinet member, Robert C. Weaver, to head the new department. Providing an additional $1.1 billion for roads, health clinics, and other public works was the Appalachian Regional Development Act. Additional bills raised the minimum wage, increased Social Security, and in 1967, expanded the modern Food Stamp program.

Perhaps most significant was the Medical Care Act of 1965. Truman's call for a comprehensive plan of medical insurance had languished facing steadfast opposition from the American Medical Association. Now LBJ had the votes to create Medicare. All seniors sixty-five years of age and older had a basic plan that provided up to ninety days of hospital care, 100 days of nursing home care, and 100 home health care visits. A supplemental plan at $3 per month covered a variety of health costs at 80 percent, beyond a $50 co-payment. Surpassing even Truman's proposal, the new law also created Medicaid, a program of free health care to the poor and indigent. The federal government set eligibility requirements and shared expenses with the states, which set the specifics of coverage. General revenues and increases in the Social Security tax, Johnson insisted, covered the costs. Perhaps fittingly, Johnson signed the legislation in Truman's hometown, the aging former president looking on proudly.

President Johnson signs the 1965 Medicare Bill with former President Harry Truman, at right. (LBJ Library)

Johnson had reason for optimism. While the OEO alone spent $750 million in its first year and twice that the following year, the tax cuts appeared to work. The gross national product increased 7 percent in 1964, 8 percent in 1965, and 9 percent in 1966. By then, more than half of families had an income surpassing $7,000. The country, Johnson assumed, could afford his programs. Medicare received positive press with over 19 million elderly citizens enrolled in its first two years, 12 million using it to defray expenses. Also, Congress heeded Johnson's pleas and passed the monumental Civil Rights Act of 1964 and the Voting Rights Act of 1965. All forms of discrimination on the basis of race, gender, or religion were now illegal, with new federal assurances of suffrage rights. The long nonviolent struggle of Martin Luther King, Jr., now had real results, which all assumed would soon quell protests. The Great Society, it appeared, was coming to fruition.

Johnson remained on the attack, pressing the Great Society beyond the war on poverty. New consumer protections, such as automobile safety requirements, became law. A new Department of Transportation controlled millions of dollars for highways and mass transit. A slate of bills to protect the quality of the nation's air, water, and land brought America into the modern environmental age. Immigration legislation jettisoned national quotas. In some of his last major successes impacting the poor, Johnson signed the Demonstration Cities and Metropolitan Area Redevelopment Act and additional housing legislation. The former encouraged central planning in the construction of entire communities while the latter called for the rehabilitation of over 6 million low-income housing units by 1978.

Aided by prosperity, congressional majorities, and sympathetic courts, the Great Society ensured Lyndon Johnson's place in history. It was, according to the magazine *Congressional Quarterly,* a legislative grand slam. Whether history recorded Johnson in a positive or negative light, however, remained to be seen. No one could yet gauge the relative success of his efforts. The turning point in history was the possible success of Johnson's War on Poverty—it would either lead to the Great Society or languish.

ACTUAL HISTORY

If Johnson hoped that the Great Society would bring the nation together in the consensus he craved, it did not take him long to face reality. Confronted with unrestrained liberalism, Republicans cried socialism, and the ardent brand of Goldwater conservatism grew. Among the fierce political debates that followed, Johnson could point to some real progress. The new highways, consumer protections, and environmental regulations won strong bipartisan support. The skies and water became cleaner and the people safer. Even Republicans had difficulty challenging the popularity of such programs as Head Start, which quickly enrolled almost 2 million children.

The larger War on Poverty was not so clear-cut. In one sense, poverty plummeted from 40 million in 1959 to 25 million in 1968, a decrease from 22 percent of the nation's families to 13 percent. African American families saw their income rise to 60 percent of white families. Only 23 percent of black families earned less than the poverty line by the end of Johnson's term, down from over 40 percent at the outset. Poor Americans witnessed a 30 percent reduction in infant mortality and a three-year increase in life expectancy. Undoubtedly, as the Bureau of the Census noted, this improvement had much to do with continued economic growth. As Republicans argued, a rising tide raised all boats. Who, the Democrats then countered, could deny the influence of at least some Great Society programs?

The reality was that despite continued economic growth and the largest single federal effort in history to address the problem, poverty persisted. Millions still languished in miserable slums, ignorant and malnourished. African American unemployment was still double the rate for whites, and among inner-city black youth—the focus of so much of Johnson's efforts—crime and unemployment was triple the level of whites. As if to underline this point, the civil rights movement continued an uncomfortable trend. Having achieved legal equality, a new, younger generation of black leaders pressed for social and economic equality, a tougher challenge not so easily eradicated by a stroke of a pen. Protests did not diminish; they intensified. No longer facing planned, nonviolent campaigns aimed to win the hearts and minds of mainstream Americans, the nation now woke to spontaneous and often violent unrest. Johnson knew this; indeed, he hoped his programs would nip the trend in the

President Johnson meets with civil rights activists at the White House on August 6, 1965. (LBJ Library)

bud. As early as 1965, riots had gripped the Watts area of Los Angeles, five days of flames and destruction televised in color around the world. Thirty-five people died and over 600 buildings were destroyed. The next summer, even though the War on Poverty was in full swing, riots flared in Chicago, New York City, Cleveland, and a number of smaller cities. In July 1967, riots in Detroit lasted for weeks and took the lives of forty people. By the end of Johnson's term, major uprisings had occurred in such states as Indiana, Wisconsin, and Connecticut. The 1968 assassination of Martin Luther King, Jr., caused a riot in Washington, D.C., with dark clouds of smoke blowing over the nation's capital.

By that momentous year, which also included the assassination of Robert Kennedy and a major riot at the Democratic National Convention, it was becoming sadly apparent that the Great Society had real problems. While some programs worked smoothly, persistent administrative disruptions hampered others. Johnson had dramatically expanded the federal bureaucracy but had not changed its culture. Each department and agency worked as its own autonomous fiefdom, each with its own clientele, traditions, and loyalties. Duplication, corruption, and competition were common. On the other hand, adherence to planned procedures made the system unresponsive to emergencies and even to slow changes in technology and the economy. The Job Corps, for example, housed urban black youth in rustic dorms that appeared more like barracks. There they often learned factory skills that were already obsolete. Surveys in 1967 found that 28 percent of graduates were still unemployed six months after completing their training. The Neighborhood Youth Corps employed over 2 million young people but frequently paid them for work already completed or other low-paying, make-work jobs. The media highlighted cases in which school officials found themselves flooded with equipment no one wanted or even knew how to use. Bureaucracy, it seemed, was not very capable of adapting to changes brought on by progress and innovation as was the private sector.

While much of the housing legislation proved beneficial, public housing often took the form of massive high-rise buildings that afforded a poor environment to raise children and gave residents no incentive for upkeep. In addition, projects were frequently in areas that offered minimal employment and inadequate transportation. When communities began urban renewal projects, real estate developers, investors, and moderate-income families often reaped the lion share's of the benefits. Poor blacks were simply moved out of downtown locations to more remote areas. In this way, some critics argued that the programs actually increased racial tensions.

In addition, the traditional powers in the cities—the business executives, mayors, and their political machines—often resisted any institutional change. CAPs were a case in point. City governments saw the program as another way to practice patronage and dispense services, with Washington picking up the tab. Local activists, however, used their new leverage to demand money for programs that did not benefit traditional vested interests. Simply put, they wanted the money spent differently. Tensions between CAPs and local governments simmered. The situation got so bad in Chicago that Mayor Richard J. Daley demanded absolute control over the allocation of funds and accused OEO activists of fostering class struggle. In some cities OEO workers led voter registration drives or rent strikes to pressure local leaders, with political warfare the result. In the end, OEO finally folded in 1974.

Medicare and Medicaid had their own problems. Within ten years of their start, they had provided over $32 million in medical care for the elderly and the poor. There is no doubt that the programs saved the lives of thousands. At the same time, however, the American Medical Association had allowed passage of these bills only after shaping the programs in ways that contributed to skyrocketing health care costs. Physicians' fees and hospital costs soared after enactment. By 1975, the costs of the programs had grown more than 500 percent.

With the problems of the Great Society growing more apparent, liberal Democrats and conservative Republicans pointed to different culprits. Liberals complained that the programs never really addressed the root cause of poverty: unequal income distribution. While spending on social welfare jumped from 7.7 percent of the gross national product just prior to Johnson's presidency to 16 percent just after, approximately three-quarters of the payments went to the non-poor. Medicare, for example, helped all elders regardless of income. Increases in Social Security affected all. Liberals noted that while the total costs for the Aid to Families with Dependent Children program had grown to $5 billion annually, this was only one-sixth of the amount spent on Social Security. Several independent studies, for example, calculated that the Job Corps demanded an expenditure of $11,000 per trainee to be truly successful, a figure far

ANOTHER VIEW   A Similar Future

A successful war on poverty might not have altered the modern political dynamic to any great extent. The Vietnam War would have continued to rage, with no additional funds from a booming economy making any great difference. No influx of new monies would have changed the corrupt South Vietnamese regime or made it more popular among the Vietnamese people. Johnson's escalation of the war would have engendered criticism and protest even if his policies had eradicated poverty. A counterculture continued to grow after all, the product of a youthful baby boom generation coming of age as much as the problems of economic inequality. America would have remained a divided nation, regardless of Johnson's efforts on behalf of the poor. In addition, an end to poverty might have engendered its own problems—for example a flood of new, poor immigrants. This would have further divided the nation. All of this would have frustrated Johnson to the point that he still would not have run in 1968. Nixon still would have won the White House, and Watergate with its many ramifications would still have occurred.

surpassing actual allocations. To detractors, the war on poverty was a phony war; it had not failed but rather had never really begun. At the same time, conservatives complained that the War on Poverty undermined the old Protestant work ethic; it encouraged a dependency on government. Because many low-wage jobs did not provide health insurance, employment often meant the loss of Medicaid. This, they argued, was an incentive not to work. Because marriage often decreased welfare payments, the programs discouraged the formation of traditional families.

Whatever one's political affiliation, no one could deny that the Vietnam War profoundly impacted the War on Poverty. Initially, Johnson and most Americans assumed that the country could afford both "guns and butter." As the 1960s passed and the war escalated, however, the costs rose as quickly as the death toll. As early as 1966, the government was spending almost $22 billion annually on the war. Every dollar, of course, was money that might have gone to the Great Society. In that year, for example, the total cost of the War on Poverty was $1.2 billion, a huge figure but one that still paled by comparison with war expenditures. In addition, disagreements over the war began to split Johnson's liberal coalition, in essence a wedge that affected all policies. Just before his death, King summed up this reality. The Great Society, he said, was killed on the battlefields of Vietnam.

In the end, perhaps Johnson laid the groundwork for his own demise. He did not anticipate the cost of the war, and he simply let expectations grow too high. In almost every instance, in every speech, he seemed to imply that an end to all poverty was not only possible, but achievable in the near future. A letdown was inevitable.

The Vietnam War was now spawning its own violent domestic protests, and combined with criticism of the Great Society, events were too much for Johnson. To the surprise of the nation, he announced that he would not seek reelection in 1968. With a divided Democratic Party arguing over the war, the stage was set for the election of Republican Richard Nixon. Nixon's election that year was due somewhat to Johnson's

War on Poverty. Nixon's vague promises to enforce law and order implied a new, unsympathetic view of protesters, whether such protests agitated for peace or help for the poor. In this sense at least, Nixon represented the beginnings of a backlash to Johnsonian liberalism.

Once in office, Nixon attempted a significant revision of the federal welfare apparatus. His solution, the Family Assistance Plan (FAP), was a novel approach that promised to replace most of the established programs, including Aid to Families with Dependent Children, with a guaranteed annual income for all families. The FAP promised a family of four $1,600, although additional money was possible depending on how much the family earned. For the first time the government offered financial assistance to all low-income earners, not simply services for those who met specific qualifications. As the administration argued, even a family with an income almost twice the established minimum might benefit because of its tax refund and food stamp provisions.

The plan hardly represented the elimination of direct federal efforts to combat poverty, which many of Nixon's most fervent conservative supporters anticipated. Resistance grew in Congress as an unlikely alliance developed between the FAP's Republican critics and liberals, who argued that Nixon's minimal standards actually left the poor worse off than the status quo. As he wrestled with the Vietnam War, ultimately withdrawing American forces, Nixon had little time to defend the FAP and finally dropped the proposal. Focusing on foreign policy, Nixon let domestic issues slip, and after his FAP plan failed, let matters of poverty fall to the Democratic-controlled Congress. While he attempted New Federalism, which called for federal funds in block grants rather than specific federal mandates, he acquiesced to Democrats as they expanded the existing system. Benefits under Medicare and Medicaid grew, and the government finally indexed Social Security payments. Now benefits automatically grew with the rate of inflation.

In addition, new policies began to develop to address racial inequities. Through a series of administrative and court decisions in the 1970s, affirmative action assumed that the government could do more than eliminate discriminatory barriers to individual opportunity; it needed to ensure that a representative number of people from different groups had a reasonable chance for acceptance. This, supporters argued, compensated for historic discrimination and the subtle and hidden racism that persisted. Affirmative action slowly grew as busing students to achieve racial equity in schools increased. Both proved controversial. Affirmative action raised the questions of quotas and reverse discrimination. What should happen if one applicant from a favored group received opportunities not afforded a better qualified competitor? Questions of busing were simpler. Was it fair to bus one child across town to an inferior school just to achieve racial equity? Not surprisingly, such divisive issues ensured that protests continued. In Boston, for example, violence erupted in a protest over busing. These were not easy questions. In one sense, the policies augmented a black middle class. In another, however, resentment festered as the playing field tilted.

A new era of identity politics had begun. Growing from the civil rights movement, other groups began to stress their separate identity. Latinos, Native Americans, gays and lesbians, Asian Americans, and feminists, among others, applied a similar critique to their own situations. Out of this pride in their own distinctive values and cultures came a new assertiveness. Earlier activists had stressed assimilation; now it was almost a doctrine of separation. Litigation exploded, frequently warranted but hardly a homogenizing force. In short, each focusing on his or her own arguably detracted from the unified effort necessary to combat poverty effectively.

As controversy swirled around the continued welfare state, more fundamental threats to the War on Poverty grew. The Vietnam War had significantly increased the national debt, and now, conservatives wielding the budget knife held all the momentum. More significantly, American support for Israel in the Yom Kippur War of 1973 angered the oil-rich Arab states, who united in an oil embargo of America. The long-feared energy crisis had arrived. The United States had grown dangerously dependent on foreign oil and thus the embargo proved quite effective. Prices skyrocketed and consumers faced long lines at the gas pump. Higher fuel prices, in turn, led to rising costs elsewhere. By the end of the decade, inflation wracked the nation, reaching as high as 18 percent. Real wages stagnated for most Americans and actually dropped by 25 percent for young males. Many freshly minted college graduates could now anticipate earning what high school graduates had in previous generations. With unemployment rarely below 7 percent, the public spoke of stagflation.

Nixon struggled with these developments, at one point even resorting to unsuccessful wage and price controls. He had little time or inclination for combating poverty, especially with questions dogging him over his connections to an apparent burglary at the Democratic National Committee headquarters. These questions ultimately proved more than annoying, of course, as they launched the infamous Watergate scandal. Tied in with the cover-up of the crime, Nixon resigned in disgrace in 1974, the first president ever to do so. It was one of the low points in American history. His successor, Vice President Gerald R. Ford, was a capable public servant but was unable to alter the fundamental dynamics of the economy. His slogan "WIN: Whip Inflation Now" did little to change the nation's bleak outlook. In 1976, the anti-incumbent mood swept former Georgia governor Jimmy Carter into the White House. The first Democrat since Johnson, Carter had no intention of reigniting the economic liberalism of his party predecessors and offered no new social welfare initiatives. He did not join his colleagues in advocating universal national health insurance or promoting full employment bills but rather placed his faith in deregulation and in tighter monetary policies. The nation's long post–World War II economic boom was now clearly over— and the nation still had millions of poor to prove it.

Johnson's War on Poverty was a product of this boom, its end the death knell of collective efforts to eradicate poverty. The War on Poverty depended upon optimism, a genuine faith that the federal government could positively affect the lives of the poor. Now the optimism was gone, the victim of a decade of frustration. The Vietnam War was a failure; the government was corrupt; the economy was mired in stagflation. The time appeared right for a new approach, a fresh start. The time was right for Ronald Reagan.

KEY CONCEPT Supply-side Economics/Reaganomics

The popularity of supply-side economics grew from a disillusionment with Keynesian economics and its emphasis on monetary controls and government action to boost consumer spending during recessions. A term first coined by economist Herbert Stein, supply-side economics involved incentives to producers of goods and services, as well as their investors. It assumed that business cycles were caused by lack of credit more than weak demand. Common examples of supply-side incentives included tax cuts for wealthier corporations and individuals, reduction in capital gains taxes, investment tax credits, rapid depreciation allowances, and universal tax-deferred investment retirement accounts. Ronald Reagan adopted a version of supply-side economics first articulated by economist Arthur Laffer. Now known as Reaganomics, this theory of Laffer's argued that reducing tax rates would actually augment federal tax revenue by increasing work, savings, and investment. Reaganomics remains popular in the administration of George W. Bush.

For Reagan, the key to helping the poor was not government but the free market. Deregulation and tax cuts stimulated investment and ultimately jobs—supply-side economics to its supporters and trickle-down economics to its detractors. Government should get out of the way, Reagan insisted. Slashing domestic spending and emasculating most Great Society programs that remained, Reagan exuded confidence. He rebuilt the military and with his sunny, affable personality was undeniably popular. Defeating Carter in 1980, Reagan easily won reelection in 1984. By this point his economic program was, at least in one sense, quite successful. Higher interest rates curbed inflation, and after a recession passed in 1982, the economy once again boomed. The apparent success led to the 1988 election of his vice president, George H. W. Bush. While promising a more compassionate Republicanism, Bush largely followed the playbook of his mentor. Only when he raised taxes late in his term did conservatives complain.

If Bush began to distance himself somewhat from Reaganomics, he did so for a reason. There was, after all, another side to the Reagan legacy. As the economy boomed in the largest peacetime expansion in American history, increased defense expenditures exploded the national debt. In addition, ironically, the number of Americans in poverty actually increased from 11.7 percent in 1980 to 15 percent in 1992. While millions prospered, a minority simply fell further behind. By 1992, the richest 5 percent saw their percentage share of the nation's aggregate family income increase to 17.6 percent, up from 15.3 percent in 1980. The poorest 20 percent, however, saw theirs decline from 5.1 percent to 4.4 percent. Justifying neo–laissez faire policies, conservatives stressed the complicity of the poor in their situation, the mythical welfare queen driving a Cadillac.

It was not Social Darwinism reborn, however, because the new conservatives stressed the importance of private charity. Bush, for one, spoke of a thousand points of light to characterize volunteers. While charitable organizations had indeed become more efficient by the 1990s, overly bureaucratic administrations and redundancy still remained. Large food corporations had themselves become more efficient in processing damaged goods and now marketed them in wholesale rather than making donations. Charities simply could not keep up. The problem compounded when a movement grew to de-institutionalize mental heath care. Soon mentally ill patients swelled the homeless populations in many large cities. Frustrated with government inaction and their continued plight, thousands rioted in Los Angeles in 1992, costing sixty people their lives and once again exposing the forgotten underbelly of prosperous America.

Prosperity continued to breed conservatism. The 1992 election of the first Democrat since Carter, Bill Clinton, hardly revitalized liberalism. Touting himself as a New Democrat, Clinton reflected the conservative consensus on poverty. While he tried unsuccessfully to institute universal health care, he signed the Personal Responsibility and Work Opportunity Act of 1996. This monumental legislation represented a dramatic reversal of the social policy that Johnson had championed a generation before. It abolished the government's pledge to ensure a minimum level of subsistence and replaced it with a system of grants to states. Recipients could count on two years of job training, but then, barring an unusually high unemployment rate, faced a curtailment of benefits. The law also set a lifetime limit of aid at five years. If there were any doubts before that Johnson's War on Poverty was over, they were quickly laid to rest.

Entering the twenty-first century, the poor remained, although the will to address the problem did not. Poverty remained a part of American life, although it was conveniently forgotten by the majority. It was as if the Michael Harrington book that had so inspired Johnson's War on Poverty still applied; not much had changed. Americans wrung their hands when Hurricane Katrina in 2005 exposed the horrible conditions of the poor in New Orleans, but then went about their business. Poverty was here to stay.

ALTERNATE HISTORY

Johnson might have moved quickly to address the problems of the Great Society, and perhaps, might have achieved his goal of eradicating poverty. In his years in the Senate, Johnson had been the master tactician. He had involved himself in every legislative detail and knew exactly when to use flattery or threats. He had employed the "Johnson treatment," which used his large frame to intimidate opponents. As president, Johnson continued to use such tactics to his advantage, cornering senators or congressmen in the Capitol. Had he involved himself to a greater degree within the bureaucracy itself, however, he might have corrected the redundancy and corruption so prevalent in many of his programs. Had he been more personally involved in the actual implementation of his legislation, he might have intimidated mayors such as Richard J. Daley or wooed community activists as part of a successful mediation.

Better administrative controls would have recognized that the Great Society's large public housing projects needed to be near affordable public transportation, that tenants in such projects needed an ownership interest to ensure the required maintenance. Redevelopment would not have simply dispersed poor minorities and broken up neighborhoods but rather would have given real credence to CAPs. Revisions in the food stamp and other welfare programs would have ensured that the majority of funds went to the truly needy and not become middle-class entitlements. Programs with proven records such as Head Start would have seen their budgets expanded. Throughout it all, Johnson might have taken a broader perspective. Rather than rapidly implementing a wide range of programs in the fear of losing his political mandate, he might have moved more slowly, working harder to win political consensus. If Republicans had felt more included in the process, resistance could have diminished.

This would have provided a real opportunity to correct the problems of Medicare and Medicaid. Working with the American Medical Association, negotiating with doctors and their lobby personally, Johnson might have restricted some of the soaring hospital and physician fees associated with these programs. This, in turn, would have restricted the costs to the states and private businesses, ensuring adequate health care for the elderly and indigent. Unlike in recent years, more employers could have afforded to keep decent health insurance for their workers. Hospitals would have no longer faced treating such large numbers of uninsured Americans in their emergency rooms and thus would have reduced their charges. In the end, more Americans would have received preventive health care, thereby avoiding long-term disability and disease. The benefits of this government-based health insurance program might have eventually led to the passage of a universal health insurance plan, such as the one Clinton unsuccessfully proposed. Unlike today, when over 40 million Americans are uninsured, all Americans might then count on the care they needed.

The success of Johnson's War on Poverty would have had implications far beyond simply health care. Since minorities were disproportionately in poverty, racial relations would have dramatically improved. Infant mortality and crime rates would have dropped more than they did, while literacy would have increased even further. Expanded education would have opened new avenues for advancement, with potentially new industries the result. There would have been more African American college graduates and, in time, a much larger black middle class. Areas with large black populations, such as the South, would have enjoyed an even greater economic boom. The last remnants of segregation would have diminished more quickly than they did. With increased buying power, African Americans would have enjoyed more economic clout while businesses that catered to that market would have prospered.

Contentment would have muted the rise of more militant civil rights leaders. Riots in such places as Watts, Chicago, or New York City might never had occurred. If protests had developed, they would never have spread so rapidly; there simply would not have been the anger that fueled them. Without scenes of violent protest, Americans would have enjoyed a greater sense of community and unity. Without poverty, there would have been more equity in schools, and thus less need for busing. Every student might have found a suitable school near his or her own home, with no need for protests such as occurred in Boston.

Affirmative action would have been unnecessary. With everyone prospering, the problems of quotas or reverse discrimination would have been negligible. There would have been less identity politics and its accompanying resentment. All of this would have meant less litigation. Martin Luther King, Jr., might have felt no need to continue his campaign past the Civil Rights Act of 1964 or the Voting Rights Act of 1965. Legal segregation ended with these monumental laws, after all, while the success of the Great Society would have addressed many of the remaining social and economic inequalities. Retiring to a simple life of a minister, or perhaps writing his memoirs, King might never have faced an assassin's bullet. America would never have experienced the riots that rocked the nation after his death.

The inner cities might have witnessed a renaissance. Rather than having abandoned housing and dilapidated buildings, downtowns would have remained vibrant. Restaurants, entertainment venues, and an array of service industries would have spread throughout refurbished apartment buildings and condos. Cities that suffered a particularly high rate of exodus, such as Detroit or Washington, D.C., would have seen their populations remain stable or even grow. This, in turn, would have affected congressional representation. Meanwhile, because sleek mass transit would have transported workers easily, suburban sprawl might have slowed, resulting in more appropriate land use. Combined with the Great Society's already successful anti-pollution laws, the nation's environment would have benefited.

Surging government revenues from a successful War on Poverty would have dramatically expanded possibilities. Simply put, more people working would have meant more money from taxes. The booming economy would have decreased the deficit and, in time, created years of surpluses. The happy question then facing lawmakers would have been how to spend the money. Pleasing conservatives, the government might have reacted by lowering tax rates or granting rebates. This, in turn, would have provided a further economic stimulus. On the other end of the political spectrum, the government might have launched a number of new federal ventures, such as increased foreign aid. This would have solidified American allies in the Cold War and improved the economies of the underdeveloped world. A flourishing international trade might have resulted. At the very least, the United States would have been able to fund new defense systems without running into the red and billing future generations.

When the Arab oil embargo resulted in the energy crisis of the 1970s, Americans might have had the funds for a true program of energy independence. They would have had the ability, after all, to pay for new domestic drilling or for the development of alternative fuels. They could have paid compensation for workers displaced as the economy moved away from fossil-based fuels, or they could have funded a massive conservation program. Without as much dependence on the oil of Middle Eastern nations, the United States might have enjoyed more flexibility in its policies toward that volatile region.

In an alternate history, Lyndon Johnson might have been regarded as one of the greatest men to have served in the office of president. (Library of Congress)

In one scenario, at least, the additional revenue might have aided in the defense of South Vietnam. There would have been more money for economic aid or for the military. Without poverty or as much racial or ethnic tension, protests against the war might have appeared more benign. While a number of other factors were certainly at play, a more united America might even have succeeded in stemming the advancement of the communist troops and accomplished a permanent division of the nation, similar to that which took place in Korea.

The success of the War on Poverty certainly would have confirmed the wisdom of Keynesian economics, which would have remained the guiding economic principle of the nation. Johnson most likely would have run and won in the 1968 election. If the Vietnam War had persisted, the election would have undoubtedly still been close. Nevertheless, economic contentment would have trumped international distress. Johnson would not have been regarded as a tragic figure but, in many respects, as one of the greatest presidents in American history. There might even have been a Johnson monument in Washington. Johnson's victory over poverty would have ensured the continued dominance of the Democratic Party, which could have justifiably campaigned as the champion of the everyday people. Richard Nixon probably never would have won the presidency, and there never would have been any need for his FAP. More important, there never would have been a Watergate scandal. The nation would have been spared that agonizing ordeal, with all of its ramifications. Without Watergate, any number of political scenarios might have unfolded. Ford most likely would have remained in Congress, never having gained the true national spotlight. Without public disgust at political corruption, Carter might have remained in Georgia. Leading Democrats such as Senator Edmund Muskie of Maine or Senator Ted Kennedy of Massachusetts might have won the White House. They would have been, after all, the established leaders of a dominant political party.

It is reasonable to assume that if Johnson had run for a second term, he would have retained Hubert Humphrey as his vice presidential candidate. Known as a strong liberal with a record of support for civil rights legislation, Humphrey might very well have run for and been elected president in 1972. Three days after Humphrey's inauguration, Lyndon Johnson would have died, on January 23, 1973. The national mourning for Johnson, like the earlier mourning for Kennedy, could easily have provided the new president, Humphrey, with the emotional and political tools to further advance the Kennedy-Johnson civil rights and anti-poverty agenda.

A booming economy, soaring surpluses, and the dominance of the Democratic Party probably would have denied Ronald Reagan the presidency. The new conservatism so powerful in recent years would have remained a minority view. Reaganomics would have stayed a theory, and there never would have been the welfare reform legislation of 1996.

In the end, an America without poverty would have been an America much different from the country today. It is difficult to predict with certainty what would have unfolded because the United States has never seen an end to poverty. The possibilities, nevertheless, are endless.

J. Brooks Flippen

Discussion Questions

1. Is poverty inevitable in a capitalist society like the United States?
2. Was the War on Poverty doomed because of its goals, or because of a variety of administrative failures?
3. Can poverty be addressed and eliminated by the establishment of bureaucracies, or only ameliorated?
4. What factor do you think was most significant in stalling the War on Poverty? Was it lack of political will, the focus on the Vietnam War, internal flaws in the method itself, or some other factor?
5. Who have had more success in battling poverty, conservatives or liberals?

Bibliography and Further Reading

Beschloss, Michael R., ed. *Taking Charge: The Johnson White House Tapes, 1963–1964.* New York: Simon and Schuster, 1997.

Branyon, Robert L., and R. Alron Lee. "Lyndon Johnson and the Art of the Possible." *Southwestern Social Science Quarterly* 45 (December 1964): 213–225.

Burton, Emory. *The Poverty Debate: Politics and the Poor in America.* Westport, CT: Greenwood Press, 1999.

Conklin, Paul K. *Big Daddy from the Pedernales: Lyndon Baines Johnson.* Boston, MA: Twayne, 1986.

Dallek, Robert. *Flawed Giant: Lyndon Johnson and His Times, 1961–1973.* New York: Oxford University Press, 1998.

Dugger, Ronnie. *The Politician: The Life and Times of Lyndon Johnson.* New York: W.W. Norton, 1982.

Frezzo, Mark. "Keynesian Economics." In Cynthia Northrup, ed., *The American Economy.* Santa Barbara, CA: ABC-CLIO, 2003.

Goodwin, Doris Kearns. *Lyndon Johnson and the American Dream.* New York: Harper and Row, 1976.

Harrington, Michael. *The Other America: Poverty in the United States.* New York: Macmillan, 1962.

Hooks, Bell. *Where We Stand: Class Matters.* New York: Routledge, 2000.

Page, Benjamin, and James Roy Simmons. *What Government Can Do: Dealing with Poverty and Inequality.* Chicago: University of Chicago Press, 2000.

Rodgers, Harrell R. *American Poverty in a New Era of Reform.* Armonk, NY: M.E. Sharpe, 2000.

Sicilia, David B. "Supply-Side Economics." In Cynthia Northrup, ed., *The American Economy.* Santa Barbara, CA: ABC-CLIO, 2003.

TURNING POINT

What if President Johnson had not engaged in escalation and South Vietnam had fallen to communists in 1966?

INTRODUCTION

The Vietnam War—sometimes called simply "the conflict in Vietnam," as no declaration of war was ever made by the United States—was, on one level, a war fought between communist North Vietnam (the Democratic Republic of Vietnam) and South Vietnam (the Republic of Vietnam). On another level, it was drawn into the international politics of the Cold War and became a proxy war fought between the United States (and its allies) and North Vietnam's communist allies, the Soviet Union and the People's Republic of China.

In the United States especially, the language of proxy wars drove policy: the war was fought not simply against the Vietnamese but against forces of communism threatening to conquer all of Southeast Asia. The Korean War had been fought for similar reasons, and the first American military advisors to the South Vietnamese army were deployed only two years after the Korean War armistice. The American involvement in Vietnam escalated over time from the provision of noncombatant advisors to the use of special forces in special situations to ordinary troops in defensive combat—until finally, in the biggest wave of escalation, offensive troops were deployed in great number.

After World War II, both the scope and the specifics of the international community had changed. The old European empires came to an end, the United States—bolstered by newly demonstrated military might and a powerful postwar economy—was the leading superpower, and the conflict between capitalism and communism took center stage. The United States abandoned its previous policies of isolationism and took an active role in global politics, NATO (North Atlantic Treaty Organization), and the United Nations, while the Soviet Union offered its support to communist movements around the world. In the years immediately after the war, China and Greece both fought civil wars between communist and conservative factions, with the communists winning in China (except for a small amount of territory) and losing in Greece. The People's Republic

ANOTHER VIEW   As Goes Vietnam…

There's no compelling evidence to support initial fears that if Vietnam had fallen to communism, the rest of Southeast Asia would have followed. But perhaps drawing the war out exhausted North Vietnam's capabilities and demonstrated an American commitment to anti-communism that dissuaded expansionism and similar aims. What if a 1966 withdrawal had in fact led to an expansion of Southeast Asian communism?

Cambodia and Laos would have fallen quickly, both possessing their own internal communist movements. If it remained clear that the United States would leave Southeast Asia to fend for itself, the region could have become the proving ground for a different sort of proxy war, a Sino-Soviet proxy war, with the People's Republic of China and the Soviet Union vying to adopt and create satellite states. Burma (now Myanmar) would have followed Cambodia and Laos. Thailand would have had to be invaded by force and would have been a difficult defeat, but serious support from either the Soviets or the Chinese would have made it a winnable war.

A greater conflict would have been inevitable: Burma borders India and Bangladesh.

Malaysia and Indonesia, south of Thailand, would have spread communism close to Australia and would have virtually surrounded U.S. allies, including the Philippines, the oil-rich Sultanate of Brunei, and the former British colony the Republic of Singapore. War would have been unlikely. More plausibly, like the situation in Eastern Europe, some definite boundaries of containment would have been set up, with Western intermediate-range missiles based in adjacent countries. American relations with India would have become more important, and Australia would have become more active strategically. Perhaps most important to the long term, American attention would have remained focused on Asian communism to a degree it did not in actual history, where Soviet communism was so often treated as the sole power at the other end of the table. The domino world would have been far less relieved by the collapse of the Soviet Union, though its satellites in Southeast Asia would perhaps have converted to free markets, breaking up the solid bloc of communist states in the region.

of China was a large and powerful communist presence, the very existence of which greatly affected the international perception of communism as a force that would spread across the globe one nation at a time, with countries falling to communism like aligned dominoes.

The "dominoes" continued to fall from efforts by the Soviet Union as well, with communist governments established across Eastern Europe in Bulgaria, Hungary, Poland, and Romania. Germany was divided into East and West, communist and capitalist, as was its capital city Berlin. Communist parties grew in power and support in Central America, Belgium, Czechoslovakia, Finland, and Italy, and the Soviet Union briefly created a Kurdish communist state within the borders of Iran. It is easy to see why the Western world developed a paranoia toward communism, given how quickly it grew in power in some parts of the world—and that paranoia was a guiding force behind the events of the Korean War in the early 1950s.

World War II had ended the Japanese occupation of Korea that had persisted since 1910, and in its aftermath the United States and the Soviet Union jointly occupied the country, creating two states—one in the north, one in the south—each of which claimed jurisdiction over the other. The Soviet-backed northern state was communist and dictatorial, nationalizing its industries, which were more heavily concentrated than in the largely agrarian south. The American-backed southern state adopted a liberal democracy after the American authorities refused to acknowledge the validity of any indigenous communist government. Foreign troops withdrew by the end of the 1940s, and in retrospect it seems inevitable that the two Korean states should go to war: North Korea invaded South Korea in 1950, and although the war has never officially ended, the fighting lasted three years. During that time, South Korea enjoyed the military and economic support of the United States, the United Kingdom, Canada, Turkey, and groups operating in the name of the United Nations; North Korea had the support of the Soviet Union and the People's Republic of China.

Approximately 600,000 Korean soldiers died, and three times as many civilians. American troops were for a period instructed to treat Korean civilians on a battlefield as hostiles, and numerous refugees were killed under suspicion of being communist spies. North Korean and Soviet forces, meanwhile, violated numerous Geneva Convention proscriptions, instituting mass political slaughters and mistreating its prisoners of war, sometimes in "re-education camps." The fighting ended with the creation of a demilitarized zone between North and South Korea, which has persisted into the twenty-first century.

Only six years after the Korean War, the Cuban revolution established a communist government led by Fidel Castro—who, like many communist revolutionaries, included American statesmen like Franklin Delano Roosevelt among his heroes—and the newly communist Cuba began to establish a relationship with the Soviet Union. Cuba is extremely close to the United States and had long enjoyed friendly American relations; the proximity of a Soviet-friendly communist state did not sit well with any American administration. In 1961, newly inaugurated President John F. Kennedy authorized the Bay of Pigs invasion, first recommended under the Eisenhower administration: a plan to overthrow Castro. The attempt failed badly, resulting in the execution of many Cuban exiles, the resignations of leading Central Intelligence Agency (CIA) officials, and the necessity of negotiating with Castro for the release of more than 1,000 prisoners.

A year later, Soviet nuclear missiles were deployed to Cuba, where they were to be installed after the United States installed similar warheads in Europe and Turkey. For thirteen days, war—or at least military action directly against Soviet missiles and forces—seemed possible, and after a naval blockade was established by American forces, Soviet Premier Nikita Khrushchev offered Kennedy two deals: the missiles would be withdrawn if the United States agreed not to invade Cuba, or, as the second deal demanded, if the United States additionally removed its missiles from Turkey. Kennedy agreed to both conditions, though kept the removal of missiles from Turkey secret for political reasons. He would later credit the Cuban missile crisis with keeping the United States out of Vietnam during his term of office (at least to the extent it would become involved under the Lyndon Johnson administration).

A French colony since the nineteenth century with a long history of struggle against China after gaining independence from it in 938 C.E., Vietnam was briefly occupied by Japan during World War II. For most of the period of occupation, Japan allowed the French bureaucrats who had been operating the colonial government to continue to do so, but late in the war the Japanese imprisoned the French and granted Vietnam nominal independence. After the Japanese surrender, a nationalist group led by Ho Chi Minh tried to establish a Vietnamese government, but it was effectively dissolved when Chinese and British troops arrived to supervise the Japanese exit from the region. French control was reestablished, and negotiations with Minh failed. In 1950, the Soviet Union and the People's Republic of China recognized Ho Chi Minh's communist state of the Democratic Republic of Vietnam, located in the northern part of the country. When the French withdrew later in the decade, the anti-communist Republic of Vietnam was established in the south, and the Geneva Accord called for elections meant to unify the country.

Ho Chi Minh, born Nguyen Sinh Cung in 1890, was raised a Confucian (a follower of Chinese philosopher Confucius) and spent his twenties traveling the world; reportedly he took odd jobs in England, Boston, New York City, and France, where he became a communist in the years following World War I. He helped in the formation of the French Communist Party and petitioned various statesmen to consider the plight of the Vietnamese in what was then known to the West as French Indochina. In 1930 he founded the Communist Party of Indochina and followed that with the Vietminh independence movement eleven years later, fighting for independence first from the Japanese and later from the French. It was the Vietminh who put him in power in the lull between Japanese and French rule. Ho Chi Minh took inspiration not only from communist victories of the past but also from America's revolutionary origins, and he believed that the American government and people should be sympathetic to Vietnam's status as an oppressed colonial holding. Before the Vietnam War, he made many appeals for aid to American presidents, and when he declared the founding of Vietnam's new independent government, he quoted from the American Declaration of Independence and played the "Star-Spangled Banner."

As a response to Ho Chi Minh's new communist government, the founding of South Vietnam was strongly tied to the Cold War and the U.S. need to establish an anti-communist base in Southeast Asia. The United States and South Vietnamese president Ngo Dinh Diem opposed the Geneva-required elections, arguing that they would be rigged by northern communists; Diem retained American-supported power as a result, but Ho Chi Minh's state continued as well. Diem's popularity among his own people is a matter of historical debate; American intelligence and diplomacy at the time paid little attention to indications that Diem was unpopular even among those who did not support and were not compelled by the northern communists. It is difficult as a result to be sure of the extent of Diem's support among not only southern Vietnamese but also nonsocialist Vietnamese. When Diem's anti-Buddhist policies escalated (he publicly suspected a general Buddhist-communist alliance), the United States privately agreed not to interfere with a coup meant to remove Diem from power. He was assassinated in the process, twenty days before President Kennedy's own assassination.

This was a crucial point for both Vietnam and the United States: American complicity in the coup and in the circumstances that resulted in Diem's assassination entangled the two countries together. The new South Vietnamese government needed the American military to defend itself; the Americans needed an anti-communist government to defend in Vietnam.

IN CONTEXT   Veterans

A side effect of the anti-war movements was the poor treatment of many veterans when they returned home from the Vietnam War, or when on furlough. Especially after My Lai and journalistic coverage of some of the atrocities committed by Americans in Southeast Asia, veterans faced the prospect of jeers and abuse as they returned to their native soil. Vietnam veterans had, on average, seen more combat than veterans of previous wars; had received better training and were more likely to be educated; but they were often treated and portrayed practically as criminals. At a time when recreational drug use was on the increase in the United States, soldiers found themselves in a country where drugs were cheap and widely available, and by the 1970s heroin use in particular was significantly higher among soldiers than in the civilian population.

Fewer than 1 percent of the soldiers exposed to Agent Orange received compensation. The many soldiers suffering from post-traumatic stress disorder (PTSD)—previously called shell shock and encompassing "flashbacks"—rarely received treatment for, or even acknowledgment of, the condition. Scientists realize now that the apparent increase in PTSD among Vietnam veterans compared to veterans of previous wars is probably due in part to the greater combat exposure of Vietnam veterans. World War II was still a recent memory for many, and though the Korean War had not been a success, it had at least been relatively brief. Popular culture portrayed the Vietnam veteran as a loner, an outsider, on the edge—movies like *Billy Jack* and *First Blood* made him a vigilante of sorts, but eventually in the 1980s, the archetype was absolved, with TV shows like *The A-Team* and movies like *Missing in Action* portraying the soldiers in Vietnam as misunderstood heroes whose government had abandoned them. The war was an especially popular subject for movies in the mid to late 1980s, with *Platoon* cited by critics as the best and most accurate of that wave of blockbusters.

Following the establishment of South Vietnam, the American government began to lend the country military assistance to defend itself against North Vietnam. Military advisors had previously worked with the French during their control of the area, but in 1955, President Dwight D. Eisenhower authorized the deployment of the first advisors sent specifically to train the South Vietnamese military (ARVN, the Army of the Republic of Vietnam). This was the source of some early criticism of American involvement in Vietnam: the same military forces trained by American advisors were responsible for the persecution of various religious groups throughout the country, including Buddhists and the Caodaiists, members of a syncretic religion combining elements of Buddhism, Catholicism, Taoism, and Confucianism.

Three years later, North Vietnam invaded neighboring Laos—Laos and Cambodia would continue to be involved in the moves of the Vietnam War—and South Vietnamese communists formed the National Liberation Front of South Vietnam (NLF) to fight a guerrilla war against the South Vietnamese government, which called the NLF the Viet Cong (for Vietnamese communist). The United States responded by sending more advisors to South Vietnam, the first of many escalating moves. Eisenhower's successor, Kennedy, authorized the use of chemical weapons in Vietnam, including the famous Agent Orange. It and the other dioxin-based "rainbow herbicides" were used from 1961 to 1973, decimating more than a tenth of South Vietnam. The rainbow herbicides have been the subject of much controversy, not only because of birth defects among the Vietnamese after the use of these chemicals in the country but also because of the exposure of U.S. soldiers to the chemicals, resulting in cancer, genetic damage, and other ailments.

TURNING POINT

American involvement in Vietnam was slow to escalate, with each American president inching things along as the war progressed. At the end of 1958, when North Vietnam invaded Laos, it seemed to lend some credence to the notion that if communism was "allowed an inch, it would take a mile." The essential American policy, though, was one of containment: the enforcement of isolation on a communist regime, in the hope that it would not only fail to spread—halting the so-called domino effect—but would wither and die. Confining communism to existing communist countries was the principal goal of American foreign policy throughout the early decades of the Cold War.

As the war continued, containment took more and more resources. In 1961, Kennedy authorized the Special Forces of the U.S. Army to wear green berets—with which they quickly became synonymous, thanks in part to the 1968 pro-war movie *The Green Berets* directed by and starring John Wayne—and assigned them as special advisors to the South

Secretary of Defense Robert McNamara points to a map of Southeast Asia during a press conference in 1965. (Library of Congress)

KEY CONCEPT   Transcript of Gulf of Tonkin Resolution (1964)

Eighty-eighth Congress of the United States of America

At the Second Session

Begun and held at the City of Washington on Tuesday, the seventh day of January, one thousand nine hundred and sixty-four

Joint Resolution

To promote the maintenance of international peace and security in southeast Asia.

Whereas naval units of the Communist regime in Vietnam, in violation of the principles of the Charter of the United Nations and of international law, have deliberately and repeatedly attacked United States naval vessels lawfully present in international waters, and have thereby created a serious threat to international peace; and

Whereas these attackers are part of a deliberate and systematic campaign of aggression that the Communist regime in North Vietnam has been waging against its neighbors and the nations joined with them in the collective defense of their freedom; and

Whereas the United States is assisting the peoples of southeast Asia to protect their freedom and has no territorial, military or political ambitions in that area, but desires only that these people should be left in peace to work out their destinies in their own way: Now, therefore be it

Resolved by the Senate and House of Representatives of the United States of America in Congress assembled, That the Congress approves and supports the determination of the President, as Commander in Chief, to take all necessary measures to repel any armed attack against the forces of the United States and to prevent further aggression.

Section 2. The United States regards as vital to its national interest and to world peace the maintenance of international peace and security in southeast Asia. Consonant with the Constitution of the United States and the Charter of the United Nations and in accordance with its obligations under the Southeast Asia Collective Defense Treaty, the United States is, therefore, prepared, as the President determines, to take all necessary steps, including the use of armed force, to assist any member or protocol state of the Southeast Asia Collective Defense Treaty requesting assistance in defense of its freedom.

Section 3. This resolution shall expire when the President shall determine that the peace and security of the area is reasonably assured by international conditions created by action of the United Nations or otherwise, except that it may be terminated earlier by concurrent resolution of the Congress.

Vietnamese. Secretary of Defense Robert McNamara recommended sending 200,000 troops in response to NLF attacks and the concern that the NLF's actions in South Vietnam would make defense against North Vietnam even more difficult.

A year later, Kennedy signed the Foreign Assistance Act, which reinforced the American policy of assisting countries "on the rim of the communist world" when they were threatened by communism. Though Kennedy's feelings were informed by unsuccessful talks with Khrushchev and the growing belief that Southeast Asia would be the battleground of a Soviet/American proxy war, the "communist world" in this case was the People's Republic of China. American policy makers would be criticized for decades by experts on Southeast Asia for their apparent belief that a communist Vietnam would be a puppet or satellite for communist China—despite the millennia of struggle between the Vietnamese and their former Chinese overlords.

By 1963, some Americans were already calling for Vietnam to be fought to a clear victory or abandoned. Arizona Senator Barry Goldwater advocated an aggressive approach to Vietnam, which became part of his platform in his 1964 presidential campaign against Johnson, Kennedy's vice president and successor after his assassination. Johnson won the election, and the decision of how to deal with Vietnam fell to him. The Gulf of Tonkin incident in early August 1964 would prove to be, at least in the public view of things, the turning point of the war. From August 2 to August 4, the North Vietnamese were alleged to be responsible for a pair of attacks on the USS *Maddox* and the USS *C. Turner Joy,* both of them destroyers in the Gulf of Tonkin. The attack on the *Maddox* occurred in a part of the gulf the United States maintained was in international waters while the North Vietnamese claimed it as part of their territory. Whatever the accuracy of the territorial dispute, the *Maddox* was struck by only a single bullet, after evading a fired torpedo. There apparently was no organized attack.

Secretary McNamara, though, characterized the incident as an unprovoked attack and presented a case for retaliation to Congress, which passed the Gulf of Tonkin Resolution. The resolution granted Johnson the ability to take all necessary steps, including the use of armed force in Southeast Asia, and allowed the Vietnam conflict to progress and escalate without a declaration of war.

ACTUAL HISTORY

Johnson escalated American presence in Vietnam quickly and steadily, under the supervision of General William Westmoreland, who he appointed commander of military operations in Vietnam. From 1964 to 1968, the American military presence rose from 16,000 soldiers to 500,000 at the time of the Tet Offensive. The first combat troops arrived in South Vietnam on March 8, 1965: 3,500 Marines joining the 20,000 advisors present. The rapid increase of American troops forced North Vietnam to change its strategies (the Tet Offensive was eventually an example of its new aggressive approach).

Bombing was a cornerstone of the escalation plan. All in all, the United States dropped more bombs in Vietnam than it did in World War II. From 1965 to 1968, Operation Rolling Thunder conducted a sustained bombing campaign against North Vietnam (followed in 1972 by Operation Linebacker and Operation Linebacker II). By destroying North Vietnamese surface-to-air missiles and bases of operations, McNamara and Westmoreland hoped to destroy the morale of the North Vietnamese as well.

Under Johnson's direction, measures were taken to avoid possible attacks on citizens and soldiers of other countries, such as the Soviet advisors working with the North Vietnamese

U.S. Air Force F-105 Thunderchief pilots bomb a military target through low clouds over North Vietnam on June 14, 1966. (National Archives and Records Administration)

military. Zones heavily populated by civilians were eventually approved for attack, though, in order to maintain the pace of escalation. Both the Air Force and the Navy participated in Rolling Thunder, but by the time of the Tet Offensive, McNamara was no longer confident the war could be won from the air. His management of the operation and Johnson's call for pauses in the bombing while diplomatic approaches were attempted have both been cited as likely factors in the operation's failure.

In 1965, the Soviet Union began supplying North Vietnam with anti-aircraft munitions, in response to Rolling Thunder and American air strikes. That August, Operation Starlite launched the first major ground battle (air and naval units were also involved) without South Vietnamese troops: nearly 6,000 Marines struck a Vietcong base. Though American casualties were only one-twelfth of the Vietnamese casualties, the Marines failed to destroy the Vietcong 1st Regiment, as had been hoped. The win was decisive enough to discourage the Vietcong from large-scale battles in the future, and most Vietcong actions were guerilla-style, with small units. (Starlite was supposed to be named Satellite; a clerical error during a power outage misnamed it at the last minute.)

By 1967, an increasing percentage of the American public was unhappy with the American involvement in Vietnam—not just those participating in protest movements but moderates as well. Johnson's reassurances that the enemy's losses were greater than America's did not appease them, especially when many questioned the wisdom and practicality of being in Southeast Asia to begin with. American successes were generally considered in terms of body count rather than tactical objectives, a metric muddied by the issue of civilian casualties and the frequent difficulty of positively identifying Vietcong, and the reports of successes and victories from American officials clashed with the public's perception that the war was dragging on with no apparent progress. Two major events of 1968 exacerbated this: the Tet Offensive and the My Lai massacre.

The Tet Offensive was a North Vietnamese/NLF attack launched in Saigon (the capital of South Vietnam) on the eve of January 30, 1968—Tet, the celebration of the lunar new year. Related operations continued sporadically for the next year and a half, but the immediate attacks on Saigon were the most important. A cease-fire had been declared from January 27 to February 3 for the holiday, but during this time the NLF struck a number of strategic targets in Saigon, including the American embassy and President Thieu's office. The soldiers included many Vietcong members who had been secretly employed in the city, and the attack on the embassy was especially noteworthy because the guard had not been informed of the attacks elsewhere in the city, and as such had not been reinforced.

The fighting in Saigon lasted three days, ending quickly in most places. The North and the NLF achieved none of their tactical goals, but the mere fact of the attack—and the vulnerability of the American embassy—seemed to fly in the face of Westmoreland's earlier assurances of American dominance and his declaration that American troops could leave Vietnam as early as 1969. The war very clearly was far from being won, and Johnson's approval rating plummeted.

The My Lai massacre made things worse. After the Tet Offensive, U.S. intelligence believed that members of the 48th battalion of the NLF had taken refuge in the village of My Lai, in the Quang Ngai province of South Vietnam, home of many NLF members and target of frequent bombing by Rolling Thunder. Charlie Company, 1st Battalion, 20th Infantry Regiment, 11th Brigade, Americal Division was assigned to destroy the village on March 16, 1968, and told to assume anyone present was Vietcong or a communist sympathizer. No obvious NLF members were found, but hundreds of civilians were killed, including babies and the elderly. Some were thrown into ditches and executed with automatic weapons; others were reportedly killed with hand grenades. The killing continued until a U.S. Army helicopter intervened, its pilot—Hugh Thompson, Jr.—demanding that the attack end and promising to open fire on Charlie Company if they persisted. Charlie Company's soldiers reported that they acted as instructed, and that every Vietnamese in the village was to be considered a deadly threat; it is unclear whether intelligence included women and children in the attack order.

My Lai was initially reported as a U.S. military victory, with a small number of admitted civilian casualties; later, soldiers accusing the military of casual brutality against Vietnamese civilians sparked an investigation by Major Colin Powell (future secretary of state) and a separate investigation by Congressman Morris Udall. Twenty-six men were charged with premeditated murder and related crimes for their participation in the My Lai massacre. The American public was outraged, with the numbers of conscientious objectors among potential draftees soaring and the peace movement reaching its peak of strength. Only Lieutenant William Calley, Charlie Company's leader, was convicted; he served less than four years of house arrest at Fort Benning before being released. In contradiction to the standards set by war trials in the aftermath of World War II, Calley's sentence was reduced because of his belief that he was following orders (though his commanding officer was cleared of charges, and no charges were brought against the men who had given the orders to destroy the village).

For some, the poor command of Charlie Company was a symptom of a problem beginning to plague the American military in Vietnam: the brightest, most competent officers were being replaced due to injury and attrition by increasingly less competent men. Whether this was in fact the case or if the errors lay with the chain of command or other areas, it had a poor effect on public perception. The image of American soldiers killing babies became emblematic for the anti-war movements, which were no longer limited to small groups of college students. The chant "LBJ, LBJ, how many kids did you kill today?" was cried out at many demonstrations, and the unpopularity of the war undoubtedly contributed to Johnson's decision not to run for reelection. Senator Robert Kennedy, brother of President John Kennedy, joined the race for the Democratic nomination when Johnson dropped out, and was assassinated by Sirhan Sirhan. Johnson's vice president, Hubert Humphrey, ultimately took the nomination and lost to Eisenhower's vice president, Richard Nixon, who ran on an anti-counterculture platform and promised to hand the reins of the Vietnam War over to South Vietnam. Unlike many anti-war factions, Nixon presented at least the premise of a plan to extract troops from the country without losing the war in the process.

President Lyndon B. Johnson awards the Distinguished Cross to First Lieutenant Marty A. Hammer. (Library of Congress)

Nixon took the notion of the Vietnam War as a proxy war and flipped it around: rather than simply confronting the communist world on the Southeast Asian battlefield, he aimed his diplomatic efforts at the Soviet Union and China, successfully "opening" China to American relations and trade for the first time since the Chinese adoption of communism. While the friendlier relations with these two superpowers eased fears of the Vietnam War escalating to a World War III–scale conflict, the effect on the war itself was slim, and both communist nations continued to support North Vietnam financially and politically.

Nixon ordered an incursion into Cambodia (where communist Khmer Rouge extremists were taking refuge near North Vietnamese bases) to destroy Vietcong resources. The incursion inspired multiple protests across the United States, including a demonstration at Kent State University, which resulted in the killing of four students and the injuring of nine others by the Ohio National Guard.

As a result of the Cambodian incursion, the Khmer Rouge (the communist party in Cambodia) was forced to consolidate its power elsewhere in the country. Ultimately it seized control of Cambodia under Pol Pot, an extreme Maoist whose treatment of his people was far more vicious than anything Ho Chi Minh was accused of. Laos was also invaded later by South Vietnamese forces assisted by the United States in a failed attempt to close the Ho Chi Minh Trail, North Vietnam's supply route to the south. The peripheral involvement of Cambodia and Laos in the Vietnam conflict is one reason some are reluctant to use the term *Vietnam War,* as it diminishes the scale of events.

The USS *New Jersey* bombards targets on South Vietnam's central coast in March 1969. (U.S. Navy)

In 1972, on the eve of the presidential election, in which Nixon was opposed by anti-war candidate George McGovern, National Security Advisor Henry Kissinger announced that peace was imminent. By then, American troop presence was below 30,000, and the prospect of peace seemed to imply that the rest of the troops would be home soon. The announcement proved premature. When peace talks stalled, Operation Linebacker II focused bombing on Hanoi, and it was three more years before the last U.S. forces would return home—defeated. In the spring of 1975, with the South Vietnamese economy destabilizing because of the withdrawal of U.S. fiscal assistance and troop presence, North Vietnam successfully invaded and conquered by force. The last U.S. troops evacuated Saigon on April 30, as South Vietnamese troops surrendered. On July 2, 1976, the two countries were united as the Socialist Republic of Vietnam, and Saigon was renamed Ho Chi Minh City.

Roughly 60,000 American troops died over the course of the Vietnam War, with another 150,000 injured. Between 2 and 5 million Vietnamese were killed, probably more than half of them civilians. More than 40,000 Vietnamese have been killed by unexploded bombs and other hazards in the postwar decades. Almost half of South Vietnam's population was displaced, many of them relocating to the United States and settling in the "Little Vietnams" and "Little Saigons" of many cities, in some cases making up the bulk of the Asian population.

In 1975, communist revolutionaries finally succeeded in overthrowing the government of Cambodia, after years of struggle and the

IN CONTEXT   Aftermath of the War in Vietnam

Many South Vietnamese fled the country during the war or immediately after the fall of Saigon—especially the educated or skilled who could secure work elsewhere, creating a detrimental effect on the country's pool of intelligence and skills. Many of those who remained were sent to concentration camps if they had connections to the toppled regime, as the government went about its task of converting South Vietnamese institutions not only to a postwar economy but also to a communist system. For the next twenty years, refugees from Vietnam, Cambodia, and Laos fled by boat, seeking asylum anywhere they could find it and contending with the Thai pirates who roamed the sea to rob the refugees of their recently liquidated assets. Refugee camps were set up in neighboring countries for some of the 2 million refugees left homeless by their escape. The United States permitted resettlement to, among others, the half-Vietnamese children of American servicemen and their mothers or caretakers, which resulted in a black market as unqualified Vietnamese sought to buy these rights for themselves.

Meanwhile, Vietnamese agriculture suffered extraordinary setbacks due to the dioxins used by the United States military. Many children have been born in both South Vietnam and North Vietnam with dioxin-related birth defects. Additionally, nearly 7 million unexploded bombs, land mines, and other devices remain in Vietnam—6 million of them American. This presents an extraordinary hazard for the Vietnamese, and the task of finding and removing them will be a lengthy one.

near-indifference of the international communist community. Pol Pot, the prime minister of Democratic Kampuchea (as his administration renamed Cambodia), massacred thousands of ethnic Vietnamese when the Vietnamese government refused to cede land Pol Pot claimed had been stolen centuries earlier. Because Pol Pot's government was supported by the People's Republic of China, Vietnam appealed to the Soviets, who supported an invasion of Cambodia. Both Vietnam and the Soviet Union—which felt threatened by China's growing influence in the region—would benefit from a Vietnamese-dominated Southeast Asia. Pol Pot's regime was ended in January 1979, and a month later the Chinese government announced that it intended to invade Vietnam in retaliation. With most of Vietnam's most experienced troops still in Cambodia, 200,000 Chinese troops invaded the north. They didn't advance far and retreated soon; both sides claimed victory in this so-called Sino-Vietnamese War, with the Vietnamese successfully repelling the invasion and the Chinese claiming that breaching the borders of Hanoi was their only tactical goal, a punitive measure.

The United States, meanwhile, continued its policies of containment, which extended to supporting any regime that opposed communism—which in South and Central America often meant especially right-wing ones, such as the repressive military regime of General Augusto Pinochet in Chile, which was strongly supported by the United States with both military and economic aid. In general, though, the tensions between the Soviet Union and the United States relaxed from the late 1960s to the start of the Reagan-Thatcher era, a phenomenon or period called détente. Under détente, East Germany was recognized by the Western world, and President Richard Nixon was successful in restoring American relations with the People's Republic of China, an achievement sometimes overshadowed by his poor handling of the protest movements and his resignation from office in the aftermath of his illegal cover-up of the Watergate scandal and assorted other misdoings related to his reelection campaign.

Watergate struck another blow to the public's perception of the presidency, from which it has perhaps never recovered. Public support of détente, too, began to crumble when the Soviets invaded Afghanistan in 1979 and Iranian college students took sixty-six Americans hostage for fourteen months. Neoconservative Ronald Reagan was elected president due in no small part to his position that détente was a form of unacceptable appeasement of the Soviets and communism in general, and the perception of incumbent President Jimmy Carter as weak because of the ongoing hostage situation. Reagan's vice president, George H. W. Bush, who succeeded him as president, continued many of Reagan's policies and coasted on his inertia, essentially creating a twelve-year "Reagan era."

Though tensions tightened in the 1980s, the *glasnost* and *perestroika* liberal policies of Soviet Premier Mikhail Gorbachev not only eased those tensions but paved the way for the dissolution of the Soviet Union into constituent free-market states. By the end of 1991, the Soviet Union and the Warsaw Pact had ceased to exist, Germany was reunified, and the Cold War that had never been declared had officially been pronounced at an end. Some historians have characterized a "short twentieth century," framed by Russia's adoption of communism in 1917 and abandonment of it in 1991, with the implication (probably correct) that the existence of a Soviet communist state influenced the major world events within that window.

The same year that the Soviet Union dissolved, the United Nations Security Council declared war on Iraq after its invasion of Kuwait, leading to the brief Gulf War, which (including Operation Desert Shield, a defensive operation to prevent the invasion of Saudi Arabia) lasted less than seven months. It was the first "real" war the United States had fought since Vietnam. In the sixteen intervening years, military actions had been limited to brief engagements like those in Grenada and Libya. It was also the first war fought since the draft had been abolished and thus fought with a purely voluntary army.

Eleven years after the Gulf War, President George W. Bush referred to an "axis of evil" in his State of the Union address, an axis consisting of Iraq, Iran, and North Korea. One year later, Iraq was invaded against the wishes of the United Nations. By 2006, the situation of U.S. troops in Iraq reminded many of Vietnam, and studies suggested that international opinion of the United States was at an all-time low. President Bush described the war as one small part of a larger ideological conflict, using language similar to that of the Cold War era.

In 1995, Vietnam and the United States reestablished diplomatic and trade relations, and the United States opened a new embassy in that country. By the twenty-first century, Vietnam had begun establishing itself as a tourist destination, and the influx of Vietnamese to the United States has popularized Vietnamese restaurants and, in some cities, sandwich shops selling *bahn mi*, a sandwich served on a rice-flour baguette that reflects both Vietnamese cuisine and the years of French occupation.

ALTERNATE HISTORY

But what if Johnson had not escalated the U.S. involvement in Vietnam?

What if National Security Agency (NSA) intelligence had been more accurate, and the Gulf of Tonkin incident had never given Johnson, McNamara, and Westmoreland the justification they needed to secure the executive branch's ability to expand American military commitment indefinitely, in the name of anti-communism? Some other rationale could have been found, but perhaps Johnson would have instead responded to the growing anti-war sentiment in the country, and reevaluated his certainty of victory.

Instead of deploying more combat troops, Johnson could have withdrawn them or converted more of them to advisors, aiming to meet one of the frequently stated objectives of the war: preparing South Vietnamese forces to fight the war for themselves and reducing the war to a purely Vietnamese concern. The bulk of the American presence could have been withdrawn by early 1966.

The problem with that scenario is that the South Vietnamese made no real progress during the period of American military involvement, and the eventual withdrawal of the American advisors would have left them in much the same position they had been in before that period, albeit with better weaponry. In retrospect, it is hard to say what went wrong. Some historians think the American military was not familiar enough with the style of war being fought to provide effective training. The lack of strong leadership among ARVN officers is often cited as a problem as well.

It would probably have made little difference when troops were withdrawn, from a Vietnamese perspective: the outcome of the war would have been the same, though an earlier defeat would have greatly reduced civilian casualties and the damage caused by the rainbow herbicides. The difference in the United States, though, is palpable. When Johnson would have run for reelection in 1968, the war would have been over for two years. In actual history, Johnson withdrew from the race in the midst of primary season after Eugene McCarthy's anti-war campaign took a chunk out of his support; here in this alternate history, there are no such concerns. George Wallace, governor of Alabama, would have run as an independent on a pro-segregation campaign, sweeping so much of the Deep South that the Republican Party—long unpopular in the South as the party of Abraham Lincoln—would have been encouraged to court the southern vote in the future. With Johnson running, Robert Kennedy would have stayed out of the race—and would have avoided being assassinated by Sirhan Sirhan. Johnson might not have won reelection by an overwhelming majority, but he would have won. Republican opponent Richard Nixon would have lacked the "silent majority" in support of the war in Vietnam, and the issues dividing the parties would have been less clear-cut, less dramatic. America would have stayed the course and stuck with Johnson. As a side effect, without Bobby Kennedy's assassination, the Secret Service would not have been prompted to take on the protection of presidential candidates among its other duties.

The protest movements would have focused on issues other than the war, continuing to grow out of and take cues from the civil rights movement, and there would have been no Kent State incident to crystallize conflicts and make young people seem an embattled minority. While some movements might have suffered from the lack of a clear and dramatic target like the Vietnam War, this would have been mitigated by the lack of anti-war movements to draw attention away from such causes. The civil rights movement would have progressed essentially the same as in actual history. In his second term, Johnson would have been better able to address issues such as prison reform and the recommendations of the National Advisory Commission on Civil Disorders he would have created in 1967.

In 1972, the big issues in the presidential campaign would have been civil rights and the economy, which while still nominally healthy would no longer have been as robust as in the years immediately after World War II. Protest movements, the New Left, and the sexual revolution would have made many Americans uneasy with the changing times, and the presidential candidates would have reflected this: Democrat Bobby Kennedy would have been a comfortable choice, reminding people of his brother. Republican Strom Thurmond (like Ronald Reagan, a former Democrat) explicitly would have invoked simpler times, when the federal government did not send troops to interfere with states' rights. Wallace's primary campaign as a Democrat would have been disappointing even in the South—too many "Dixiecrats" would have rallied around Thurmond, who had led the walkout at the 1948 Democratic National Convention when President Harry Truman endorsed a civil rights platform.

The general unease would have brought a new cynicism to politics, and "character" would have become a key issue in the 1972 election. Thurmond would have been condemned by liberals and moderates for his record-setting filibuster of the 1957 Civil Rights Act, his outspoken opposition to integration, and rumors of a his having had a child out of wedlock with an African American woman who worked for his family. Bobby Kennedy would have faced rumors of involvement with actress Marilyn Monroe and accusations of inconsistencies in his voting record, in which it appeared that he was prone to supporting the continuation of anything his brother had started as president (such as the involvement in Vietnam). His Catholicism would have been an issue as well, given the changes in the Catholic Church at the end of the 1960s brought about by the Second Vatican Council. The candidate would have frequently been asked how he felt about various Catholic reforms, many of which would have been unpopular with conservative Catholic Americans, who feared the Church was too swayed by contemporary social trends.

In the end, Kennedy would have won the election. The focus of his foreign policy would not have been the communist threat but unrest in the Middle East and especially the policies of apartheid (segregation) in South Africa. The first piece of major legislation passed under the Robert Kennedy administration would have called for economic sanctions against South Africa until apartheid was ended, though it would not have been until after he left office that this would finally come to pass. Other major accomplishments of Kennedy's presidency would have included the ratification of the Equal Rights Amendment guaranteeing protection from discrimination based on race, sex, or creed; concessions toward the Native American community and a major overhaul of the Bureau of Indian Affairs; and a new wave of anti-poverty programs seeking to aid the American poor, something that occasionally would have alienated his middle-class supporters who would have been tightening their belts. While president, Kennedy's memoir about the Cuban missile crisis—during which he was attorney general in his brother's administration—would have been an international best seller. Toward the end of his first term of office, Kennedy would have held a conference with the governors of the southern states, seeking to ease tensions over states' rights issues. Some would have seen this as simple preelection pandering; others would have credited the move with successfully defusing Wallace's hopes in 1976, and indeed the Alabama governor would have declined to run.

The end of American involvement in Vietnam would have helped forestall rampant inflation—though the United States would still be competing for resources with nations now recovered from World War II. The administration would not have been exacerbating the problem with the massive expense of the war. Industries would have faltered as other countries entered the market—Japan's growing strength in the automobile and electronics industries, for instance—but the blow would have been softer, until the beginning of the energy crisis in 1973. Between some Arab nations refusing to sell oil to allies of Israel and others tripling or quadrupling their prices, the United States would have felt a sharp economic sting. The classic big, wide American car would have plummeted in popularity, replaced by cheaper and more efficient German and Japanese automobiles. Community centers and other free facilities would have closed in cold climates because of the cost of heating oil. Kennedy would have proposed electric car and solar power initiatives but would have been met with resistance from industry and special-interest lobbyists. By the end of the 1970s, an electric car would have become popular in California, first among the left-leaning rich of Hollywood and later among those who followed their lead.

In 1976, the energy crisis would not have abated, and energy and the economy would have been the principal issues in the election. Kennedy would have won the Democratic primary with the ease to which a popular incumbent is accustomed, and he would have faced a close race against California governor Ronald "Dutch" Reagan, whose campaign would play up his cowboy image and Hollywood past in an attempt to match the Kennedy charisma. Though he would have lost, Reagan would have fared much better than most expected, and some might have suggested that his choice of Nixon—previously defeated by both Johnson and the elder Kennedy—as running mate could have been his only misstep. Kennedy's second term would not have been as successful as his first: the American public would have wanted a Kennedy who was strong, decisive, and charismatic, and the climate would simply make those things difficult.

By 1977, when his second term would have begun, Kennedy would have been fifty-one years old. Though still young by presidential standards, Bobby would not have been the young man his brother was in 1960. Kennedy would have been unable to adequately deal with the situation in the Middle East, and accusations of being "soft on OPEC" (Organization of Petroleum Exporting Countries) would have deliberately mirrored the "soft on communism" accusations of earlier in the Cold War. In 1980, Vice President Jimmy Carter would have stepped aside to let Edward Kennedy run for the president's office, but Kennedy would have failed to even win the Democratic primary, which would have been taken by the conservative Washington senator Henry "Scoop" Jackson. Jackson would have lost the election to George H. W. Bush, former director of the CIA, who would have beaten Reagan in the Republican primary and taken him on as a running mate. Bush would have been the first Republican president since Eisenhower, and his election would have seemed to signal a change in the seasons, a shift in focus.

An economically dissatisfied American public might no longer have been as comforted by détente as they once were: the Soviet Union still would have existed, after all, as would the People's Republic of China. Communist regimes would continue to be established in all corners of the world. Bush's foreign policy would have focused, necessarily, on the Middle East and retaliations for the Iranian hostage crisis—but the former CIA man would have encouraged secret wars against the smaller communist governments and the creation of right-wing governments indebted to the United States. Several Arab and Latin American leaders could have been eliminated through assassination, including Libya's Muammar Gadhafi and Iraq's Saddam Hussein. New agreements would have been reached with the OPEC nations, though Bush would have refused to withdraw any support from Israel. Apartheid would have finally ended in South Africa, which Bush would have credited to his newly strengthened sanctions.

In 1984, Bush would have been reelected with a new running mate, Senator Jack Kemp; Reagan would have retired voluntarily, though it would have been an open secret that the Republican Party had concerns about his age. The former football player Kemp would have been better suited to the vice presidential position. Bush's opponent, Walter Mondale, would have won only seven states. In actual history, Bush was not quite the statesman Reagan was, and was far less effective at dealing with foreign leaders, especially Soviet Premier Gorbachev. Bush would not have indulged in the rampant defense escalation of Reagan, and the first movement toward the cessation of the Cold War would have been a cooperative one between Bush and Gorbachev. Despite the Soviet Union's opposition to Israel, it would have thrown its lot in with the United States in dealing with the OPEC nations, and a healthier oil economy would have finally been constructed, even as West Germany would have begun to mass-manufacture highly energy-efficient electric cars. Bush would have spoken publicly of the necessity of ending American dependence on foreign oil, and treaties with the Soviet Union would have included the possibility of American business access to Soviet oilfields.

In this alternate history, the Democratic Party would have been stronger than in actual history, thanks to its two-decade dominance of the presidency, and Kemp would have been defeated in 1988 by Colorado Senator Gary Hart. The Reverend Jesse Jackson would have become the first black vice presidential candidate and might have been shot to death while stumping for votes in Selma, Alabama. Governor George Wallace would have condemned the assassination and promised the death penalty, having either turned over a new leaf or responded to the shifting of political and social winds. Hart's fellow Coloradan Patricia Schroeder, a congresswoman, would have replaced Jackson—a move many considered risky, but Hart could have banked on enough "sympathy" votes that he could afford a female running mate. There would have been grumbles among the Democratic Party leadership, but mostly about his picking someone from his own state.

The inertia of the Bush and Gorbachev years would have carried into Hart's presidency, and the Cold War would have all but evaporated. The Soviet Union and the Eastern European communist nations would have converted to free-market economies by the end of Hart's first term of office, a term marked primarily by efforts to rebuild an economy still suffering from the oil crises of a decade earlier and by swiftly declining race relations in the wake of the Jackson assassination. After the Chinese

Reverend Jesse Jackson, center, at a jobs protest in 1975. In an alternate history, Jackson could have run for vice president. (Library of Congress)

government's violent actions against pro-democracy protesters in 1989, American sanctions would have been swift and would have been approved by much of the Western world. When Hart would have run for reelection in 1992, the last months of his campaign would have been troubled and distracted ones, as U.S.-China relations deteriorated. China would have reacted strongly to U.S. sanctions and would have decided to reclaim Taiwan, the island province where capitalist refugees had set up a separate government. Taiwan would have had the support of the United States and most of the Western world, specifically included in mutual defense treaties.

Although Hart would have been successfully reelected, the fear that he might not have been aggressive enough to face international hostilities would have contributed to the sweeping Republican wins in House and Senate races, not only in 1992 but also in 1994. The neoconservative Republicans would have pushed through legislation calling for increased defense spending as well as social reforms, such as restrictions on abortion, a "protection of marriage" act that implicitly outlawed same-sex marriages, and federal protection for school prayer. In 1993, the United States and its United Nations allies would have faced a newly aggressive China massing missiles and troops against Taiwan. Fears of Chinese military strikes would have been acute, and the dissolution of the Soviet Union would have made it difficult to verify what military technology the Soviets might have shared with the Chinese.

The face-off would have lasted until 1999, and for the first time in decades, American men would have been drafted into military service—as would be a limited number of American women. The situation would have ended in something of a stalemate, with Hart's successor, President Albert Gore, unwilling to commit American troops to a land war in China, at least in the numbers that would have been required to make victory even plausible. A continuing target of China, Taiwan would have remained independent and home to a number of American military bases. In the first decade of the twenty-first century, a Cold War would have continued between the United States and China.

Bill Kte'pi

Discussion Questions

1. If the United States had withdrawn from Vietnam during the presidency of Lyndon Johnson, clearly the nature of American politics would have been affected and different presidential candidates might have been nominated and elected than in actual history. Reviewing the nominees and presidents listed in this chapter, are some choices more likely than others? Do you believe the presidential elections would have gone as described or do you think they might have followed a different pattern?

2. Considering that Vietnam, in actual history, has retained a communist government that is opening its doors to some free enterprise, what sort of political economies do you think would have evolved if the

domino countries of Southeast Asia had been taken over by communist regimes in the 1970s?

3. One of the consequences of the Vietnam War in actual history was that the American people became extremely hesitant to endorse any prolonged U.S. military involvement overseas during the 1980s and 1990s. If the United States had withdrawn from Vietnam before incurring thousands of casualties there, how would that have affected U.S. foreign and military policy in the later decades? Do you think the United States would have been more or less inclined to commit troops in trouble spots abroad?

4. The anti-war campaigns of the 1960s and 1970s among youth helped provide a rallying point for protests on a wide variety of issues, ranging from sexual liberation and environmental concerns to disarmament. If the war had not been drawn out, how would that have affected the youth movement more broadly?

5. If Ronald Reagan had not been elected president in 1980, as he was in actual history, it is unlikely that the expensive arms buildup of his era would have occurred. Reagan supporters believed that Reagan's nuclear arms policy and his endorsement of the Strategic Defense Initiative ("Star Wars") forced the Soviet decision to accept arms control and end the Cold War. Do you believe that internal changes within the Soviet Union would have brought an end to the Cold War even if Reagan had not been elected in 1980?

Bibliography and Further Reading

Anderson, David L. *Columbia Guide to the Vietnam War.* New York: Columbia University Press, 2004.

Downs, Frederick. *The Killing Zone: My Life in the Vietnam War.* New York: Norton, 1978.

Herring, George C. *America's Longest War: The United States and Vietnam, 1950–1975.* New York: McGraw-Hill, 2001.

Karnow, Stanley. *Vietnam: A History.* New York: Penguin, 1984.

Langguth, A. J. *Our Vietnam: The War 1954–1975.* New York: Simon and Schuster, 2001.

McNamara, Robert S. *In Retrospect: The Tragedy and Lessons of Vietnam.* New York: Vintage, 1996.

Myers, Thomas. *Walking Point: American Narratives of Vietnam.* London: Oxford University Press, 1988.

Ninh, Bao. *The Sorrow of War.* New York: Riverhead, 1996.

Nolan, Keith W. *The Battle for Saigon: Tet 1968.* New York: Presidio Press, 2002.

Palmer, Bruce. *The Twenty-Five Year War.* Lexington: University Press of Kentucky, 2002.

Spector, Ronald. *After Tet: The Bloodiest Year in Vietnam.* New York: Vintage, 1994.

Young, Marilyn B. *The Vietnam Wars: 1945–1990.* New York: HarperCollins, 1991.

TURNING POINT

What if civil rights leader Martin Luther King, Jr. had escaped assassination and had become a force in the Democratic Party?

INTRODUCTION

Despite the issuance of the Emancipation Proclamation during the American Civil War, many African Americans and other minorities continued to endure inequality for the next century, especially in the South. Local statutes known as Jim Crow laws were passed that effectively barred people such as African Americans from fully executing their constitutional rights, such as voting.

Groups, including the Ku Klux Klan, terrorized and persecuted African Americans, carrying out lynchings and other acts of violence. Segregation was common in the South, and African Americans were not always guaranteed their rights in other parts of the country either. Many felt that Congress needed to pass new laws to guarantee these privileges. Eventually, African Americans decided that they could not rely on whites to act on their behalf and that leaders of a movement to bring about this change needed to emerge from within their own community. The most effective person to bring about this change was Martin Luther King, Jr., and he was born on January 15, 1929, in Atlanta, Georgia.

Both King's father and grandfather were pastors at Ebenezer Baptist Church in Atlanta. He grew up attending segregated schools. A bright student who had a way with words, King entered Morehouse College in Atlanta at the age of fifteen and earned a B.A. in sociology in 1948. Having decided to follow his father and grandfather in the pulpit, he headed to Crozer Theological Seminary in Chester, Pennsylvania, where he was influenced by the theological writings of Paul Tillich and Reinhold Niebuhr. King earned a bachelor of divinity degree from Crozer in 1951 and moved further north to continue his education, opting for Boston University's Ph.D. program in systematic theology. While he was in Boston, King met Coretta Scott, a student from Alabama. They were married on June 18, 1953.

In 1954 the young couple moved back to Coretta's home state of Alabama, where King served as pastor of Dexter Avenue Baptist Church

Coretta Scott King at the Democratic National Convention in 1976. She was married to Martin Luther King, Jr. in 1953. (Library of Congress)

in Montgomery. He completed his Ph.D. at Boston University in 1955. That same year, the Kings' first child, Yolanda Denise, was born. But 1955 was a momentous year for King and the civil rights movement for two reasons. In Mississippi, a young African American named Emmett Till was brutally murdered after he whistled at a white woman. The men who boasted of killing him were acquitted by an all-white, all-male jury. The other event, which more directly involved King, occurred in December when Rosa Parks refused to move to the back of the Montgomery bus she was riding. She was expected to give her seat near the front of the bus to a white passenger. In accordance with the local ordinances at the time, Rosa Parks was arrested and convicted for violating the law.

Earlier that year, King had been appointed to the executive committee of the Montgomery Chapter of the National Association for the Advancement of Colored People (NAACP). The secretary of the chapter was Rosa Parks. The Parks incident caused an uproar, resulting in an organized Montgomery bus boycott. King was elected president of the Montgomery Improvement Association. His intellect and gift for oratory made him a natural for a protest movement such as this. Throughout 1956, the members of this group organized and ran a car pool so that those who normally would take the bus could join the boycott and still get to work, shops, or home. King personally endured multiple arrests on trumped-up charges and convictions; his house was bombed. After a year, the U.S. Supreme Court declared the enforced segregation of the buses unconstitutional.

In response to this decision, African American churches in Montgomery became the target of bombing campaigns. The resolution of the Montgomery bus boycott, even if it was more symbolic than pragmatic, was a watershed moment for King. It helped to catapult him into the national consciousness and paved the way for his future advocacy of nonviolent means of conflict resolution. In 1957 he appeared on the cover of *Time* magazine, his son Martin Luther III was born, and he organized a conference in Atlanta for pastors of southern African American congregations, which resulted in the formation of the Southern Christian Leadership Conference (SCLC). King was elected president of this group. It was conceived as something of an alternative to the NAACP, which had long been involved in lobbying and litigation efforts. Initially, the SCLC sought to effect change by promoting voter registration among African Americans. This effort met with mixed success. Another important event that year took place in Little Rock, Arkansas, where the National Guard was called in to prevent an effort to integrate the public schools.

In 1958, King was stabbed in an assassination attempt. He had always been interested in the potential of nonviolent protest movements to bring about change, and after recovering in 1959 he traveled to India to meet with followers of the late Mahatma Gandhi, an advocate of nonviolent protest. Upon his return, he decided to move back to Atlanta to be closer to the SCLC headquarters and to serve as co-pastor of his father's church. Meanwhile, in 1960 African American students began participating in sit-ins at lunch counters that were ordinarily reserved for whites only. These students acted independently of King and his organization, but they contributed to the overall civil rights movement. The same can be said for the freedom rides of 1961, in which students challenged racial segregation on buses traveling between Montgomery, Alabama, and Washington, D.C. While King supported these student efforts, he did not actively participate in them. Acts of violence were committed against those who participated in the freedom rides, and King was criticized for not being more directly involved. This led to tension between the SCLC and the Student Nonviolent Coordinating Committee (SNCC). King felt that the approach adopted by the students was at times too militant.

In 1962, James Meredith became the first African American to attend the University of Mississippi. For him to do so without incident, federal marshals were assigned to escort him to class. That same year, King led demonstrations against segregation in Albany, Georgia. Once again, for his efforts he was arrested and jailed, and as with earlier efforts it did not yield the desired results. However, he learned from his experiences, and the next year, 1963, would prove to be a watershed year for the civil rights movement largely due to his work.

In the spring of 1963, he organized the SCLC-led boycott of merchants and mass demonstrations in Birmingham, Alabama, a place where segregation ran rampant. The demonstrations garnered widespread media coverage. King wrote his famous "Letter from a Birmingham Jail" here, despite his wife having given birth just two weeks earlier to their fourth child, Bernice Albertine. When the authorities in Birmingham used violence to counter the protests, President John F. Kennedy called for the consideration of civil rights legislation. The murder of a leader of the Mississippi NAACP, Medgar Evers, further underscored the urgency of

The Congress of Racial Equality conducts a march in memory of African American youths killed in a Birmingham, Alabama, church bombing in 1963. (Library of Congress)

getting something done. With momentum on his side, King and the SCLC led a March on Washington for Jobs and Freedom. The SCLC worked in concert with other organizations, such as the NAACP and the SNCC. A number of singers, such as Bob Dylan; Joan Baez; Peter, Paul, and Mary; and Marian Anderson also performed at the event that was held on August 28, 1963, at the Lincoln Memorial in Washington, D.C. In all, over 200,000 people were in attendance to hear King give his "I Have a Dream" speech. He and the other leaders met with President John F. Kennedy and Vice President Lyndon Johnson afterward, where they were assured that the administration was committed to the civil rights legislation effort.

Another year of triumph for King was 1964. In January, he was named *Time* magazine's Man of the Year. Although President Kennedy was assassinated just a few months after the March on Washington, Johnson made good on his promise and used his considerable talents and influence to ensure that the Civil Rights Act was passed in 1964. This act strengthened existing laws by prohibiting discrimination based on race or religion in public establishments. Johnson signed it into law on July 2, 1964, just weeks after three white volunteers were murdered for showing their support for civil rights in Philadelphia, Mississippi. The year wound down with King becoming the first non-Anglican to preach from the pulpit of St. Paul's Cathedral in London and the youngest man awarded the Nobel Peace Prize.

In 1965, a follow-up to the Civil Rights Act, the Voting Rights Act, was passed. This was in large part a response to demonstrations in Selma, Alabama. The SCLC and SNCC organized voter registration drives and demonstrations in this city. Some of the demonstrators were killed by

---

KEY CONCEPT   Cold War Paranoia

During the time of King's activity, the 1950s and 1960s, many people in the United States were in the grips of fear and paranoia. The United States was adamantly opposed to communism, the form of government that was practiced in the Soviet Union. The years following World War II up until the fall of the Soviet Union are known as the Cold War. Both the United States and the Soviet Union, with their competing philosophies, had the capability of inflicting immense damage through the use of nuclear weapons. There was great fear that communist influence would undermine the U.S. government.

In the 1950s, a U.S. Senator, Joseph McCarthy, accused many prominent individuals of being secret communists. The House Un-American Activities Committee held public hearings in an effort to expose people as communist sympathizers. Many of the charges were baseless, but just having been accused tended to damage people's reputations. Meanwhile, some Americans felt that they had the right as citizens to have communist sympathies.

At the same time, the FBI, led by J. Edgar Hoover, became increasingly powerful. Hoover taped the activities of and created secret files on anyone whom he believed was a threat to the national security of the United States. As a result, the privacy of many innocent people was compromised. Martin Luther King, Jr., was on the FBI watch list, as were numerous other activists who criticized any of the policies of the U.S. government. Some of King's followers were known to have been involved with communists, and it is believed that the FBI used this information to intimidate King. Because of the pervading attitude of fear, some people who might have been sympathetic to King may have shied away from supporting him.

---

state and local troopers, who attempted to block the demonstrators from marching to the state capitol in Montgomery. These acts of violence met with outrage and spurred the passage of the legislation.

In 1966, King shifted his sights to improving the quality of life of blacks in the North. He concentrated his efforts on the city of Chicago, where he temporarily moved his family. In this city, blacks suffered from severe economic exploitation and discriminatory housing practices. King's SCLC-led demonstrations were met with hostility. In the end, a truce was negotiated with Chicago Mayor Richard J. Daley. A young man named Jesse Jackson was one of the men who worked with King in Chicago.

King's influence on the civil rights movement declined, and his efforts to lead the SCLC were becoming frustrated. Urban unrest was on the rise, and the U.S. involvement in the Vietnam War was intensifying. King was critical of the Johnson administration's stance on the war. For years, J. Edgar Hoover's Federal Bureau of Investigation (FBI) had been keeping King under surveillance, with the knowledge of Attorney General Robert F. Kennedy.

A drawing of Martin Luther King, Jr. at the height of his influence in 1968. (National Park Service)

ANOTHER VIEW   The Legacy of Malcolm X and the Nation of Islam

The life and legacy of Malcolm X, one-time member of the Nation of Islam, is an interesting counterpoint to King's. Although his contemporary, Malcolm X came from a different part of the country and lacked the family stability that King had enjoyed.

Malcolm X was born as Malcolm Little on May 19, 1925, in Omaha, Nebraska. His father was a Baptist preacher. The family moved to Lansing, Michigan, where Malcolm grew up. His father was active in civil rights locally, and the family suffered at the hands of a local white supremacist group. Their home was burned, and the elder Little died in what was ruled an accident. Malcolm, an intelligent child, drifted to the Northeast where he engaged in a life of petty crime and served time in jail. While in prison, Malcolm converted to Islam and changed his last name to X. He joined the Nation of Islam, which was led by Elijah Muhammad. This group was a proponent of separation and self-sufficiency from white America, as opposed to the full integration that people like Martin Luther King, Jr., advocated. Malcolm, as the articulate and militant spokesman for the Nation of Islam, criticized King and groups such as the SCLC. Many people were attracted to the Nation of Islam as a result of Malcolm X's dynamic personality. Like King, he was targeted by the FBI. He became disillusioned with Elijah Muhammad's leadership and left the Nation of Islam in 1964. He made a pilgrimage to Mecca, Saudi Arabia, called a *hajj*. He formed his own Muslim group, the Muslim Mosque, Inc., a group that was more open than the Nation of Islam. He changed his name once again, this time to El-Hajj Malik El-Shabazz. On February 14, 1965, his house was firebombed, but the family was unhurt. On February 21, 1965, Malcolm was assassinated, allegedly by members of the Nation of Islam in New York.

Malcolm X waiting at a Martin Luther King, Jr., press conference in 1964. (Library of Congress)

King had experienced differences with groups such as the NAACP and SNCC, but the civil rights movement, particularly among African Americans, was becoming increasingly fragmented. The Nation of Islam leader Malcolm X had criticized King and the SCLC before leaving the Nation and being assassinated in 1965. Following this, Stokely Carmichael emerged as leader of the Black Power movement, which adopted some of the attitudes espoused by Malcolm X.

In 1967 President Johnson nominated NAACP lawyer Thurgood Marshall to a seat on the U.S. Supreme Court. Meanwhile, King started planning a Poor People's Campaign for the following year. Unfortunately, he did not live to see it.

TURNING POINT

On April 3, 1968, in Memphis, Tennessee, Martin Luther King delivered his last speech, "I Have Been to the Mountaintop." He had come to the city in support of striking sanitation workers. On the evening of April 4, 1968, King was shot and killed on the balcony of the Lorraine Hotel in Memphis.

The nation was stunned. Violence and looting broke out in some cities, and over forty people were killed. Indeed, some, such as Stokely Carmichael, called for violence in response to King's murder. Ralph Abernathy, King's long-time assistant, was chosen to succeed him as head of the SCLC and gradually order was restored.

King's funeral took place in Atlanta on April 9. Vice President Hubert Humphrey, Jacqueline Kennedy, Richard M. Nixon, U.S. Supreme Court Justice Thurgood Marshall, and Robert F. Kennedy (who was himself assassinated a couple of months later) were among the more than 100,000 who attended the funeral.

Days after Robert Kennedy's assassination, James Earl Ray was arrested at London's Heathrow Airport, allegedly on his way to South Africa. In his possession was a forged Canadian passport. Ray, a thief, had escaped from prison in Missouri the year before, and he had just robbed a London bank. He was charged with King's murder and extradited to Tennessee. In 1969, Ray confessed to the murder of King, a confession that resulted in no trial

The aftermath of a riot in Washington, D.C., following the assassination of Martin Luther King, Jr., in 1968. (Library of Congress)

and a ninety-nine-year sentence. Days later, Ray recanted his confession and claimed he had been set up as part of a conspiracy.

But what if Ray had missed?

ACTUAL HISTORY

The years following King's death saw the civil rights movement he led become even more fractured. Opposition to U.S. involvement in the Vietnam War intensified. In the 1970s, feminism and gender equality became a major civil rights issue. The National Organization for Women was modeled after some of the African American civil rights organizations. Cesar Chavez campaigned for the rights of migrant workers in California. The *Roe v. Wade* Supreme Court decision legalized abortion. The U.S. Supreme Court also ruled that capital punishment was constitutional. Affirmative action policies were implemented in schools and workplaces. In the 1980s, the Americans with Disabilities Act was passed, a significant piece of civil rights legislation. Gay rights dominated the civil rights agenda in the 1990s and into the twenty-first century.

Ralph Abernathy did not prove as effective a leader of the SCLC as King had been. Shortly before he died, Abernathy published his memoirs, *And the Walls Came Tumbling Down*. In this book, he revealed that King was guilty of infidelities, which caused Abernathy to be ostracized by his former associates before his death in 1990.

Jesse Jackson emerged as the dominant African American voice after King. He was involved in groups such as the Rainbow Coalition and Operation PUSH (People United to Serve Humanity). He ran for the Democratic nomination for president in 1984 and 1988. Jackson, a proponent of nonviolence, has been involved in a number of controversies.

One of King's associates in the SCLC, Andrew Young, was elected mayor of Atlanta and was named U.S. ambassador to the United Nations during the Jimmy Carter administration. Young, also a devotee of nonviolence, later resigned from his post following his controversial meeting with a member of the Palestinian Liberation Organization. Another of King's associates, Marion Berry, was elected mayor of Washington, D.C., both before and after he was convicted of drug possession.

The legacy and spirit of King lives on in many ways. The Martin Luther King Papers Project is part of the Martin Luther King, Jr., Research and Education Institute based at Stanford University. In the 1990s, scholars revealed that King had plagiarized portions of the dissertation he wrote for his doctorate from Boston University. The fact that other scholars, including Stephen Oates, Stephen Ambrose, and Doris Kearns Goodwin were also found to have plagiarized portions of their published works somewhat muted the impact of this to King's reputation and academic credentials.

The King Center was founded by King's widow and is based in Atlanta. The Lorraine Hotel in Memphis, where King was assassinated, is now the site of the National Civil Rights Museum.

In 1983, President Ronald Reagan signed into law the creation of a new federal holiday in honor of King; it is celebrated on the third Monday of January, which usually occurs close to King's birthday. The creation of this holiday was met with opposition in some quarters. It was observed for the first time in 1986 and was observed by all fifty U.S. states for the first time in 2000. In Utah the holiday is known as Human Rights Day and in Arizona as Civil Rights Day.

A number of places have been named for King, including avenues in major cities across the country and perhaps dozens of public schools. In 1986, a motion was passed renaming King County, Washington, which includes the city of Seattle, for Martin Luther King, Jr. The main branches of the public libraries of Washington, D.C., and San Jose, California (including the San Jose State University Library) are named in honor of Martin Luther King, Jr. The hit song "Pride (in the Name of Love)," celebrating King's beliefs, was written and recorded by the Irish rock group U2 in 1984.

James Earl Ray escaped from prison in 1977. He was caught and spent the rest of his life behind bars until his death in 1998. In 1993, a man named Loyd Jowers claimed that he had been offered money by someone in organized crime to help arrange the King assassination, and that the killer was not Ray. Most found his claims baseless. However, the King family believed him, and in 1997 King's son Dexter met with James Earl Ray in prison and announced that the King family did not believe that Ray was responsible for King's assassination. In 1999, a Memphis jury found Jowers guilty of involvement in a plot to kill King in a case brought forward by the King family. Jowers died in 2000.

Rosa Parks died in 2005 and became the first woman to lie in state in the nation's capitol. Her funeral was attended by former President Bill Clinton and many others. On March 29, 2006, the House of Representatives of the state of Alabama unanimously passed a bill pardoning Parks for her arrest over half a century earlier.

King's children are still alive and remain active in furthering their father's legacy. Martin Luther King III was the leader of the SCLC from 1997 to 2004. Coretta Scott King died in 2006. Her funeral was attended by U.S. presidents George W. Bush, George H. W. Bush, Bill Clinton, and Jimmy Carter.

The FBI files on Martin Luther King, Jr., have been sealed until 2027.

ALTERNATE HISTORY

A would-be assassin's bullet could have narrowly missed killing King on April 4, 1968, while he was in Memphis, Tennessee. The alleged culprit would have been apprehended a few months later, not, however, before a copycat would have succeeded in killing Robert F. Kennedy. True to character, King would have condemned the violence, but he would not have allowed these actions to deter him from his mission. Although the Poor People's Campaign would have been a mixed success, it would have kept King and his movement in the limelight. King would have gained even more publicity at the Democratic National Convention that year, where he would have joined demonstrators against the Vietnam War. King would have been increasingly critical of the U.S. involvement in the war.

King's followers would have continued to be concerned about his safety, but King would have felt that it was important to press forward. In 1969 he and other civil rights leaders would have met with President Nixon to urge him to reconsider his policies in Vietnam and the impact both the war and the draft would have been having on ethnic minorities. When the year passed with no progress on these fronts, King would have stepped up his criticism of Nixon. The FBI would have continued its surveillance of King.

For his part, he would have managed to energize a number of groups to support the Democrats in 1972 against Nixon. He would have been active in voter registration drives. Democratic nominee George McGovern would have been impressed with King, and in some quarters it would have even been rumoured that King was under consideration for a vice presidential slot. Although this would not have come about, King would have delivered a searing address at the convention excoriating the Nixon administration. The election would have been close, largely due to King's support of McGovern. The third-party candidate, segregationist Alabama governor George Wallace, would have made a stronger-than-expected showing. Ultimately, Nixon would have eked out a victory. His second term, however, would have been short-lived as he would have been forced to resign due to the Watergate scandal, as in actual history.

For King and the Democrats, Nixon's resignation would have been a moral victory. Many African Americans would have been mobilized in the previous election and would have felt that momentum was on their side. With American forces withdrawn from Vietnam and Nixon out of office, King could have been offered the chairmanship of the Democratic Party. Nevertheless, he still would not have been successful in all the causes he championed. He would have campaigned repeatedly to overturn the Supreme Court's death penalty ruling but would have made no progress in this area.

King would have been an enormous help in getting Georgia governor Jimmy Carter elected president in 1976. Carter would have repaid the favor by naming King U.S. ambassador to the United Nations. He would have served in this post for a few years before turning his attention to an issue of international importance—the apartheid regime in South Africa. King would have long been a supporter of Nelson Mandela, the South African dissident jailed for his stance against South African segregationist policies. King would have learned from experience that when he spoke truth to power and took a stance that others feared to take, he usually got results in the long term. He would have been critical of the violent intents of the Black Power movement, for instance, and in so doing he would have gained the respect of many people.

King would have traveled the world in an effort to gain support for the release of Mandela and the end of the apartheid regime. During the Ronald Reagan presidency, he would have shadowed Reagan. For example, when Reagan voiced his opposition to the Berlin Wall, King would have reminded everyone of the situation in South Africa. He would have become such an effective gadfly in his criticism of the administration that many people would have encouraged him to run for president. He would have demurred, but in 1984 Walter Mondale, the Democratic nominee, would have named King the first black vice presidential candidate in U.S. history. This would have been met with furious opposition in some quarters, but for the most part it would have electrified the campaign.

Ultimately, in one of the closest elections in U.S. history, Reagan would have won a second term, but in a show of solidarity and on the advice of people close to him, Reagan would have named King a special envoy to South Africa. It would have been an unprecedented step. Despite the many problems that Reagan would have encountered in his second term, King's effective work on the South African issue would have resulted in Nelson Mandela's release from prison in 1986 and would have seen the country abandon its racist policies in 1987.

By 1988, King would have been an influential leader of the Democratic Party. He would have run for and won the Democratic nomination for president, and he and his vice presidential nominee, Mario Cuomo, would have had a strong campaign. Even so, King would have been once again on the losing end of one of the closest elections in U.S. history, as George H. W. Bush took the presidency.

King would have been at a crossroads, with many wondering if he would reenter presidential politics, but he would have surprised everyone by returning to his roots at the SCLC. He would have written several well-received books and supported Bill Clinton's presidential campaigns. At one point, Clinton would have offered King the position of secretary of state, but he would have refused. However, he would have served as an informal advisor to Clinton.

In particular, King would have been successful in getting the administration to pay attention to the genocide in Rwanda. He would have been deployed to troubled hotspots around the globe such as Northern Ireland, Yugoslavia, and Israel. Although he would have garnered publicity for these efforts, he would not have effected great changes, with the possible exception of Northern Ireland, where his presence would have been appreciated. State department officials would have tended to find King's presence more of a distraction or hindrance than a help. King, for his part, would have considered it important to spread the gospel of nonviolence around the globe, as he would have realized that whatever publicity and goodwill he earned in one part of the world would reflect well on his other efforts.

However, as time went on King would have turned his attention to domestic causes such as campaigning against the violence among African American young men. Unlike his earlier campaigns, he would have relied on his personal magnetism and persuasion rather than mass demonstrations. However, he would have participated in the Million Man March (a demonstration by African Americans), despite some well-publicized differences with Nation of Islam leader Louis Farrakhan. King would have been effective in urging stronger paternal role models among African Americans. He would have also been a leader in getting hate crimes legislation passed.

Some people would have urged King to support causes such as reparations for African Americans for slavery, but he would have felt that this was not a wise course of action. He would have supported affirmative action policies, but not as fervently as some would have wished.

With the election of George W. Bush and the outbreak of the Iraq War, King would have reentered politics in 2002 and would have easily won a Senate seat in Georgia, confounding many in a southern state that would have become a Republican stronghold over the years. King would have continued to court controversy, but at this point he would have achieved so much that attempts to discredit him would have been unsuccessful. Consequently, he would have emerged as the most vocal and effective critic of the government's lack of response to the Hurricane Katrina disaster. He would have skewered the Bush administration over its mishandling of the recovery efforts, and throughout Bush's second term would have continued to hammer away at his policies.

King would have rallied the Democrats to victory in the midterm elections in 2006, but he would have surprised everyone again by announcing that he would not seek reelection and would retire from political life. The years would have been taking a toll, and he would have wanted to make sure he left the SCLC and his other interests in strong shape before he died. King would have passed away peacefully in his sleep at age seventy-eight in 2007.

Glenn Robert Gray

Discussion Questions

1. Martin Luther King, Jr., advocated and used the tactic of nonviolent demonstrations as the preferred means to achieve goals of social justice. Do you think that method is more or less effective in the United States than the use of the courts and the legislatures?

2. In the alternate history suggested in this chapter, Dr. King became very active as a political figure in the Democratic Party. What factors do you think would have made it likely that he would have emerged as such a leader? What factors would have worked against his success as a regular Democratic Party political leader?

3. Within the span of a decade, four major leaders in the United States were assassinated: John F. Kennedy, Martin Luther King, Jr., Robert F. Kennedy, and Malcolm X, while attempts were also made on the lives of George Wallace, Gerald Ford, and later, Ronald Reagan. What factors do you think led to so many assassinations and attempted assassinations?

4. Martin Luther King, Jr., is memorialized with a national holiday and with the naming of streets and places. Do you think his memory would be more or less honored if he had not been assassinated?

5. What factor do you believe most accounted for the public following that Dr. King developed? Do you think it was his oratory, his education, his tactics, or his beliefs?

Bibliography and Further Reading

Abernathy, Ralph David. *And the Walls Came Tumbling Down: An Autobiography.* New York: HarperCollins, 1989.

Branch, Taylor. *At Canaan's Edge: America in the King Years, 1965–1968.* New York: Simon and Schuster, 2006.

Branch, Taylor. *Parting the Waters: America in the King Years, 1954–1963.* New York: Simon and Schuster, 1988.

Branch, Taylor. *Pillar of Fire: America in the King Years, 1963–1965.* New York: Simon and Schuster, 1998.

Burns, Stewart. *To the Mountaintop: Martin Luther King Jr.'s Sacred Mission to Save America, 1955–1968.* New York: HarperCollins, 2004.

Carson, Clayborne. *The Autobiography of Martin Luther King, Jr.* New York: Warner, 1998.

Garrow, David J. *Bearing the Cross: Martin Luther King, Jr., and the Southern Christian Leadership Conference.* New York: William Morrow, 1986.

King, Martin Luther, Jr. *A Call to Conscience: The Landmark Speeches of Dr. Martin Luther King, Jr.* Boston: Little, Brown, 2001.

Kotz, Nick. *Judgment Day: Lyndon Baines Johnson, Martin Luther King Jr., and the Laws that Changed America.* New York: Houghton Mifflin, 2005.

Pepper, William F. *An Act of State: The Execution of Martin Luther King.* New York: Verso, 2003.

Posner, Gerald. *Killing the Dream: James Earl Ray and the Assasination of Martin Luther King, Jr.* New York: Random House, 1998.

Washington, James Melvin, ed. *A Testament of Hope: The Essential Writings of Martin Luther King, Jr.* New York: Harper and Row, 1986.

↻ TURNING POINT

The North Vietnamese Tet Offensive was a climax of the Vietnam War. What if the United States had invaded North Vietnam in retaliation?

INTRODUCTION

The Vietnam War, controversial since its official beginning in 1965 and its end in 1975, could be seen as a continuation of Vietnam's centuries-long resistance against conquerors and colonial powers, the longest of them being China. It could be traced from the revolt of the Trung sisters in 40 C.E. against the Chinese. When the Chinese defeated them, the sisters committed suicide. Then came other well-known, iconic resistance leaders like Trieu Au, Tran Hung Dao, and Le Loi.

The Chinese were the first foreign power that the Vietnamese incessantly resisted. Though China called Vietnam "Annam," meaning "the pacified south," the Southeast Asian land had been a hotbed of rebellions and uprisings throughout history since the Trung sisters' revolt. Vietnam finally gained recognition from the Chinese in the fifteenth century with the efforts of Le Loi, a wealthy landowner who served the Chinese and then turned against them. Over the centuries, indigenous rule of the country soon came down to a toss-up between two powerful families, the Trinh and the Nguyen. They divided the country roughly into what later became North and South Vietnam.

The first contact with the French was when the Nguyen emperor Gia Long enlisted their help against the Chinese in 1802. Then he turned on the French and expelled them. In the 1850s, Napoleon III sent a military force to establish what was to be known as Cochinchina, and along with Laos and Cambodia, Vietnam became part of what was called French Indochina.

Later on, the person who was to be the Vietnam War's most influential figure appeared in 1919 at the Versailles Treaty, demanding Vietnam's independence. He was born Nguyen Sinh Cung but went through many name changes until settling on the name he immortalized: Ho Chi Minh. A staunch communist, he and his school friend Vo Nguyen Giap, who was later to become North Vietnam's chief military leader, formed the Vietnamese Communist Party in the 1930s. During World War II, when

ANOTHER VIEW   French Defeat at Dien Bien Phu

One of the major influences on the occurrence of the Vietnam War was the French defeat at Dien Bien Phu in 1954. With French colonial rule ended in Vietnam, a major power holding back the communists from attempting to take over their country was gone.

What if the French had somehow won the day at Dien Bien Phu? Or what if the French had checked Ho Chi Minh's forces successfully and prevented them from building up enough strength to challenge the French at Dien Bien Phu?

We would probably have seen no Gulf of Tonkin incident or U.S. participation in Vietnam. If the French had retaken Vietnam, strengthened by their victory over the Vietminh, history would have seen a French-controlled Vietnam retain influence over the region. They would have dealt with subsequent raids and attacks from Vietminh units, but never with the widespread scale and effect of the U.S. war. American aid would have been minimal, and the European powers would have taken the brunt of the fight with the communists.

---

the Japanese marched into the country in 1942 and took over without a fight, the two leaders formed the Vietminh, which resisted the Japanese forces until the end of the war.

With the end of World War II, control of the country eventually returned to the French, and Ho Chi Minh and his party initially cooperated with the French. After an incident in which a French boat crew was arrested by the Vietminh, hostilities erupted, developing into the French Indochina War of 1946–1954 (also called the First Indochina War; the American war can be called the Second Indochina War). In a foretaste of things to come, the Vietnamese defeated the French in the climactic battle of Dien Bien Phu, thus freeing Vietnam from foreign powers. This finally gave Ho Chi Minh and his party the power to establish their own independent country, the so-called Democratic Republic of Vietnam (also called Tonkin or North Vietnam), taking their seat of power in Hanoi.

However, the French did not want to give up their territory so easily and still held on to the regions around Saigon; they called a conference to decide the fate of Vietnam. The Geneva Conference of 1954 oversaw the formation of two Vietnams. A borderline at the 17th Parallel was drawn by Allied Powers (United States, France, and Britain). Initially supposed to be under the control of the French, the South's government was placed under the control of Vietnamese emperor Bao Dai. He was then deposed by his prime minister, Ngo Dinh Diem, who proclaimed himself president of South Vietnam.

The division of Vietnam was originally meant to be temporary before the nation was

Ngo Dinh Diem (front), president of South Vietnam, is flanked by Lady Bird Johnson in 1961. (LBJ Library)

unified once the populace had chosen its leaders. Ho Chi Minh first tried to unite the two countries himself by asking for an election at the Geneva Conference for Vietnam. Diem and the United States refused, certain that Ho would win. Seeing the Democratic republic in the South refuse to undertake this unification measure meant to Ho Chi Minh that there was no other recourse but to use force to achieve his dream of a united Vietnam.

The North Vietnamese created a group called the NLF (National Liberation Front) in the south, incorporating people from the south who were opponents of Ngo Dinh Diem. This group acted in tandem with the PRP (People's Revolutionary Party), the Southern branch of the North's Lao Dong or Communist Party, to form a guerilla army; this was to be known as the PLAF (People's Liberation Armed Forces) or Vietcong. The Vietcong found it easy to gain the cooperation of some peasants in the south because of the South Vietnamese government's unpopularity, which stood in contrast to Ho Chi Minh's stature as an icon of Vietnamese independence. This group and the North Vietnamese Army would be the main opponents the United States had to face in the coming storm of war.

The two Vietnams started fighting a civil war with each trying to seize control of the other and unify Vietnam in their own way. At this time South Vietnamese army units were inexperienced and inept in combat, which was among the reasons the United States poured in assistance. In January 1963, the Vietcong defeated an ARVN (Army of the Republic of Viet Nam, South Vietnam's army) unit at the battle of Ap Bac. Another serious defeat was suffered at Don Xoai in 1965. In both cases, the ARVN was routed by a foe they outnumbered. In October 1963, Diem was deposed and killed in the last of the many attempted coups d'etat against him. He was replaced by Duong Van Minh. In the 1967 elections, Nguyen Van Thieu became president, a position he held until 1975.

Nguyen Van Thieu, standing before a world map, served as president of South Vietnam during the Tet Offensive. (LBJ Library)

ANOTHER VIEW   Gulf of Tonkin Incident

Intelligence failure is often the reason for the mistakes of the U.S. government and military. It certainly applies to the Gulf of Tonkin incident, when military leaders thought that certain navy ships were under attack by the North Vietnamese naval forces when in fact no such attack had happened. Further analysis a few decades later indicated that the information regarding the event had been mishandled as it was passed around, and exaggerations and changes that occurred were the result of honest errors. If this incident had not been overblown as it was, the Vietnam War might not have escalated. Perhaps U.S. aid would have continued in the form of advisors, and there would have been no basis for deploying American troops in the area. If North Vietnam had later made an open incursion into South Vietnam, then the United States would have escalated. An open incursion into South Vietnam would have been more believable to the American public as a reason to prosecute the war, and anti-war sentiments would have been greatly reduced.

Finally came the catalyst for the United States. The press reported that on August 4, 1964, U.S. destroyers USS *Maddox* and USS *C. Turner Joy* were attacked by North Vietnamese patrol boats in the Gulf of Tonkin, near the North Vietnamese coast. U.S. President Lyndon B. Johnson used this incident as a basis for escalating U.S. involvement in the conflict between South and North Vietnam. He asked Congress to pass the Gulf of Tonkin Resolution, which authorized him to increase the amount of U.S. military forces to Vietnam. Later, reports of the incident were proven to have been questionable. But now the die was cast. The United States was committed to preventing the threat of communism from expanding in the Southeast Asian region.

President Lyndon Johnson signs the Gulf of Tonkin Resolution, giving him the power to increase U.S. forces in Vietnam. (LBJ Library)

Since the French defeat in 1954, the United States had already been involved in Vietnamese affairs, being an ally of France. The United States helped the Vietnamese during World War II and the French in the First Indochina War. In addition, U.S. involvement in the region was based on the domino theory, first named by President Dwight Eisenhower—a belief that if Vietnam were to fall, the other countries around it would fall to communism. This would set off a chain reaction of nations falling to communism until America itself was under threat of communist invasion.

Since the end of the French war, the U.S. Special Forces, popularly known as the Green Berets, were being sent to Vietnam to train South Vietnamese troops in combat techniques. On October 21, 1957, Green Beret Harry Cramer became the first American soldier to die in Vietnam, due to an accidental explosion.

Another incident that led to active U.S. action was on February 7, 1965, when a U.S.

KEY CONCEPT   The Domino Theory

The domino theory was the idea that if South Vietnam were allowed to fall to communist North Vietnam, the rest of Southeast Asia would follow, succumbing to the juggernaut of communism. With the Cold War at its height, the expansion of communism was one of the great paranoias of the time. It was a strong fear that was influenced by the Russian victory in World War II and the communist takeover of China in 1949. The Western world was increasingly worried over the spread of communism in even a small area. That small area, if completely taken over, could be a stepping stone for communism to spread over to the U.S. mainland. The fear was that from Southeast Asia and the Philippines, communism would jump over to Indonesia, Australia, and the Pacific Islands. With only a body of water as the remaining obstacle, the communists could land next on U.S. shores.

Aviation Battalion at Camp Holloway near the city of Pleiku was attacked by over 300 Vietcong during the night. The Vietcong mortared the bases and escaped, leaving seven dead and 100 wounded. The Vietcong attack was done in violation of a cease-fire, called for the Tet or Lunar New Year celebrations that year. It foreshadowed the coming offensive.

Numerous American advisors were already in the country, around 15,000 by the end of 1963. The first delivery of committed ground troops happened on March 8, 1965, at the beach near the town of Da Nang. The landing was met by an ironic reception committee in the form of village girls who put garlands around the necks of the soldiers. But a few days earlier, March 2, around 100 U.S aircraft had been ordered to strike targets in North Vietnam, marking the start of the famous Rolling Thunder bombing campaign from the air.

By the end of 1965, there were 184,000 U.S. troops in the country. By 1966 this number had grown to 385,000, and by 1967 there were 486,000. But whatever the strength of the U.S. forces at the start of the war, they were ill-prepared for what they were to confront later. The commander of U.S. forces in Vietnam, General William Westmoreland, hoped to meet the North Vietnamese and Vietcong in a conventional battlefield, fighting in open fields and in masses. He hoped these types of battles would later lead to an invasion of North Vietnam. But the North Vietnamese used insidious techniques and hit-and-run tactics. They would strike suddenly from hidden places then fade away in the night. They used local people as informants and planted disguised spies. They used guerilla warfare techniques, which most U.S. soldiers at the time had no experience with.

Though the Chinese were formerly enemies of Vietnam, Ho Chi Minh and his general Vo Nguyen Giap borrowed heavily from Mao Tse-tung's writings on guerilla warfare. They used this type of fighting to great effect, especially in the early days of the war, taking advantage of the relative inexperience of new U.S. troops coming in. The main strategic thinker for North Vietnamese forces was Vo Nguyen Giap. He wrote a book called *People's War, People's Army*, which outlined the very strategies used by his armies.

ANOTHER VIEW Guerilla Warfare

It is arguable that the use of guerilla warfare won the war for the Vietnamese. Long accustomed to their jungle environment, they knew how to operate on their own turf and work it to their advantage. All they needed was to frustrate U.S. efforts at achieving accurate body counts to create uncertainty among U.S. ranks and doubts in their own combat efforts. If earlier in the war, say 1963, the United States had immediately understood the techniques of guerilla warfare and let their own troops turn those tactics on the enemy, they would have achieved better results. For example, if patrols had sneaked through the jungle as the Vietcong did, they would have been better prepared for surprise attacks and would even have been able to surprise the enemy at times. This would also have eliminated the need for extreme measures, like tree bulldozing, use of Agent Orange, and napalm bombing.

The tunnel system of Cu Chi, as well as other tunnels, could have been more effectively disabled if the U.S. forces had not just destroyed the tunnels as they were found. Since the tunnels were booby-trapped, the U.S. forces did not need to penetrate deeply into tunnels every time. The "tunnel rats" could have set their own booby-traps at entrances for Vietcong going in and out. This way, the Vietcong would have become cautious even of their own tunnel system, and their operations would have been hampered.

The rotation policy of troops also had a great effect on the war's outcome. After one year, troops in combat were shifted home and replaced by inexperienced men; thus, a fighting force had to start all over again in learning the enemy's tactics. The draft system meant that training was rushed and sparse, so the soldiers sent were almost totally unprepared for the changing face of combat. The experienced troops were unable to pass on their knowledge to these new fighters. Had those more experienced troops remained longer and been able to teach the newer troops how the war in Vietnam was fought and how the enemy worked, there would have been fewer casualties and more successful operations.

These successful guerilla strategies that the North Vietnamese Army (NVA) and the Vietcong used depended on a wide network of tunnels dug under the jungle. The tunnel systems were virtual underground bases; troops could sleep in them, supplies could be delivered there, and attacks could start from them, using well-camouflaged entrances near some U.S. bases and posts. In fact, some of the tunnels could be found almost directly under U.S. firebases. One of the most famous tunnel systems was the one under Cu Chi, forty miles northwest of Saigon.

Unknown to the U.S. forces, these tunnels were being used to support a massive attack plan in the making, one that was also supposed to lead to an uprising against the South Vietnamese government and the United States. Supplies, troops, and instructions were being moved through these tunnels to NVA and Vietcong units all over the country. The plan was to be enacted during a time when there was a lull in the fighting and when the United States and South Vietnamese would least expect any attack. The time was Tet, the Lunar New Year festival celebrated by the Vietnamese. A cease-fire had been announced for the holiday so that people could forget the ongoing war for a while and observe their tradition in peace.

Meanwhile, as preparations for the Tet attacks went on, Westmoreland continued the search-and-destroy policy, directing his forces to draw the

KEY CONCEPT   Vietcong

The Vietcong was a separate organization from the North Vietnamese Army (the People's Army of Vietnam). "Vietcong" is actually an abbreviation of Viet Nam Cong San, which means "Vietnamese communist." The term was spread into use by officers of the South Vietnamese military and was never used by the group itself. The group's actual name was the National Front for the Liberation of Vietnam, originally all-communist in its founding but then expanded to include all kinds of people opposed to the U.S.-backed Vietnamese regime. It was mainly composed of peasants, teachers, clerks, and other ordinary people in South Vietnam who were opposed to rule by the United States, which they considered another foreign hostile power like the French.

The Vietcong were nearly annihilated by the U.S. and South Vietnamese forces in the Tet Offensive, contrary to what the American public thought at the time. Thus, more than three-fourths of the combat effort fell to the North Vietnamese Army, with the Vietcong playing relatively minor roles.

enemy out into the open. But time and again the Vietnamese would continue to use their guerilla doctrine and very often elude their pursuers. Even when the Cu Chi tunnels were discovered, U.S. forces destroyed only the end portions of the system, while the more vital sections and many other tunnel systems were never found.

Back in the home front in late 1967, President Lyndon Johnson stepped up a propaganda campaign to inform the American people that the United States was winning the war. Thus, at this stage, the American public expected that the war was going well—and that there would be no surprises.

Intelligence, though, had been gathered that indicated a massive attack was coming. Unfortunately, both U.S. and South Vietnamese top-ranking officials found the idea of an attack on Tet doubtful because it would be a sacrilege on such a sacred holiday. In addition, almost half the South Vietnamese forces were on leave for the holiday. Another factor was that peace talks were under consideration at the time, so military action was reduced. But the situation was ripe for a surprise attack.

Foreshadowing the coming attack, two unusual battles occurred in 1967. One was on October 29, when a Vietcong regiment took over and tried to hold a small town. Though it failed, this was not the usual pattern for the communist forces; their general mode was to attack, then go back into hiding. Another was in November, when four NVA regiments tried to hold against U.S. forces at the town of Dak To for twenty-two days. Documents were soon found that instructed the communist forces to make the U.S. forces spread as thinly as possible. Experts in the military, including Westmoreland himself, warned that this was an indication of a major offensive to happen on Tet. But these warnings went generally unheeded.

Soon, the Lunar New Year Eve (Tet Nguyen Dan) arrived. Most people were now bent on having a good time. Even South Vietnamese president Nguyen Van Theiu was vacationing at a house in the provinces. Only a vigilant few stayed on and readied themselves for what was to be one of the biggest events of the war.

TURNING POINT

On January 30, 1968, the eve of Tet, the Lunar New Year, around 84,000 NVA and Vietcong troops staged simultaneous attacks all over South Vietnam. Mortar and shell fire opened up on the cities of Saigon, Khe Sanh, Hue, and other major urban centers, and bases like those at Da Nang. The eve of Tet was usually celebrated with firecrackers, so when people heard the first gunshots, they dismissed them as firecrackers. But as the shots continued and the differences in the sounds became apparent, the people realized that they were under attack—in their own hometowns.

U.S. and South Vietnamese forces scrambled to defend against this surprise attack. Some skirmishes resulting from the Tet Offensive lasted until the next year. After the offensive, though it was declared a victory by the Allies and a reason to escalate U.S. involvement, the American public was shocked by images of their embassy in Saigon damaged and a South Vietnamese police officer summarily executing a whimpering Vietnamese prisoner, among other reports from the battle. This made the public perceive that the war was being fought unsuccessfully, and some demanded a withdrawal of U.S. forces.

The turning point here is whether the U.S. government sees the invasion attempt as a reason for escalating the war or for pulling out of it. Had the American people and government believed that they had actually won the Tet Offensive and fewer had protested the war, and had the American press presented the Tet Offensive differently, U.S. forces could have made the offensive a reason to push escalation to the ultimate level and conduct an invasion of North Vietnam.

ACTUAL HISTORY

As the NVA and Vietcong forces almost simultaneously launched their attacks on the eve of the Tet celebrations, U.S. and South Vietnamese forces found themselves poorly prepared. The surprise of the assault was compared to that of the Germans during the Ardennes Offensive during World War II and the Japanese attack on Pearl Harbor.

Among the primary targets was the capital of South Vietnam, Saigon itself. Within Saigon, six targets were swarmed over by the communist forces: the presidential palace; the U.S. embassy in Saigon; Tan Son Nhut Air Base; the Vietnamese Navy Headquarters; and the national broadcasting station. The NVA sent thirty-five battalions to claim these targets. Some of the members of these battalions worked as cab drivers in the city. Some disguised themselves as local Saigon police who deployed themselves near the radio station. They carried a tape of Ho Chi Minh's speech meant to arouse the people to revolt against the United States. This attack however failed as an ARVN officer at the station cut power to it, preventing the broadcast.

Examples of other places under attack were the U.S. base at Da Nang, Ban Me Thuot, Quang Nam, Dalat, My Tho, Can Tho, Ben Tre, Nha Trang,

Kontum, and Khe Sanh. All in all, eight provincial capitals, five of the six autonomous cities, and fifty-eight other major towns were stormed in the Tet Offensive. The base at Khe Sanh was one of the places where Westmoreland had predicted an attack would come. While it had been under siege days before, intelligence had hinted at a coming offensive, so Westmoreland ordered the defenses of Khe Sanh to be increased. However, as Khe Sanh was farther off in the country, in hindsight it was believed that the attacks here were one of the distractions to draw forces away from Saigon and other major targets. Khe Sanh was also one of the most media-covered events during this crucial time in the war.

The attack on the U.S. embassy was to be the most publicly visible part of the Tet Offensive. In the middle of the night of January 31, 1968, Vietcong soldiers blew a hole in the embassy wall and overpowered the guards. Contrary to what was perceived in the news, they entered the compound but never entered the building. Thus the communist forces were trapped on the embassy grounds, unable to take their objective; then U.S. and ARVN forces arrived and wiped them out some hours later. Reporters who were at the scene during the recapturing efforts had the impression that the embassy itself was taken and that this reflected incompetence on the part of the U.S. and ARVN forces. Along with the other factors leading to the battle, like the Vietcong buying a nearby house for the operation and smuggling arms through supposedly secure checkpoints in Saigon, the embassy battle was perceived to be a microcosm of the whole war.

Among the more significant battles of the offensive was Hue City, which was to be immortalized as one of the bloodiest battles of the war. Ten NVA battalions attacked Hue City and carried on what would later be discovered as a brutal massacre of civilians in the area. The NVA forces took over, and U.S. forces fought for almost a month to clear the city of them. U.S. marines had to work the NVA out, house by house, because of the ban on artillery strikes to prevent heavy damage to the sacred city of Hue. The civilian massacre, estimated to have cost about 3,000 lives, gained little publicity after the offensive; thus it was generally missed in the news because of other, more sensational events.

However, despite the pressure applied all over the country by the communist forces, none of them succeeded in the end. All attacks were eventually repulsed, and the NVA and Vietcong lost. Communist forces suffered about 45,000 casualties, according to U.S. estimates. The Vietcong were almost annihilated, and they would never play a major role in the war again. Most of the work now had to be done by the NVA. The communists never got the uprising in South Vietnam that they hoped to incite through the offensive.

After the embassy battle, reporters and news people were called in by Westmoreland for a press conference. Westmoreland's announcement was one of victory. But television reports of ruined buildings, bodies of Vietnamese on the streets, and battered, weary soldiers stood in contrast to the general's announcement.

Protests against the war mounted. The soldiers who fought in the Vietnam War were portrayed by anti-war activists as cruel, cold-blooded killers of a defenseless people. When the public was leaked confidential documents about the war (the Pentagon Papers), with information that included decision-making processes during the Tet Offensive and the

Vietnam War protestors at the March on the Pentagon in 1967. (LBJ Library)

whole war, the American public became convinced that the Vietnam War was a losing proposition. Reports continued coming in of high casualties, and increasingly Vietnam veterans found themselves alienated from a public that saw them in a negative light.

One of the most reputable reporters of the time, Walter Cronkite, went to Saigon immediately after the Tet Offensive, and his visit impressed on him that the United States was losing the war. On February 27, 1968, he told the world on his news broadcast that the Vietnam War was likely to end in a stalemate. Cronkite's report, along with the constant barrage of photojournalism and television reporting, increased American horror at the war and contributed to a growing disillusionment with the war's goals.

The Tet Offensive ended with 3,895 U.S. troops dead and the South Vietnamese losing 4,954. The civilian casualties were much greater, with 14,000 dead, 24,000 wounded, and 800,000 who lost their homes to the offensive.

Westmoreland used the incident as a reason for bringing in reinforcements, sending in a request for 200,000 troops. But his request ran into a brick wall; U.S. senators and legislators saw the issue as the public did and decided that Vietnam was not worth fighting for. No new troops came. With the Tet Offensive and the Vietnam War's negative impact, Lyndon Johnson declined to run for president again. In 1968, Richard Nixon, a former supporter of the war, became his successor. Seeing the unpopularity of the war, Nixon promised to pull all American troops out of Vietnam.

Westmoreland was also replaced as the leader of U.S. forces in Vietnam by World War II veteran General Creighton Abrams. Under Abrams, the policy of Vietnamization was implemented. A steady pullout of U.S. forces began to leave all matters to the Vietnamese, much to the chagrin of the South. The message was this: the United States had intervened far enough, and it was time to leave the Vietnamese alone.

With the negative outlook on the war now becoming mainstream after this event, U.S. soldiers found it increasingly difficult to cope with the change of culture in their home country. Vietnam veterans who had finished their tour sometimes came home to face alienation and rejection from the people in their own hometown. This was furthered by the cultural revolutions of the 1960s.

Unpopularity continued to soar with more mistakes and further incidents rubbing in the message. On March 16, 1968, the whole world was shocked when a Vietnamese village of women and children were slaughtered by U.S. troops, an event that came to be known as the My Lai massacre. Another event was the disastrous Hamburger Hill action starting May 11, 1969. Despite having secured the objective in the end, the

General William Westmoreland meets with President Johnson (right) following the Tet Offensive in 1968. (LBJ Library)

attempts to take target 937 resulted in numerous lives lost, often due to miscoordination and incompetent planning.

Hamburger Hill also showed military planners that Westmoreland's goal of drawing the enemy out into the open was unachievable. It was difficult to fight an enemy that could go in and out of hiding at will and appear anywhere he wanted. Thus, Vietnamization became the favored policy and it proceeded. Roles and equipment once used by U.S. forces were given to ARVN troops.

Even more significant—and closer to home—were the protests mounted by the American public. As early as April 21, 1965, a Buddhist monk had set himself on fire (a suicidal practice called self-immolation) in Saigon to protest U.S participation in Vietnam's conflicts. Later that year in Washington, D.C, two Americans, Norman Morrison and Roger Allen Laporte, self-immolated in protest against the war. However, cooler heads were more successful in their less fatal protest methods, with well-known figures like Martin Luther King, Jr., Norman Mailer, and Dr. Benjamin Spock in their ranks.

But the worst event among the demonstrations was the shooting of Kent State University students during a campus protest in 1970. Because of the violence that had accompanied some of these incidents, the Ohio National Guard was called in as a precaution at Kent State. But in a tense moment, National Guard troops fired on the demonstrators with live

IN CONTEXT   Cultural Unrest in the United States

At the same time the Vietnam War was raging, the seeds of change were being sown in homeland United States. Men and women with long hair, floral-patterned clothes, and peace sign accessories were gathering conspicuously in various spots across the nation and spreading a new, colorful, yet potentially disturbing culture among the youth. With a mix of modern rock music, frequent sexual activities, prevalent drug use, and rebellion against conventional morality, the psychedelic culture was exploding and shaking up the foundations of U.S. culture.

This cultural explosion contributed to the morale drop among the troops in Vietnam. Returning troops would be shocked to find these "flower people" coming up to them and calling them murderers or butchers. Members of this subculture were to be found among anti-war protesters, vehemently decrying the war as another extension of U.S. imperialism and the war-mongering political culture. Not only moral foundations were disturbed, but the foundations for waging the Vietnam War were also shaken. The culture of "peace" that the psychedelic culture claimed to stand for was totally against the rationales for the war. This culture clash contributed to loss of support. Some of this culture found itself among the soldiers deployed in Vietnam. Soldiers sported peace signs on their helmets, weapons, and vehicles, and a noticeable number went absent without leave or refused to follow orders to protest the war. Even veterans had joined some anti-war protests.

ammunition. Four students died, and ten were wounded. Two of the four who died were not even part of the protest. The public outcry against the war strengthened now that casualties included the Americans' own children at home.

In September 1969, the famed North Vietnamese leader Ho Chi Minh died, and control was passed on to Vo Nguyen Giap. Although Giap's strategies had failed on the battlefield, they succeeded in bringing the Americans to the negotiating table. Peace talks continued throughout 1972; these were often deadlocked, with each side making demands that the other side refused to give.

Later on, however, representatives of the United States and North Vietnam met again in Paris on January 23, 1973, and the Paris Peace accords were signed on January 27, the same day Lieutenant Colonel William Nolde became the last soldier to officially die in the Vietnam War.

U.S. participation in the war was declared over. Though some military personnel remained in a few U.S. bases, they very rarely participated in actual combat. The South Vietnamese were left to fend for themselves. For almost two years, the ARVN withstood as much as they could against the numerous and politically united North Vietnam, but internal problems like corruption and desertion, and a stronger NVA overcame them in the end. By this time, Richard Nixon had resigned as a result of the Watergate scandal, and Gerald Ford was now president. In December 1974, the U.S. Congress passed the Foreign Assistance Act of 1974, which cut off all U.S. aid to Saigon and voided the peace terms set under Nixon's administration.

In March 1975, the central highlands fell to the NVA, then Pleiku, Kontum, and Hue City. By April, the ARVN had collapsed in chaos, and there was relatively little opposition to hold back the NVA from rolling in. President Nguyen Van Thieu resigned and left his doomed government to General Doung Van Minh, fleeing to the United States; on April

27,100,000 NVA troops surrounded Saigon, which had only 30,000 ARVN troops left to defend it.

With defeat imminent, many South Vietnamese politicians and prominent people fled the country. The United States finally launched Operation Option IV, the evacuation of Saigon. It was a picture of chaos in newspapers and on television as Vietnamese from all corners of the city crowded the embassy, fearing being left behind. Finally, on April 30, 1975, the last U.S. Marines and evacuation helicopters left Saigon, just as the NVA soldiers in tanks broke down the gates of the presidential palace and embassy. President Duong Van Minh surrendered Saigon to NVA colonel Bui Tín, and a year later, North and South Vietnam were combined into the Socialist Republic of Vietnam. Saigon was renamed Ho Chi Minh City.

Many battles could claim to have affected the war greatly, but the point where the downhill run began was the Tet Offensive. While actually a combat victory for the United States, it was at the same time a political failure.

One of the after-effects of the war was the emigration of the "boat people." After the Vietnam War ended, many families, sometimes whole villages, took to the sea in flimsy boats and rafts in an effort to escape the economic distress and oppressive regime in Vietnam. They fled to places like Hong Kong, Thailand, Australia, and the Philippines, eventually moving to the United States, France, and other countries, creating sizable communities that exist to this day.

With the pullout of the United States, Southeast Asia became a hotbed of communist activity. The domino theory became true in a limited sense. When South Vietnam fell, the neighboring countries of Cambodia and Laos fell to communism as well. In Cambodia in particular, when the Khmer Rouge came to power, millions of people perished under what is known as the "killing fields" event when the regime purged intellectuals and anyone who idealized Western democracy. The killings stopped when the Khmer Rouge were overthrown in 1979, an event ironically brought about by an invasion from Vietnam.

However, other Southeast Asian countries like Thailand, Singapore, and Indonesia never fell to communist influence, and so the domino theory was not entirely true. Laos remained under communist control, but Cambodia, after the overthrow of the Khmer Rouge, became a democracy. Some still argue that the U.S. presence in Vietnam in a way checked the dominos from falling in Southeast Asia.

Vietnam in the 2000s remained under communist control, but with the collapse of the Soviet Union, it softened to influences from the West, and some Western industries set up operation in Vietnam. Yet the mark of the Vietnam War remains on the people, both Vietnamese and American, as one of the most controversial conflicts in history.

U.S. soldiers lead prisoners of war to a collection point in September 1968. (U.S. Army)

ALTERNATE HISTORY

Had the aftermath of the Tet Offensive been interpreted differently, instead of a call for reduction there could have been a call for further escalation of U.S. involvement. One key was the presentation of the event in the American press. If the press had reported that the Tet Offensive was a success despite the losses and that the embassy was not really taken, the American people's view of the war might not have been so negative, and they might still have approved of the war's prosecution.

The Tet Offensive could have been interpreted as a patriotic call for escalation, and the press and Walter Cronkite could have presented the event as an alert to the threat of communism, pointing out that it was a powerful and surprising menace but could be crushed any time the democratic powers choose to do so.

If the victory after the Tet Offensive had been interpreted in this way, Lyndon Johnson would have been seen in a positive light and could have been reelected president in the next election. Nixon would have never have stepped into office, and "Watergate" would not have become a part of our vocabulary. Congress would have granted Westmoreland's request for more than 200,000 men and more weapons and war materiel. Angry at the damage and surprise caused by the Tet Offensive, Johnson and his advisors would have decided to mount an invasion of North Vietnam.

With more men coming in and more reports being studied more carefully, a change in American tactics would have been necessary. While Westmoreland would still not get the large-scale conflicts that he had hoped for, he would have had the forces needed to mount an invasion of North Vietnam itself. A study of the enemy's tactics would have revealed that the search-and-destroy missions would have had to be supplanted with counter-guerilla tactics—turning the guerilla tactics around on the communist forces.

The plan would have probably involved the U.S. Special Forces (Green Berets) and the Special Operations Group (SOG) doing covert probing missions into North Vietnam to report on the enemy's forces. With the true purposes of the Cu Chi and other tunnels discovered, some military experts would have suggested that instead of destroying them, U.S. forces should take them and use them for U.S. purposes. Part of the battle for North Vietnam would have involved a lot of tunnel fighting, and "tunnel rats" would have gained prestige in these conflicts.

With things looking better for the United States in the war, many peripheral events would have never happened or would have happened differently. For example, the My Lai massacre would not have been a part of our history. Hamburger Hill, one of the most wasteful incidents of the war in terms of lost lives—and apparently for nothing—would have been most carefully rethought, and the hill would have been captured in a different, less expensive way. Had the Vietnam War ended at this point, the reception of Vietnam veterans at home would probably have been vastly different from what it was.

With the large forces gathered and new tactics applied, the invasion of North Vietnam would have been under way by November 1968. While it moved forward, the Soviets and Chinese would definitely have been disturbed by the American advance.

China would have decided to participate to help North Vietnam as it had North Korea in the Korean War, though the assistance would have been minimal. Russia, on the other hand, would have considered the U.S. invasion a serious threat and would have sent a small amount of troops to assist in defense of the country, though a full commitment of troops would not have been made at this time.

Later, the Vietcong would have been eliminated or disbanded by North Vietnam to consolidate manpower into the NVA. The NVA would have borne the brunt of all the assaults, as in actual history, only this time they would have been overwhelmed and certainly would have gone to their allies for help. The Chinese, seeing the Vietnamese as ancient enemies that could lure them into an entanglement with the West, would have withdrawn their support and stayed quiet, unwilling to force the heavy hand of the Americans. The Russians would have seen the American threat in Vietnam as significant and would have stepped up support, both in materiel and advisors. Ho Chi Minh would have perceived a growing threat not just in the American invasion but also the Russian presence in Vietnam, akin to colonial interference of past days.

At this point, Ho Chi Minh would have died and the spirit of the NVA people would have been crushed, so dependence on the Russians could have increased. Yet the Soviets, after the Cuban missile crisis, would have been wary of U.S. actions and would have tended to avoid any more direct confrontation. Peace talks would have been called between the two superpowers with their Vietnamese partners beside them. Hints of nuclear war would have come up in the talks, but none of the two superpowers would have been willing to continue such threats after their experience in the Cuban missile crisis. The two parties could have reached an agreement that would have resulted in a Korea-like partition, with a line dividing the two countries, leaving a communist North and democratic South.

The Vietnam War would have ended in a stalemate between the two Vietnams, and they would have reverted to their status before the war. The Soviets would have withdrawn from North Vietnam and left the North Vietnamese to their own devices. But U.S. forces would have stayed in South Vietnam and set up large bases to prepare for any threat from the Soviets or the North Vietnamese. A constant buildup would have occurred with new and advanced equipment being positioned there. Equipment such as the F-15 Eagle, F-16 Falcon, and AH-64 Apache would have been deployed in Vietnam and would have had their first taste of combat in skirmishes in that country.

With Vietnam becoming another pivot for the Cold War after Korea, it would also have become one of the watchposts of the Southeast Asian region. While an uneasy peace would have settled between the North and South Vietnams, the two Koreas would have continued with the same type of uneasy balance they had lived with for years. The 1980s would have been filled with tension over the potential dangers of the Asian front. Westmoreland, with his success in Vietnam, would have been president of the United States and would have approved massive aid programs to Southeast Asian allies.

As the Cold War moved on in the 1980s, the Soviets would have begun to feel that they could try an invasion in their Southeast front, but not in Afghanistan; rather, it would have been in Vietnam. Afghans would have been allies supporting the United States in defending against Soviet incursions. Osama Bin Laden would have become a soldier watching the northern Afghan border.

The Soviet Union would still have been closed to the outside world, and the feeling of paranoia and worry about the Cold War conflict so common in the 1950s would have remained strong at this time. The democratic world would have been nervously watching what the Soviets would do next. Singapore, Thailand, Cambodia, the Philippines, and other Asian countries near Vietnam would have been dominated by the two superpower flashpoints: the Koreas and the Vietnams. No southeast Asian nation would have been known for phenomenal growth, like Singapore and Thailand.

In the 1980s, with the possibility that Ronald Reagan would not have been president, the economic boom that was felt in real history would not have happened with a Vietnam War victory. There would have been no tremendous recessions in the market, but the looming threat from the Soviets would have kept the stock market from rising too far. However, the military program like that embarked on in the 1980s would certainly have still moved at full steam.

A lot of veterans certainly would have greater prestige today than in actual history. More Vietnam veterans would have occupied positions in U.S. government.

By the early 1990s, the U.S. bases in the Philippines would have been forced out of the country by the Mount Pinatubo volcanic eruption, as in actual history. But they would have had a place to go: South Vietnam. It is likely that with South Vietnam in U.S. control, the majority of the Clark facilities in the Philippines would have been moved there, thus making Vietnam the primary deployment position in Southeast Asia.

North Korea, with a strong Soviet Union still behind it, would have developed and tested nuclear weapons successfully in the 1990s—and shared the technology with North Vietnam. They would have been developing weapons in secret, along with chemical and biological weapons. Discovery of this would have been a cause of panic in the Southeast Asian region, and tension would have led to another standoff between South Vietnam and North Vietnam.

In the aftermath of this nuclear confrontation, Southeast Asia would have had a near economic crash from the panic, but it would have recovered. The year 1997 would have never seen an Asian currency crash but would instead have seen a steady economy influenced by an American-backed Vietnam. Cold War tensions would have caused this changelessness.

The later 1990s, however, could also have seen a resurgence of anti-imperialism against U.S. rule, with Asian people lobbying for a withdrawal of U.S. occupying forces. These would not have been effective though, as the paranoia against communism would have overcome any dislike for the United States.

However, when the 2004 tsunami happened, it could have been a catalyst for the communist militaries from North Vietnam and North Korea to mount attacks, seeing that the United States would have been distracted by relief and assistance operations. The two countries could have simultaneously mounted attacks in certain areas but would eventually have been beaten back by U.S. forces. The Soviet Union could have intervened but would still have been afraid to take direct action against the United States, and would have instead dissuaded the two Asian communist countries from furthering their offensives. Fear of nuclear war would reemerge, sufficient to cause massive troop concentrations in south and east Asia.

China would also have felt pressure from the Allied presence and would have given hints of hostility throughout the 1980s and 1990s. It would not be open to capitalism as it has become in actual history. Instead, South Vietnam would have become the center of outsourced industries. "Made in South Vietnam" could have become one of the more popular tags associated with merchandise. In this alternate history, because of continued U.S. presence in Southeast Asia, China and the Soviet Union could have had closer ties.

However large these development in foreign affairs might have become, all nations since World War II would have remained tired of large-scale warfare and would have avoided the occurrence of massive confrontations as much as possible. Instead, military action on a smaller scale would have continued, similar to the operations in Iraq and Afghanistan in the 2000s in actual history. Several skirmishes would have occurred near the borders of each divided country, but efforts would have been made to prevent their escalation into another world war.

With communism remaining a visible threat into the 1990s, the shift of the "world enemy" from communism to terrorism would not have happened. Some communists would themselves have taken the terrorist role. Cuba would have been a major player in this, as well as some leftist and socialist elements in South America. Thus the Cold War would have maintained its momentum well into the 1990s and even the 2000s, and only by then would there be a significant resolution to avoid all-out conflict.

Instead of experiencing a gradual decline and collapse, the Soviet Union could have realized its delicate condition in the 1980s and 1990s and focused on internal reforms to correct the systems that kept them from winning against the Western powers. Instead of focusing on projects like the Chernobyl nuclear plant, resources would have been diverted to more important military needs. The late 1980s and 1990s would have been a time of a secret nuclear arms race.

By the 2000s, tensions between the Soviets and Chinese and the United States and its allies would have reached an impasse. Yet, the prevalent attitude would still have been to avoid nuclear war at all costs because of the potential damage to both sides; the situation that might have erupted could have been a repeat of the Cuban missile crisis of 1962.

With South Vietnam in the strong hands of the United States, the Soviets would have considered it foolish to challenge U.S. and allied forces directly. They would have called a truce and focused on economic development, and the truly hostile country that would have remained would have been China. In the 2000s, China would have become the last great power able to challenge U.S. supremacy. (Operations near Taiwan could have erupted into a situation similar to the Gulf of Tonkin, with Taiwan eventually becoming another Vietnam.)

But even without conflict in Taiwan, China might have decided to tighten its own defenses against the possibility of U.S. invasion from Southeast Asian bases. With U.S. economic as well as military power looming over the horizon, China would have placed heavy defenses along its borders near U.S.-allied territory.

Established as an unstoppable world power with its success in Vietnam, the United States would have been in a position to establish itself as a much larger military power as well as an economic powerhouse, even by today's standards in actual history. Communist terrorists would have attempted to destabilize U.S. security around the world. The war on terrorism today would certainly have never been undertaken and instead "terrorism" would refer to small cells of communist groups operating from Cuba and South America. They would have tried to smuggle arms and supplies, or even drugs, into the United States to fuel unrest-causing groups or gangs.

All in all, the Tet Offensive's complete lack of success in both its physical and psychological effects would have resulted in communism not succeeding throughout Vietnam. This communist defeat could have brought about Soviet intervention to end the war in peaceful but uneasy terms, and would have led to the extension of the Cold War well into the 1990s and maybe even today. Tensions would not have led to nuclear war or another major confrontation, but they would have stayed around for a long, long time.

Chino Fernandez

Discussion Questions

1. How would Vietnamese culture be different if the Vietnam War had been won by the United States? Would U.S. society be different today as well?

2. What reactions do you think the Soviet Union would have had if U.S. forces had invaded and conquered North Vietnam?

3. What would be the impact of a U.S.-controlled Vietnam in Southeast Asia? In the world?

4. What other events in Southeast Asia do you think would have happened differently had the U.S. invaded North Vietnam?

5. Would it be better in your view if the United States had retained control of Vietnam until today? Why or why not?

Bibliography and Further Reading

Arnold, James R. *Tet Offensive 1968: Turning Point in Vietnam.* London: Osprey, 1990.

Ashbrook Center. "The Tet Offensive," http://www.ashbrook.org (accessed December 2005).

Braestrup, Peter. *Big Story: How the American Press and Television Reported and Interpreted the Crisis of Tet 1968 in Vietnam and Washington.* Novato, CA: Presidio Press, 1994.

Cawthorne, Nigel. *Vietnam: A War Lost and Won.* London: Arcturus, 2003.

Ford, Ronnie E. *Tet 1968: Understanding the Surprise.* Portland, OR: International Specialized Book Services, 1995.

Karnow, Stanley. *Vietnam: A History.* New York: Viking, 1983.

Kish, G. Paul. *Obscuring Victory and Defeat: The Vietnamese Tet Offensive: An Operational Perspective.* Newport, RI: Naval War College, 1995.

Oberdorfer, Don. *Tet: The Turning Point in the Vietnam War.* Cambridge, MA: Da Capo Press, 1984.

Schmitz, David F. *The Tet Offensive: Politics, War, and Public Opinion.* Lanham, MD: Rowman and Littlefield, 2005.

Wirtz, James J. *The Tet Offensive: Intelligence Failure in War.* Ithaca, NY: Cornell University Press, 1994.

TURNING POINT

The killing of students at Kent State University in 1970 was a national tragedy. What if the incident had happened in the turbulent year of 1968?

INTRODUCTION

The mid- to late 1960s in the United States was a time of protest, dissent, and upheaval—socially, culturally, and politically. The decade began with the optimism carried over from the 1950s and shared by newly elected President John F. Kennedy. Kennedy's 1963 assassination and the expansion of the Cold War policy of containment to control the spread of communism shattered much of this optimism. As a variety of protest movements swept American society, many people began to challenge government policies and middle-class lifestyle and values. The post–World War II period had also seen a dramatic expansion of higher education, and many of the protest movements would soon find their way onto college and university campuses. The youth of the 1960s would be a lot different from the "silent generation" of the 1950s.

Many middle-class college students became active participants in civil rights, the counterculture, and other protest movements of the 1960s, bringing the political and social turmoil onto normally quiet college and university campuses across the country. No longer would administrators, professors, and students be isolated in their "ivory towers." Beside changes in the off-campus world, students sought changes in their on-campus worlds as well. They demonstrated for more democratic university administrations that would treat students as individuals rather than numbers. They also sought greater personal freedom in their course studies and personal lives. In the fall of 1964, the free speech movement swept over the campus of the University of California at Berkeley. By the mid-1960s, campus unrest was a nationwide phenomenon attracting the attention of media and society.

The New Left, a political movement sweeping the United States in the 1960s, became prominent among college and university students. Those in the movement spoke out against materialism, the Cold War, the growth of the military-industrial complex, and social and racial injustices. They advocated radical changes in American society and politics, gradually

KEY CONCEPT   The Ivory Tower and the Town-Gown Divide

The term *ivory tower* is used to denote the academic world of the university and its scholars and its separateness from the everyday concerns of off-campus communities. The term usually invokes the picture of academic scholars isolated in the worlds of their specialized research and jargon. The term's origin lies in the Bible, where it is used in chapter 7, verse 4, of the "Song of Solomon." Other early usages include that of French poet Charles-Augustin Saint-Beuve in his poem "Thoughts of August" and of American author and philosopher Henry James, who wrote a novel entitled *The Ivory Tower* in 1916. The term subsequently appeared in the works of other writers and entered into common usage.

The term *ivory tower* also often carries negative connotations, giving rise to the so-called town-gown divide between the local community and its nearby college or university and tapping into the strain of anti-intellectualism in U.S. society. Many townspeople view academic scholars as aloof and elitist. Some feel their specialized research is not necessary, not understood by the majority of people, or impractical. They also often resent students who, while bringing business to the town, also represent potential disruptions and overcrowding. Both universities and their neighboring towns usually take steps to foster good relations between the two groups to prevent the town-gown divide.

becoming more militant as the decade wore on. The most representative of the New Left organizations on the university level was the Students for a Democratic Society (SDS). After being founded at the University of Michigan in 1962, SDS saw chapters spring up on campuses all across the nation. Tom Hayden outlined their beliefs and goals in the Port Huron Statement of that same year. The U.S. involvement in Vietnam would spark the largest of the student movements to sweep college campuses in the 1960s.

The Southeast Asian country of Vietnam had been a French colony but began to seek its independence in the post–World War II period. After French forces were defeated at Dien Bien Phu in 1954, Vietnam was divided at the seventeenth parallel, an action ratified at the Geneva Convention. Communist leader Ho Chi Minh had already seized control of North Vietnam, basing his government in Hanoi. The U.S.-backed South Vietnamese premier was Ngo Dinh Diem. Ho Chi Minh wished to reunite Vietnam under communist rule, and he found support among a group of South Vietnamese rebels known as the National Liberation Front, or more commonly as the Vietcong. The United States supported the corrupt and increasingly unpopular Diem because of the Cold War policy of containment of the spread of communism and the widespread acceptance of the domino theory. Many Americans believed that if South Vietnam fell to communism, it would then spread to neighboring countries, which would fall like a row of dominoes. Diem was later deposed by a group of South Vietnamese generals, with U.S. approval, and then, assassinated.

Under the Dwight Eisenhower and John F. Kennedy administrations, the United States began providing the South Vietnamese with military supplies, economic aid, and military personnel to serve as advisors. The United States also aided neighboring Laos and Cambodia. Neither Eisenhower nor Kennedy, however, was willing to send American combat troops. Kennedy was assassinated in November 1963, and Vice President Lyndon Johnson inherited both the presidency and the Vietnam conflict. In August 1964, unclear reports of an attack on American ships in the Gulf of Tonkin in Vietnam would serve as the catalyst to greatly increase America's role in Vietnam. Congress passed the Gulf of Tonkin Resolution, granting the president the authority to take necessary measures to repel armed attacks against U.S. forces without first obtaining Congressional approval.

Johnson soon began a massive bombing campaign against North Vietnam and sent the first combat troops in April 1965, hoping to convince the North Vietnamese to abandon their attacks against South Vietnam and their aid to the Vietcong. Hanoi and the port of Haiphong were primary bombing targets. Meanwhile, increasing numbers of American combat troops fought against Vietcong who employed guerrilla-style warfare in the jungles and rice paddies of South Vietnam, measuring success through body counts. The United States did not invade North Vietnam, as it did not wish to provoke the communist Soviet Union or China into entering the conflict and possibly escalating it into World War III.

A small but growing number of students began to speak out against American involvement in Vietnam. Ultimately the anti-war protests would become, in historian Scott L. Bills's words in *Kent State/May 4: Echoes through a Decade,* "the spearhead of the radical student movement." While most research into the movement has focused on the larger and better known schools, like Harvard, Yale, Columbia, Michigan, and Berkeley, smaller schools were also active participants, including Kent State University (KSU) in northeastern Ohio. One of the earliest anti-war groups on the KSU campus was the Kent Committee to End the War in Vietnam.

Early protests at KSU took the form of weekly peace vigils organized by the Kent Committee. The events grew to include forums and educational meetings in campus dormitories and buildings as well as the stationing of information tables and distribution of informative literature. In November 1967, KSU's first Vietnam teach-in attracted approximately 200 students. The campus anti-war movement soon began to include more active tactics, such as protesting against campus recruiters—the U.S. military, police forces, and corporations that participated in military-based research.

The early KSU anti-war movement, however, only attracted a small number of followers. Most of the students, faculty, and staff supported the U.S. government and its Vietnam policy. At a 1965 peace picket march, about a dozen anti-war students were attacked by a much larger contingent of pro-war students. Both the student newspaper, the *Daily Kent Stater,* and the newspaper in the nearby town of Kent, the *Kent Record-Courier,* spoke out against the activists. Campus, town, and federal police agents watched their activities and sent informants to infiltrate the group.

The town of Kent was gaining recognition for its lively nightlife and counterculture music scene. While town residents welcomed the increased business these activities generated, many of them feared the threat to law and order. Some townspeople held stereotypical, negative views of the counterculture; some believed that all anti-war protestors used drugs and were communists, unpatriotic, and un-American. Both the town and the university administration felt that the countercultural music scene and the anti-war movement would attract outside agitators to the town and campus. Simultaneously, the anti-war movement continued to grow at KSU and the university soon had its own chapter of SDS.

TURNING POINT

The anti-war movement increased in both size and intensity as the Vietnam conflict continued and American soldiers shipped out and died in ever-greater numbers. Support for Lyndon Johnson's Vietnam policies among both students and the general public began to diminish at the same time that his Great Society domestic programs faded into the background. The Vietcong led a major offensive on January 31, 1968, during the Vietnamese Lunar New Year known as Tet. Although the attacks were eventually repelled, the violent struggle further highlighted the apparent difference between official government pronouncements that the United States was close to winning the war and the reality of the day-to-day fighting. People began to see a seeming credibility gap between public government views and reality. Several of Johnson's key advisors and cabinet members began to doubt that the war was winnable. Financing the war began to create inflation and increased budget deficits.

A variety of different anti-war protest groups formed uneasy alliances to achieve a common goal, although they often quarreled over tactics, ideological viewpoints, and strategies. Student protestors across the nation sought an end not just to U.S. involvement in the conflict but also to military-related university programs such as ROTC (Reserve Officer Training Corps) and scientific research that would aid in the development of weapons. Tactics included methods learned during involvement in the ongoing civil rights struggles, such as sit-ins, marches, pickets, vigils, petitions, and other forms of civil disobedience. Others included teach-ins featuring educational speeches, the burning of draft cards, and the harassment of military and business recruiters who came to college campuses. Meanwhile, a public backlash against the protestors as unpatriotic began to intensify as the presidential election drew closer.

President Johnson vied for the Democratic nomination with Senator Eugene McCarthy of Minnesota and Senator Robert F. Kennedy of New York. It was clear that Vietnam would hurt Johnson's chances, however, so he went on national television to withdraw from the campaign, pledging not to seek or accept his party's nomination. A common view among historians is that Vietnam ruined his political career. The campaign season would be marked by violence. Civil Rights leader Dr. Martin Luther King, Jr., was assassinated on April 4 in Memphis, Tennessee, and Robert Kennedy was assassinated on June 6 in Los Angeles, California. Race riots followed the King assassination in a number of cities. Violence also broke out outside the Chicago Democratic National Convention in August between various groups of anti-war activists and police as the public watched on television. Vice President Hubert Humphrey became the Democratic candidate.

Former vice president and California governor Richard M. Nixon became his party's nominee at the Republican National Convention in Miami. Nixon was making a political comeback, in part on his stand to restore law and order to a country in turmoil and to bring a gradual end to the war in Vietnam. He hoped to appeal to the "silent majority" or backlash voters, those who quietly supported administration policies and condemned the protestors. The popularity of Nixon and conservative American Independent Party candidate George Wallace, Alabama governor and segregationist, showed the strength of these backlash voters. On the other hand, the King and Kennedy assassinations, the violence in Chicago, and the ongoing clashes between protestors and police continued to drive more students into the anti-war movement.

Nixon won what turned out to be a close election and sought "peace with honor" in Vietnam, meaning that the process of withdrawing American troops ("Vietnamization") would be gradual. Nixon did not wish to appear to be abandoning South Vietnam. Meanwhile, the Kent State SDS chapter launched a spring offensive in April 1969 to abolish the campus's ROTC program and end university participation in war-related research. On April 8, university president Robert White refused to meet with three SDS representatives. Several hundred students then marched to the administration building, clashing with larger number of pro-administration students. Two SDS leaders, Howie Emmer and Rick Erickson, were arrested and SDS was banned from the campus.

Later that month, several hundred students marched to the Music and Speech Building to protest the closed disciplinary hearings for Emmer and Erickson. They became trapped on the building's upper floor and faced arrest by waiting police. A professor led a group of the students out through a service elevator, but more than fifty others were arrested and placed on trial for conspiracy, trespassing, and riot. The administration's method of dealing with the protestors would soon backfire, pushing many more students into the anti-war movement.

The national SDS organization split into factions at their national convention in Chicago in June. One faction, including several KSU students, formed the Weathermen and fought with Chicago police in the "Days of Rage." They would go on to bomb government and corporate offices in the 1970s.

President Richard Nixon's April 30, 1970, announcement of a U.S. invasion of suspected Vietcong strongholds in Cambodia immediately triggered a wave of student protests on college and university campuses across the country. Friday, May 1, saw spontaneous demonstrations on numerous campuses, including Kent State. During a noon anti-war rally held at a grassy meeting area in the center of campus known as the Commons, protestors gave speeches against the war and symbolically buried a copy of the U.S. Constitution. Another rally was set for the coming Monday, May 4, 1970. That evening, the protests spilled into the town of Kent, and students clashed with the town police. Bonfires were lit in the streets, and several downtown store windows were smashed. Mayor Leroy Satrom declared a state of emergency and set a curfew as police from neighboring towns came to assist in restoring order.

President Richard Nixon's announcement of the invasion of Cambodia triggered further demonstrations at Kent State University. (Library of Congress)

The following morning, rumors began circulating as townspeople and business owners surveyed the damage. Mayor Satrom called the office of Ohio governor James Rhodes to place a formal request for assistance from the Ohio National Guard, who arrived in Kent that night. That evening, the old wooden ROTC building (West Hall) on the Kent State University campus was set afire, as approximately 1,000 demonstrators watched. Some of the protestors sought to interfere with the work of the firefighters who responded to the scene by trying to cut their hoses or using other measures. Confrontations between protestors and police and National Guardsmen continued throughout the tense night, resulting in the use of tear gas. By May 3, approximately 1,000 guardsmen had been called to the campus, and Governor Rhodes arrived in Kent to hold a press conference, during which he labeled the protestors as among the worst types of people in America.

On the morning of May 4, university officials distributed pamphlets announcing that the campus rally planned for noon had been prohibited. Many students did not attend classes that day. A crowd began to gather in the hour before noon, including protestors, supporters, and onlookers. By midday, several thousand protestors and a little over 100 guardsmen were present in and around the Commons area. General Robert Canterbury decided to order the protestors to disperse. Kent State University patrolman Harold Rice used a bullhorn to make the announcement as he and several guardsmen in a Jeep sought to disperse the crowd, only to be met by shouting and rock throwing. Tear gas was fired.

The guardsmen, armed mostly with M-1 military rifles and wearing gas masks, marched across the Commons, over nearby Blanket Hill and into the parking lot near Taylor and Prentice Halls. Next they moved into an adjoining practice football field that was partially surrounded by wire fences. Many of the protestors followed, leaving the guardsmen temporarily trapped on the field as the yelling and rock throwing continued. Witnesses later claimed to have seen several guardsmen huddled together on the field, later giving rise to a conspiracy theory that they had been plotting to open fire on the protestors.

The guardsmen next returned to the summit of Blanket Hill near a pagoda, when suddenly, at approximately 12:25 P.M., a number of them fired their rifles. Some fired directly into the crowds that were gathered in and around the Prentice Hall parking lot, killing four and wounding nine others. The four students killed were rally participants Allison Krause and Jeffrey Miller, along with Sandra Scheuer and William Schroeder, two students who were walking to class when the gunfire occurred. The nine wounded were Alan Canfora, John Cleary, Thomas Grace, Dean Kahler, Joseph Lewis, Donald Mackenzie, James Russell, Robert Stamps, and Douglas Wrentmore. Faculty marshals, led by Professor Glenn Frank, then pleaded with the protestors and were able to disperse the crowd.

IN CONTEXT   International Reactions to the Shootings at Kent State

The May 4 shootings at Kent State made international as well as national headlines. European colleges and universities, like their American counterparts, had well-established student protest movements and their own violent uprisings during the 1960s. The violence at Kent State further fueled already existing dissent against American foreign policy and American involvement in Vietnam. As historian Kenneth Heineman stated in *Give Peace a Chance: Exploring the Vietnam Anti-war Movement,* "In thirteen seconds of gunfire, Kent State became an international symbol of anti-war protest and government repression." The angry reaction to the Kent State shootings led more European students to join the anti-war movement, just as it had in the United States.

Lawrence S. Kaplan, Kent State University professor of history and director of the Lyman L. Lemnitzer Center for NATO Studies at KSU, came to a similar conclusion based on his own firsthand experiences. He had been in Europe at the time of the May 4, 1970, shootings, serving as a visiting research scholar and lecturer in history at University College at the University of London during 1969 to 1970. He recalled the European reaction to the shootings that he encountered in London as well as in other European countries he traveled to while lecturing on behalf of the U.S. Information Service three weeks after shootings. He concluded from his experiences that for European students Kent State had become an international symbol of the anti-war movement.

Kent State University President Robert White and Portage County Prosecutor Ronald Kane closed the university under an injunction from Common Pleas Judge Albert Caris. It would remain closed throughout the remainder of the spring term. The National Guard remained on campus

National Guardsmen fire a barrage of tear gas into a crowd of demonstrators on the campus of Kent State University on May 4, 1970. When the gas dissipated, four students lay dead and several others injured. (Corbis)

until Friday, May 8. Rumors and confusion quickly engulfed the campus and neighboring town. As news of the shootings spread across the country and the world, so too did the confusion, shock, and outrage that followed. The variety of responses to the shootings revealed the polarization that had developed between anti-war and pro-war students and between the students and neighboring townspeople. Some townspeople and others throughout the country expressed the sentiment that the students had received what they deserved.

ACTUAL HISTORY

Hundreds of campuses nationwide experienced student strikes and shutdowns in the days following May 4. On May 14, 1970, African American students Phillip Gibbs and James Green were killed by police gunfire at Jackson State College in Mississippi. Many historians link the largely forgotten incident to Kent State. On May 3, 1971, more than 15,000 anti-war activists known as the May Day Tribe sought to shut down the federal government in Washington, D.C., through mass civil disobedience. Thousands were arrested in the largest mass arrest in American history. The May Day activities were the last major sustained actions of the anti-war movement.

In May 1970, President Robert White appointed the Commission on Kent State University Violence (CKSUV), chaired by Professor Harold Mayer. The committee met over a ten-month period, but its members were unable to agree on the causes of the May 4 events. Also in 1970, a special state grand jury issued indictments for conspiracy to commit riot and other charges against twenty-five people, most of them KSU students, along with KSU professor Tom Lough. They became known as the "Kent 25." Only five of the indicted were brought to trial and only three of the five were convicted. Charges against the remaining defendants were later dismissed. The grand jury also concluded that KSU faculty, students, and administration, as well as the KSU police department, all bore responsibility for the tragic events and that the National Guardsmen did have reason to fear bodily harm from the protestors.

President White said that the university must learn from the tragic events but also move forward with its purpose and return to normal operations. He also desired that the annual commemorations of May 4 should remain within the university community. He retired in 1971, leaving his successor and future presidents to face similar issues of remembrance and commemoration. Critics have charged that the university administration's primary goal of restoring Kent State's reputation as a peaceful institution of higher learning put public relations above all else.

Annual campus commemorations have included candlelight walks and vigils on the evening of May 3 and memorial programs on May 4, beginning in 1971. In that year, the university also founded the Center for Peaceful Change (CPC) as a memorial, and the campus library created a May 4 Resource Room. The university and various organizations have also placed several memorial plaques and sculptures on campus over the years. Questions arose about who should control the ways May 4 is

ANOTHER VIEW   Was There a Conspiracy at Kent State?

Questions of motive for the events at Kent State University in those first few days of May 1970, have never satisfactorily been answered, giving rise to a number of theories over the years. There was also a controversy over who was responsible for starting the ROTC fire on the evening of May 2. While some felt that it was the work of KSU student protestors, others claimed it was started by radical outside agitators who had come to Kent to join in the protests, or by agents of the local or national government who wished to use the fire as a justification for bringing the National Guard to campus. Conspiracy theorists point to the existence of a Federal Bureau of Investigation counterintelligence program entitled COINTELPRO, which was designed to infiltrate, discredit, and destroy various domestic protest movements. They also point to evidence that the local police and fire departments had prior knowledge of the fire and suspicious aspects of their behavior as the fire was set and as it burned.

Some of the witnesses to the events preceding the shootings later claimed to have seen several guardsmen huddled together on the football field, giving rise to a conspiracy theory that they had been plotting in advance to open fire on the protestors. Further testimony that many of the guardsmen had turned and fired simultaneously gave more credence to the theory. Those who argue against the conspiracy, however, note that the guardsmen were inadequately trained and that they were sleep-deprived over the course of the several days they spent at KSU, beginning with the night of the ROTC fire.

As for the May 4 shootings, questions arose as to whether the guardsmen fired out of panic, confusion, and self-defense or were following a deliberate plan to open fire on the students. Circumstantial evidence best fits the theory that somebody gave an order to fire, but no guardsman has ever admitted to doing so. Some theorists argued that the conspiracy went all the way to the Nixon White House. They claimed that the federal government wished to silence the rising wave of protests by using Kent State as an example of the repression that protestors could expect. Others argued that the shootings were merely the tragic result of a lack of planning on the part of the university and the National Guard and of the confusion of the confrontation that day.

commemorated, what is the proper form of commemoration, and how should the past be remembered and honored while not losing sight of the future. A variety of organizations formed to offer alternatives to the official commemorations, and some students wore T-shirts reading "Kent Police State University." Others were angered at the alternate programs, feeling that some groups were using Kent State as mere propaganda to achieve their own goals.

On the federal level, President Nixon created the President's Commission on Campus Unrest (the Scranton Committee), chaired by William Scranton, to investigate the shootings at Kent State and Jackson State. The committee held public hearings in Kent from August 19 through 21, 1970. In their final report, the committee stated that those protestors who had been involved in the events in the days leading up to May 4 were partially responsible for that day's violence. They also recognized, however, that the National Guard had served as the main catalyst for the May 4 rally and deserved criticism for their handling of the situation and use of loaded weapons.

In 1971, Attorney General John Mitchell announced that the federal government would not convene a grand jury to investigate the Kent State shootings. Kent State students and some of the families of the dead and wounded started a petition drive to reopen the case. As historian Scott Bills notes in *Kent State/May 4: Echoes through a Decade,* "They sought recognition of their claims that National Guard and state officials had acted wrongfully, violated the constitutional rights of student demonstrators, and then attempted to cover up their mistakes." In 1973, Attorney General Elliot Richardson announced that the federal government was reopening the case. This resulted in indictments against eight of the National Guardsmen. After a trial, a federal district judge acquitted all eight in November 1975.

All of the civil suits were eventually consolidated into *Krause v. Rhodes,* resulting in a fifteen-week trial in 1975. The jury decided that the plaintiffs had not been denied their civil rights and were not the victims of willful misconduct or negligence. An appeal resulted in the ordering of a new trial, as the original trial judge, Donald Young, was found to have mishandled a situation involving a threat against one of the jurors. Judge William Thomas presided over the new trial in December 1977. On January 4, 1979, there was an out-of-court settlement awarding the plaintiffs $675,000 for their injuries and suffering.

In 1977, KSU experienced a new controversy when plans for a gymnasium annex were finalized. Plans for the new annex had begun in the 1960s, and the favored location was close to Memorial Gym, near the site of the May 4 shootings. At that year's memorial program, some of the speakers spoke out against the proposed annex location. A large group led a protest march to downtown Kent and back, and a smaller group later marched to a board of trustees meeting in Rockwell Hall, occupying the hall during an overnight sit-in. The May 4th Coalition was formed and presented a series of demands to the board of trustees, but the board voted in favor of the annex. Protestors then established Tent City on Blanket Hill and held rallies to draw attention to the controversy. After a court injunction and a number of arrests, Tent City was cleared. After a number of legal challenges, construction on the new gym annex began September 19 in the presence of police guards, but no protestors. The May 4th Coalition would later split over factional differences.

The university and the nation continued to struggle with the meaning of the Kent State shootings. Kent State became a symbol of the anti-war movement and raised a number of significant questions with no easy answers. Some of the questions, such as why the National Guard turned and fired into the crowd, will most likely never be answered satisfactorily. As historian Scott Bills noted in *Kent State/May 4: Echoes through a Decade,* the shootings raised questions over "the legitimacy of dissent, the responsibility of government agencies regarding the use of force, the training and equipment of the National Guard, and the nature and use of power in America." Artists remembered Kent State in a number of tributes and documentaries, the best known being the song "Ohio," written by Neil Young and performed by Crosby, Stills, Nash, and Young shortly after the shootings.

In 1972, Nixon was reelected in a landslide, and a new North Vietnamese offensive led to the resumption of U.S. bombings in North Vietnam. Ultimately, Chinese and Soviet pressure made Ho Chi Minh's government more amenable to peace talks, and an agreement was reached in 1973 calling for a cease-fire and the removal of all remaining U.S. combat troops, among other measures. Vietnam would later be reunited under communist rule after the fall of Saigon in 1975. Congress revoked the powers granted to the president under the Gulf of Tonkin Resolution with the War Powers Act and future presidents would be hesitant to commit troops overseas in what politicians would term the "Vietnam syndrome."

ALTERNATE HISTORY

The events that unfolded at Kent State University, spreading a wave of violence and protest across campuses throughout the country, could just as easily have happened in the tumultuous year of 1968 rather than several years later in 1970. The Tet Offensive of January had already inflamed public opinion against the federal government's handling of Vietnam. The nationwide response to the assassinations of Dr. Martin Luther King, Jr., and Robert Kennedy as well as race riots and the violence outside the Chicago Democratic National Convention would have set the stage for the possibility of angry anti-war demonstrations on college campuses across the nation. More students would have been pushed into the anti-war movement just as it was reaching its height across the country.

At Kent State, a chapter of SDS had formed in 1968 to offer anti-war students a more active protest organization as an alternative to the soon to be defunct Kent Committee to End the War in Vietnam, which was viewed as more moderate. The massive Spring Offensive that had occurred at KSU in April of 1969 in response to the arrests of Howie Emmer and Rick Erickson, the banning of SDS from campus, and the closed disciplinary hearings at the Music and Speech Building would have instead become the Fall Offensive of 1968.

The arrests of over fifty students in the Music and Speech Building demonstration, combined with the university administration's subsequent inaction against those students who had accosted the demonstrators over the past several years, would have sparked a large outcry. SDS and the anti-war movement at KSU would have enjoyed a much broader base of support earlier in time. The Kent Committee would have become defunct several years earlier, as students would have become more militant and strident in their demands for justice both on and off campus. Peace vigils and teach-ins would have no longer seemed adequate in the face of administration inaction and hostility.

Student demonstrators would have organized a rally in support of SDS that would have attracted a large following. The atmosphere of tension and unrest would have spread to the town as students headed out to enjoy the vibrant nightlife. Violence would have followed in the first few days of October 1968, as it did in the first few days of May 1970. Bonfires and broken windows in Kent would have resulted in Mayor Satrom's declaration of a state of emergency and call for police reinforcements, just as they had in 1970. The burning of the KSU ROTC Building would have resulted in the arrival of the Ohio governor and the Ohio National Guard, resulting in further student anger and confrontations.

Students angry at the presence of guardsmen on campus would have planned another rally, this time set for noon on September 4, 1968. University administrators still would have banned the rally and would have used the guardsmen to disperse the crowd of protestors and spectators, with the same tragic outcome. The Kent State shootings would thus have occurred on September 4, 1968, rather than May 4, 1970. The reactionary wave of violence, student strikes, and campus closings across the country that followed the shootings would have occurred in late 1968, just as the anti-war movement was reaching its height. A general public largely unsupportive of the counterculture and the rising wave of student unrest would still have mostly favored the National Guard's actions.

The tragic events at Kent State would have become the backdrop to the 1968 presidential election, occurring in the final months of campaigning. The impending election would have forced the candidates to face the questions and issues that arose following the Kent State shootings. The reasons for the shootings, the questions of responsibility and prosecution, and the government's appropriate response all would have surfaced during the campaign debates and media questioning. Republican candidate Richard Nixon's calls for a return to law and order and a gradual withdrawal from Vietnam could have gained a greater appeal among the general public tired of the protests and shocked at the violence and turmoil threatening to divide the country. The "silent majority" would have been less silent, and Nixon would have been elected in 1968 in a landslide victory rather than a relatively close election.

The Kent State students and the families of the dead and wounded also could easily have found a much different response to their pleas for justice and accountability. The Nixon administration would have been less likely to try to block a federal grand jury investigation into the shootings, as the president would not have been in office long enough to fear the uncovering of his administration's role in the infiltration and discrediting of the anti-war movement. National Guardsmen would have been much more quickly indicted and tried for their roles in the shootings, although there most likely would have been a similar outcome as that of the actual trial. Most of the American public would still have supported their actions and would not have desired to see them punished.

Nixon would have claimed the results as a mandate that the general public supported his Vietnam policies of gradual Vietnamization of the war and of achieving peace with honor. With the anti-war movement fading, Nixon would have felt less immediate direct public

In an alternate history, Democratic senator George McGovern would have lost the 1976 presidential election to Republican Governor Ronald Reagan. (Library of Congress)

pressure to speed the process of American combat troop withdrawals. His 1970 announcement of the U.S. invasion of Vietcong supply bases in neighboring Cambodia, while still sparking anti-war protest marches, would not have resulted in a large-scale outbreak of violence, as everyone would have wished to avoid a repeat of the 1968 violence. At the same time, the anti-war movement would have appeared to be ebbing.

After the 1968 wave of violence, the anti-war movement would have drifted into factionalism several years earlier than actually occurred. A small faction of the movement would have become much more militant, giving an earlier rise to groups such as the Weathermen. A much larger number of the anti-war protestors, however, would have put their energies into electoral politics, working for peace candidates. A large number of students would have mobilized in support of the candidacy of Senator George McGovern, Nixon's Democratic opponent in the 1972 presidential election. The size and power of the student movement would have lent great grassroots support to McGovern's campaign. The contest would have appeared to be much closer, with Nixon not enjoying such a wide margin in the polls as he did in actual history.

Nixon would still have maintained a sizable following during his first term in office and would still have gained widespread praise for his historic visit to China and his policy of détente (lessening of tensions with the Soviet Union). Growing public anti-war sentiment, however, would not have been tempered by the shock and public antipathy to the growing militancy of the anti-war movement, as it would instead have become more peaceful, with most protestors now working within the system. Militant groups would have been a minority. Nixon would have found himself on the losing end of an extremely close election and would have retired from public life.

A break-in at the Democratic National Committee headquarters in the Watergate Building in Washington, D.C., would have disappeared into obscurity as a third-rate burglary. Without the damage of the Watergate scandal to hurt the Republican Party and Washington insiders, George McGovern would have lost the 1976 presidential election to California governor Ronald Reagan. Meanwhile, Kent State would still have become a symbol of the anti-war movement and the struggles over its significance and over how best to commemorate the lost lives would have continued up to the present.

Marcella Bush Trevino

Discussion Questions

1. After reviewing the details of the case presented in this chapter, what policies do you think would be appropriate for the use of National Guard troops in maintaining order during demonstrations? Should National Guard troops carry lethal weapons?

2. In the alternate history explored here, an event like the Kent State shootings occurred earlier, in 1968. Do you think that an earlier tragedy of this kind would have made anti-war demonstrations more or less effective?

3. What factor do you think accounts for the rise of Vietnam War protests in the early 1970s? Was it the unjust nature of the war or was it the counterculture's goal of targeting the establishment?

4. In an alternate history, a great many more might have been killed and injured at the student-National Guard clash that happened in 1970. Do you think the national reaction would have been different if twenty or thirty students had been killed, rather than four? Would such an event have caused more or less national sympathy with the goals of the protestors?

5. What factors account for the different nature of the protests against the Vietnam War in 1970, and those against the Iraq War in 2006–2007?

Bibliography and Further Reading

Bills, Scott L., ed. *Kent State/May 4: Echoes through a Decade.* Kent, OH: Kent State University Press, 1982.

Caputo, Philip. *13 Seconds: A Look Back at the Kent State Shootings.* New York: Chamberlain Brothers, 2005.

Casale, Ottavio M., and Louis Paskoff, eds. *The Kent Affair: Documents and Interpretations.* Boston: Houghton Mifflin, 1971.

Davies, Peter. *The Truth about Kent State: A Challenge to the American Conscience.* New York: Farrar, Straus and Giroux, 1973.

DeBenedetti, Charles. *An American Ordeal: The Anti-war Movement of the Vietnam Era.* Syracuse, NY: Syracuse University Press, 1990.

Gordon, William A. *The Fourth of May: Killings and Coverups at Kent State?* Buffalo, NY: Prometheus Books, 1990.

Grant, Edward J., and Michael Hill. *I was There: What Really Went on at Kent State.* Lima, OH: C.S.S. Publishing, 1974.

Heineman, Kenneth J., "'Look Out Kid, You're Gonna Get Hit!': Kent State and the Vietnam Anti-war Movement." In *Give Peace a Chance: Exploring the Vietnam Anti-war Movement.* Small, Melvin and William D. Hoover, eds. Syracuse, NY: Syracuse University Press, 1992.

Kelner, Joseph, and James Munves. *The Kent State Coverup.* Lincoln, NE: Iuniverse, 2001.

Lewis, Jerry M., and Thomas R. Hensley. "The May 4 Shootings at Kent State University: The Search for Historical Accuracy," http://dept.kent.edu/sociology/lewis/LEWIHEN.htm (accessed September 2006).

Michener, James. *Kent State: What Happened and Why.* New York: Random House, 1971.

Morrison, Joan, and Robert K. Morrison. *From Camelot to Kent State: The Sixties Experience in the Words of Those Who Lived It.* New York: Oxford University Press, 2001.

Taylor, Stuart, Richard Shuntich, Patrick McGovern, and Robert Gethner. *Violence at Kent State. May 1 to 4, 1970: The Student's Perspective.* New York: College Notes and Texts, 1971.

TURNING POINT

The 1963 civil rights march on the nation's capital was mostly peaceful. What if the march had been suppressed with violence?

INTRODUCTION

To understand why a civil rights march on Washington, D.C., was needed in 1963, one must go back more than 200 years. Just after June 11, 1776, Thomas Jefferson, a slave owner, wrote in the preamble of the Constitution that all men are created equal. However, there were some 500,000 slaves in America at the time.

Inability to vote was only the beginning of persecutions against slaves. Slaves were property. They could be beaten or killed without legal repercussion. Men, women, even those considering themselves married, could be separated or bred at a whim. Children could be ripped from the arms of their parents. Mulattos were often used as house slaves or sold into prostitution. Penalties for attempting escape were harsh. Long after slavery ended, the threat of beatings and death for African Americans was still very real, especially in the South.

From the beginning, slavery was a divisive issue. In the late 1780s, southern slave states were allowed to continue capturing Africans as part of the politics involved to preserve the union. Representation in Congress was in favor of the South as each slave counted as three-fifths of a person for representation purposes.

All states had to return escaped slaves, even though Vermont, New Hampshire, Pennsylvania, Rhode Island, Connecticut, and Massachusetts had made slavery illegal. In spite of such bans, the Constitution itself was misused to strengthen slavery.

In 1808, importing slaves was banned, but the illegal slave trade still flourished. In 1820, the Missouri Compromise allowed slavery there but not elsewhere west of the Mississippi River. This law would be repealed in 1854. California was made a state where slavery would be illegal, and slavery was prohibited in Washington, D.C. But undermining the positive side of this, fugitive laws were again strengthened. In 1857 the Supreme Court ruled in the *Dred Scott* decision that taking slaves into a free state did not make them free; Congress could not bar slavery from a territory, and blacks could not become citizens.

KEY CONCEPT   Terms Defined

The Union: Also known as the North, or the Yankees. The Union comprised twenty-three states: California, Connecticut, Delaware, Illinois, Indiana, Iowa, Kansas, Kentucky, Maine, Maryland, Massachusetts, Michigan, Minnesota, Missouri, New Hampshire, New Jersey, New York, Ohio, Oregon, Pennsylvania, Rhode Island, Vermont, and Wisconsin. The territories of Colorado, Dakota, Nebraska, Nevada, New Mexico, Utah, and Washington also fought against secession and slavery.

The Confederacy: Also known as the South, Rebel States, Johnny Reb, or Rebels. As a result of Abraham Lincoln's election to the presidency, on December 20, 1860, South Carolina's legislature held a special convention and voted to secede from the Union. Between January 9 and February 1, Alabama, Florida, Georgia, Louisiana, Mississippi, and Texas also seceded. Arkansas, North Carolina, Tennessee, and Virginia joined them, with Missouri also forming Confederate units. This made for eleven states and one territory supporting secession and slavery.

The Reconstruction Era: A relatively golden age for blacks just after the Civil War. Most legislation was positive. It lasted about a decade, mostly ending by the mid-1870s. African Americans voted in record numbers, electing hundreds of black officeholders. They served on juries too. Inroads were made toward desegregation. Blacks attended public schools. The climate of the country as a whole changed, however. Reasons as disparate as non–Anglo-Saxon European immigration to the north, fears of racial and religious differences there, the black movement northward, the uniting of poor white farmers for economic causes, and Republican voting realities eroded the improvements. What had started with civil rights acts ended with their overturning, with decisions such as *Plessy v. Ferguson*.

Jim Crow: Named for a black character in a minstrel show. Jim Crow refers to laws in existence between the 1880s and the 1960s that had to do with banning racial intermarriage and the imposition of segregation. Most states and many cities

Some efforts were made by slaves, freed blacks, and whites alike to resist. In 1820, the first exodus from the United States to Africa occurred when eighty-six free blacks set sail to settle in the British colony of Sierra Leone. In 1831, there was a slave rebellion in Virginia; fifty-seven whites were killed and U.S. troops were called in, killing 100 slaves. The rebellion was led by Nat Turner, who was caught, tried, and hanged. On December 2, 1859, John Brown, a white man charged with murder and treason, was also hanged in Charles Town, Virginia, for attempting to start a rebellion.

On November 6, 1860, Abraham Lincoln was elected president with Hannibal Hamlin as his vice president; by February 1861, the slave states had begun to secede, even as Kansas entered the union as a non-slave state. Six states would send delegates to elect their own president, Jefferson Davis, calling themselves the Confederate States of America. As the most anti-slavery of the four candidates running for president, Lincoln seemed to many in the slave states to represent a threat to that institution. Claiming that his election represented the end of long-standing compromises that had held the union together, seven slave states announced their secession from the United States between December 1860 and February 1861.

On April 15, 1861, Lincoln declared a state of insurrection and called for 75,000 ninety-day volunteers to enlist in the army. More states

KEY CONCEPT *Terms Defined (Continued)*

passed such laws. Depending on place, hospitals, hospital entrances, mental institutions, railroad cars, buses, restaurants, billiard parlors, bathrooms, schools, juvenile detention facilities, barber shops, amateur baseball lots, parks, bars, reform schools, circuses (ticket offices), housing, schools for the blind, prisons, militias, libraries, telephone booths, theaters, mining locker rooms, swimming, boating, and fishing facilities, and of course water fountains could all be subject to segregation.

Jim Crow laws and penalties were meant to keep whites separate from other races, discouraging any form of socializing or contact. In Mississippi, one could not even print, publish, or circulate arguments contrary to Jim Crow laws. The penalty was up to $500 or six months in jail. In North Carolina, schoolbooks could not be passed between races. Whichever race used them first got them for good. In Oklahoma, fines ranged from $10 to $50 for teaching in an integrated school. In South Carolina, no black could hold custody of a white child. The stiffest

penalties tended to deal with intermarriage and cohabitation.

Freedom Riders: Men and women who would deliberately break a segregation law so as to bring about a court case that might strike down the law they would be arrested for breaking. Many laws that came to be tested in this way involved public trasit and the riding of buses or trains. The Congress of Racial Equality (CORE), in the 1960s, and the Student Nonviolent Coordinating Committee (SNCC) organized freedom riders.

Civil Rights: Rights and/or privileges upheld by law. There are consequences for violating another person's civil rights. Freedom of assembly, speech, and the press; freedom from involuntary servitude; the right to equality in public places and to vote are all examples of civil rights included in our Constitution and its amendments.

Discrimination: Denial of civil rights based on race, sex, religion, age, previous condition of servitude, physical limitations, national origin, and sometimes sexual preference.

seceded. On May 19, Lincoln ordered all their ports blockaded. On May 29, Richmond, Virginia, became the capital of the Confederacy. The Civil War would last from these beginnings in 1861 into 1865.

On September 22, 1862, Lincoln issued the Preliminary Emancipation Proclamation, and then the Emancipation Proclamation itself on New Year's Day 1863. This short yet powerful document legally freed, after two and a half centuries, some 3 million southern slaves and allowed for the enlistment of black soldiers into the Union Army. This shortened the war, helped to eliminate stereotypes, and created black leaders. It also ended any foreign support for the South in the Civil War.

Today, monuments and plaques throughout the region commemorate the places where the proclamation was first read, often by Union officers fresh from victory on the battlefields. The black holiday Juneteenth celebrates the reading in 1865, when the last Confederate forces surrendered in Texas.

In 1863, Lincoln presented his Gettysburg Address. In part, it repeated the ideal that all men are created equal, although this time, with a very different meaning. In June 1864, he signed a bill repealing the fugitive slave laws. On November 8, he was reelected, with Andrew Johnson as his vice president.

On December 21, Sherman's Union Army defeated Savannah, Georgia, without resistance. On April 2, 1865, the Confederates evacuated their

---

IN CONTEXT   Laws, Amendments, and Court Decisions before 1963

1865 Thirteenth Amendment: On January 31, 1865, slavery was abolished in the United States. Various states soon enacted laws known as Black Codes to deny blacks their civil rights.

1868 Fourteenth Amendment: Added to counter Black Codes and confer citizenship, this prohibited states from making or enforcing laws that denied citizenship rights and protections. Life, liberty, or property could not be taken without due process.

Section Five gave Congress the power to pass any laws necessary for its enforcement. This led to the passage of many civil rights statutes during the Reconstruction Era that are still in force today.

1870 Fifteenth Amendment: Discrimination in voting based on race was outlawed. No woman would be allowed to vote until the Nineteenth Amendment passed in 1920, however. For more than a century, southern states would use poll taxes, literacy and property tests, and other tactics to deny blacks the vote.

1875 Civil Rights Act: This legislation was meant to integrate public places and ensure penalties for those who did not comply, with cases to be tried solely by federal courts. This act banned discrimination against serving on grand or petit juries and, though rarely enforced, made discriminatory practices a misdemeanor.

1883: The Supreme Court overturned the 1875 Civil Rights Act, declaring it unconstitutional to bar discrimination by individuals or corporations, finding such outside the scope of the Thirteenth, Fourteenth, and Fifteenth Amendments.

1896 *Plessy v. Ferguson:* Homer Plessy, who was one-eighth African American, was arrested testing an 1890 law on segregation of railway cars in Louisiana. Plessy's light complexion was still dark enough for him to be refused access to a white-only railway car, and when Plessy challenged the discrimination, his arrest was upheld. This far-reaching court decision allowed the doctrine of separate but equal.

1938 *Gaines v. Canada:* This decision led to the integration of graduate schools. Gaines was denied admission to the University of Missouri Law School by the registrar, Canada. The Supreme Court ordered Missouri either to supply equal accommodations or to admit Gaines. Before this, out-of-state scholarships had been given to blacks denied admission in their home states.

---

capitol at Richmond. The Union Army occupied the city the next day. On April 9, at Appomattox, Confederate General Robert E. Lee surrendered his army of Northern Virginia to General Ulysses S. Grant. On April 14, as Lincoln watched a play at Ford's Theater, John Wilkes Booth shot him; Lincoln died the next day, and Andrew Johnson became president.

Time was running out for the Confederacy and its supporters. On April 26, Booth was shot and killed. On May 10, Jefferson Davis, president of the Confederacy, was taken prisoner. On May 26, in New Orleans, Confederate General Kirby E. Smith was offered terms of surrender, accepting on June 2, formally ending Confederate resistance. By June 30, eight conspirators in Lincoln's assassination were convicted; four were later executed.

Soon after the war, the Thirteenth, Fourteenth, and Fifteenth Amendments to the Constitution were passed, stipulating voting and other citizenship rights for African Americans.

The Ku Klux Klan (KKK) was established in 1866. The Klan, along with several other such organizations, was devoted to preventing blacks from exercising their political rights. Using threats, violence, beatings, and murder, and wearing masks during their raids, Klan members

1944 *Smith v. Alright:* This decision quadrupled black voter registration. Smith, a black Texan, was refused a ballot in the white primary. S. E. Alright was the election judge. The refusal was found to be a violation of Smith's Fifteenth Amendment rights.

1946 *Morgan v. Virginia:* Interstate buses and trains were legally desegregated in this case, by a 6–1 decision. Freedom rider Irene Morgan was arrested for refusing to give up her seat on a Greyhound bus.

1948 *Shelley v. Kraemer:* Thurgood Marshall, then of the NAACP, argued on behalf of Shelley, who wished to buy a pair of St. Louis row houses. Housing had been restricted by racial covenant. About 85 percent of white-owned housing at the time in cities like Los Angeles, Chicago, and Detroit was restricted. Kraemer, attempting to enforce the covenant, failed, and integration in housing was instituted.

1952 Immigration and Naturalization Act: Naturalization of citizens was no longer dependent on race or ethnicity.

1954 *Brown v. the Board of Education of Topeka, Kansas:* "To separate black children from others of similar age and qualifications solely because of their race generates a feeling of inferiority as to their status in the community that may affect their hearts and minds in a way never to be undone.... We conclude that in the field of public education the doctrine of separate but equal has no place. Separate educational facilities are inherently unequal." (From the landmark Supreme Court decision.)

This unanimous decision struck down fifty-four years of separate but equal policies. The Supreme Court case found that segregation of schools was a violation of the Fourteenth Amendment. The ruling would extend in 1956 to end the Montgomery bus boycott. By 1966, legal desegregation would spread to restaurants, hotels, courtrooms, libraries, and public parks.

1957 Civil Rights Act of 1957: Congress created the U.S Civil Rights Commission, and a Civil Rights Division within the justice department so that voter registration suits could be brought.

1960 *Boynton v. Virginia:* Filed after freedom riders tested the law, this case integrated bus station bathrooms, cafes, and waiting rooms.

attempted to stamp out the political activists among blacks and their white Republican allies in the South. Between 1895 and 1900, about 500 blacks were lynched, mostly in southern states. In 1895, black leader Booker T. Washington encouraged an African American focus on training and economics instead of seeking desegregation and the vote.

In 1906, twenty-one people were killed in Atlanta riots, and martial law was declared. The riot was apparently spurred by publication of *The Clansmen* in 1905, a book glorifying the KKK. Incensed by the book, a group of drunken whites apparently believed newspaper claims that blacks had assaulted white women and started the first race riot in the city. In 1909, the National Congress on the Negro convened, leading to the founding of the National Association for the Advancement of Colored People (NAACP). In 1915, the KKK, repopularized, returned, and by 1923 Oklahoma was placed under martial law because of racial tensions. In 1925, the Klan marched on Washington, D.C. Legislators and the courts went back and forth over rights and not even the NAACP saw challenges to southern school segregation as viable. Instead, they tried to hang on to gains made by African Americans in educational and occupational opportunities in the North.

In the 1940s, the NAACP was about 90 percent successful in the courts, whittling away at discriminatory laws. White supremacist

ANOTHER VIEW   Women of Abolition and the Civil Rights Movement

Few women got the spotlight at the 1963 march. Notable exceptions were Daisy Bates, Mahalia Jackson, and Marian Anderson. The rest, like Coretta King, were there as wives and relegated to being supporters for the men. Many women had done the work and taken the risks for the movement, though, from the beginning.

Black abolitionists Harriet Tubman and Sojourner Truth are best known, but Frances Ellen Watkins Harper, Maria Stewart, and Harriet Jacobs also fought for the cause. White women tended to have more education, financial support, and relative freedom to move, and at least did not face being enslaved for their actions. Most came from Quaker, Unitarian, and Universalist backgrounds and, often, sympathetic families. Their greater number included Susan B. Anthony, Antoinette Brown Blackwell, Lydia Maria Child, Angelina Grimke, Sarah Grimke, Julia Ward Howe, Mary Livermore, Lucretia Mott, Elizabeth Cady Stanton, Lucy Stone, Martha Coffin Wright, and the controversial Harriet Beecher Stowe.

Stereotypes of women differed by race. White women were seen as submissive, weak, obedient, and nonsexual. Black women were portrayed as temptresses by the white men who abused them. Black men of the movement tended to want black women to be quiet and submissive, the conservative Christian stereotype.

In 1944, Howard University students staged a successful sit-in at Thompson's Cafeteria in Washington, D.C. Most were women. They were served. Among them was Pauli Murray. In 1963, at Yale University, Eleanor Holmes Norton, a noted civil rights attorney, and chairperson of the Equal Employment Opportunity Commission, would first hear of this act from Murray.

More names of the earlier 1900s included Mary McLeod Bethune; Mary Church Terrel, who helped found the NAACP and the National Association of Colored Women; Ida Wells-Barnett, who helped track lynchings; white social reformer Mary White Ovington; and even Eleanor Roosevelt.

thinking was called into question more internationally, as German Nazi propaganda pointed out American racial hypocrisy, even as the United States condemned the Nazis for anti-Semitism and "racial purity" laws. In 1941, the year the United States entered World War II, the American Red Cross refused African American blood donations. Even educated black women could not find clerking jobs outside of government, the ghetto, or black-owned businesses.

President Franklin Roosevelt issued Executive Order 8802 in 1941, declaring that defense contractors could not discriminate in hiring. Under the act, blacks were allowed into defense plant job training programs and the Fair Employment Practices Commission (FEPC) was established. Yet 1943 saw race riots in Harlem and Detroit.

Many blacks served in the war with distinction, honor, and bravery, though they could not serve as equals. African Americans have served in every conflict the nation has been involved in, including the Revolution, yet the Civil War had brought about segregation of units. In World War I, there had been the all-black 93rd Infantry Division. In World War II, there were the 92nd, 93rd, and 99th fighter squadrons: the Tuskeegee Airmen. In Korea, the 24th Infantry Division again distinguished itself. "Separate but equal" applied there, too. Housing, treatment, and ability to advance were anything but equal. White officers led black troops.

ANOTHER VIEW *Women of Abolition and the Civil Rights Movement (Continued)*

Rosa Parks is well known, but there was also Ella Baker, who risked her life urging blacks of the 1940s to join the NAACP and who ran the Atlanta SCLC; and Diane Nash of the SCLC and de facto leader of Nashville's SNCC. These women were relatively unknown, as were so many others, because the official leaders all tended to be men. Prathia Hall, Sandra Hayden, Jane Stembridge, and Connie Curry were all SNCC members, the last three white.

Some women, like Hall, did not object to the support roles to which they were relegated. Believing it made black men look strong, they allowed recognition of their own strength to become secondary. Septima Clark, a member of the NAACP since 1918, disagreed. She was not pleased with King and the SCLC for their habit of not doing the dirty work of organizing, then taking the spotlight.

In 1961 Mississippi, young teenage girls like Jessie Divens, Jaqueline Byrd, and Brenda Travis were recruited for door-to-door voter education and registration. Black women could get away with far more militancy, and the girls were strong, independent people. That did not mean that they did not get arrested when marching and suffer consequences. In refusing to give up a seat to a white woman, Jessie Divens faced a judge who threatened reform school. She flatly refused to apologize or cease her activities.

Women of the movement included freedom singers Bernice Johnson Reagon and Bertha Gober. White Joan Browning refused to give up attendance at a Georgia black church and was forced out of her college, ultimately becoming a freedom rider and SNCC member.

In 1962, Penny Patch, the only white female in the first integrated group sent into southwestern Georgia to organize, had to be careful not to be seen publicly with male coworkers, as it could cost their lives.

Eliza Thomas and Robertina Freeman were jailed in Albany, Georgia, for marching. Girls as young as eleven were arrested, beaten, and held in filthy, inhumane conditions.

In 1945, Secretary of War Robert P. Patterson appointed three generals to look into the army policy on blacks, and this became known as the Gillem Board. Before they handed down a decision assuming that segregation would continue, Isaac Woodard, a black veteran, was attacked and blinded by police in Aiken, South Carolina. President Harry Truman was outraged, and in July 1946, more so, as two black veterans and their wives were pulled from their car and shot sixty times by a Monroe, Georgia, white mob. Truman ordered the crimes investigated, stating that federal statutes would be sought for use against offenders. He then appointed the President's Committee on Civil Rights, which, with other panels in 1947, found that segregation must end.

By January 1948, Truman skipped attempts to have legislation passed in favor of issuing an executive order. On July 26, 1948, he signed Executive Order 9981, which stated, "It is hereby declared to be the policy of the President that there shall be equality of treatment and opportunity for all persons in the armed services without regard to race, color, religion, or national origin."

Throughout the rest of 1948, and into 1949, more committees, reports, and arguments went on as to how best to comply with the order. By October 1953, with the Korean War ongoing, the army reported 95 percent of blacks were serving in desegregated units.

Segregation of public facilities remained a constant irritation for blacks in Alabama and other states and a symptom of racial injustice and inequality. In 1955, in Montgomery, Alabama, Rosa Parks refused to give up her bus seat to a white man and was arrested for violating a Jim Crow city ordinance. A boycott followed, led by the Reverend Martin Luther King, Jr., and his associates. Blacks walked, leaving buses empty.

The boycott was ended by an extension of the *Brown* decision. The Coalition of Southern Congressmen resisted strenuously. In 1957, Orbal Faubus, the governor of Arkansas, called in the National Guard to prevent nine black students from attending a high school in Little Rock. The court ruled, and President Dwight Eisenhower sent in federal troops to ensure integration. The year 1960 saw four black college students protesting with sit-ins at the segregated lunch counter of a Greensboro, North Carolina, Woolworth's store. They were not served, but they stayed all day, returning with twenty-five more protesters the next. Such peaceful protesters faced violence by word and deed as they spread this action to other cities. Southern senators filibustered Congress until concessions were again made on a voting rights act.

In 1961 freedom riders spread from Washington, D.C., to the southern states, promoting rights for blacks. In 1962, President John F. Kennedy supported James Meredith, an air force veteran and the first black student at the University of Mississippi, by sending federal troops to Mississippi to end riots by whites. Governor Ross Barnett had said that he would never allow the university to integrate. Subsequent rioting left two people dead and dozens wounded.

In November 1962, President John F. Kennedy ordered an end to all federal housing discrimination and established the President's Committee on Equal Employment Opportunity with Executive Order 10925, giving numerous blacks prominent positions. Order 10925 first referenced affirmative action and freed federal funds from racial bias when they were used for hiring and employment. Also in 1962, the U.S. Supreme Court struck down segregation in all transportation facilities as unconstitutional. The Department of Defense ordered that all military reserve units, except the National Guard, be fully integrated.

In 1963 Medgar Evers, a civil rights leader, was assassinated by a sniper. Cambridge, Maryland, saw race riots and martial law. The SNCC, a racially mixed, nonviolent group, was involved in bus rides and protests in Birmingham, Alabama, as well as in other cities. In Birmingham that year, thousands of blacks risked police dogs, tear gas, billy clubs, and high-powered water hoses to take to the streets in protest of segregation and denial of civil rights. SNCC members were arrested there, taken to the Tennessee border, and moved across state lines. They then traveled to Montgomery, Alabama, where they were attacked with fists and clubs by an angry white mob. This did not stop them. Along with locals, SNCC members were sent into communities to support the African American cause overall and encourage and organize black voting. They were heavily active in Georgia, Mississippi, Arkansas, and Alabama. The U.S. Justice Department had informed the SNCC that it would not protect them but would investigate should they be harmed.

TURNING POINT

For the March on Washington for Jobs and Freedom on August 28, 1963, 100,000 people were expected to come. At first, riots had been feared. Washington, D.C.'s police chief had assembled some 5,900 men, including 350 club-carrying firemen, 1,700 national guardsmen, 300 newly sworn in police officers, and 4,000 soldiers and marines on the other side of the Potomac River in case of trouble. Interference by the KKK and the American Nazi Party were feared. Sale of alcohol was banned.

But there was no violence, and instead, 250,000 people came together from all across America. King's group, the SCLC, the SNCC, the Urban League, and the NAACP were all represented. The housewives league, Jack and Jill, and the Order of the Eastern Star, the Elks, and varied fraternities and sororities all marched, too.

Some walked to Washington, D.C. Many came by bus, train, or plane, even by roller skate and bicycle. The march was in support of a civil rights bill proposed by Kennedy after the events in Birmingham. The aim was racial equality, and both blacks and whites participated. Many faiths were represented by their clergy, and a wide cross section of Americans attended, including Protestants, Catholics, Jews, and atheists, all joining together on this day.

Included were students, working people from across socioeconomic boundaries, and many celebrities. Actors Paul Newman, Marlon Brando,

Marchers carrying signs for equal rights, integrated schools, decent housing, and an end to bias, on August 28, 1963. (Library of Congress)

Police push back against a crowd of African American protestors during the March on Washington. (Library of Congress)

Civil rights leader Baynard Taylor Rustin was the main organizer of the March on Washington. (Library of Congress)

Charlton Heston, and James Garner were there, as were Harry Belafonte, Sammy Davis, Jr., and Josephine Baker. Many popular singers of the time, including Joan Baez and Bob Dylan, were present. Gospel singer Mahalia Jackson sang just before King's speech.

The march was led by King; Roy Wilkins; Randolph King of the NAACP; Walter Reuther, president of the United Automobile Workers; and many others, both in the spotlight and behind the scenes. Chairperson of the march was A. Philip Randolph of the Brotherhood of Sleeping Car Porters, who had been banned by executive order of President Roosevelt in 1941 from making such a march at the time. Baynard Taylor Rustin, a close associate of Randolph, handled the staff, finances, travel arrangements, publicity, accommodations, and other logistical tasks.

Rustin had been involved in nonviolent protests and the civil rights movement since the 1940s. In 1963, he wrote in his socialist publication, *The Liberator*, of the great importance, beyond speeches and everything else, of black and white coming together at the Lincoln

Memorial, a quarter-million strong, carrying the civil rights revolution into the streets. The follow-through should be with nonviolent uprisings in cities across the land. It was here that King gave his "I Have a Dream" speech that included the often-quoted phrase, "I have a dream that my four children will one day live in a nation where they will not be judged by the color of their skin but by the content of their character."

Although Congress did not pass Kennedy's bill immediately, this was a major turning point. It would still take the Atlanta bombing, Kennedy's death, and President Lyndon Johnson's pushing for the passage of the bill to bring about an event that would change the face of America forever.

ACTUAL HISTORY

The 1960s were a time of upheaval and change. In 1960, only 13 percent of black men held middle-class jobs (as opposed to 51 percent of whites). By the end of the decade, this figure for African Americans would more than double to 27 percent.

In 1963, in just three months, 1,412 demonstrations were recorded by the justice department. Many people were beaten and arrested. The threat of death was very real. In Birmingham, Alabama, white supremacists bombed a church that had been a staging area for demonstrations. Four little black girls were in the basement and were killed—shocking the nation. Then, on November 22, 1963, Kennedy was assassinated in Dallas, Texas.

The Civil Rights Act of 1964, or Public Law 88–352, passed on July 2, 1964, in spite of a seventy-five-day-long filibuster. Discrimination based on race was outlawed by this act almost everywhere in America. Hiring, public accommodations and facilities, schools, and voting were all affected. The justice department gained the ability to sue on behalf of individuals. This is the single most important piece of civil rights legislation ever passed. Since 1945, such an act had been considered but had failed to pass through Congress.

Only lesser measures had passed before. Political pressures had kept Kennedy from seeking such an act, though he did attempt to extend minority rights in employment, housing, education, voting, and transportation via executive action. His assassination, however, and Johnson's pressure to see legislation passed as well as the climate of mourning and readiness in America finally spurred Congress to action. The act resolved many issues and left the door wide open for more changes to be made.

Heart of Atlanta Motel v. United States upheld the legislation, ruling that Congress had the authority to pass the Civil Rights Act of 1964, and over the next decade, some 1,500 additional lawsuits would be filed under it.

Johnson himself was a controversial, even dichotomous figure. On the one hand, he went far beyond what many initially had expected with his War on Poverty; social programs such as Medicare, the first introduced health insurance program for the poor; and civil rights legislation. The bureaucracy of his social programs was by his own admission more than he had expected. He was a Texan who early on might have supported some discriminatory causes. He was president during the Vietnam War and failed to resolve that conflict. Historians differ on whether he might

An African American confronts Ku Klux Klan members demonstrating in favor of Republican Barry Goldwater for president in 1964. (Library of Congress)

have done the right things because they were right or because they were politically expedient. The fact remains that while he, not Kennedy, was president, the most far-reaching piece of civil rights legislation in American history was pushed through.

But the violence did not end. Also in 1964, three civil rights workers were stopped for speeding in Mississippi, and disappeared. Their bodies were found buried six weeks later. There were also riots in Philadelphia, Pennsylvania, and Harlem, New York.

In 1965, two civil rights workers were slain in Selma, Alabama, where blacks were still being denied registration for the vote. Marchers were met with violence by Sheriff James Clark and his deputies. A few weeks later, on March 7, about 600 people tried to march from Selma to Montgomery. The sheriff and 200 troopers forced them back to Selma at Edmund Pettus Bridge with tear gas, nightsticks, and bull whips. Seventeen were hospitalized.

Media coverage, often lacking before the time of the march, actually interrupted the Sunday night movie on ABC to show footage of this protest march. King and his associates filed a federal lawsuit, and on March 21, the marchers went forward with the protection of federal troops. Afterward, the KKK murdered Viola Liuzzo, a white civil rights worker. Controversial black activist Malcolm X was assassinated. After years of pent-up frustration, young African Americans in the Watts, California, ghetto rioted over an alleged act of police brutality.

Johnson closed a speech in favor of the Voting Rights Act of 1965 with the words, "And we shall overcome." The 1965 act was passed and has been broadened since by various other acts and court rulings; it is considered the most successful civil rights legislation of all time. With it,

Congress outlawed just about every stratagem known by which states were denying blacks their right to vote.

Between 1960 and 1966, voter registration rose about 800 percent in Mississippi, more than 400 percent in Alabama, and more than 300 percent in South Carolina.

In June 1965, Johnson gave a speech on the necessity of affirmative action, positing that civil rights legislation alone would not be enough. Executive Order 11246, issued September 24, 1965, affected government contractors and hiring and enforced affirmative action for the first time.

Edward Brooke, a Massachusetts Republican and the first black U.S. senator in eighty-five years, was elected in 1966. Racial violence was reported in forty-three cities that year. James Meredith, having graduated college, began a 220-mile March against Fear from Memphis, Tennessee, to Jackson, Mississippi. He had hoped to show an improvement in racial climate, but was instead shot. Civil rights leaders continued the march from where he fell.

In 1967, there were more riots in Detroit, Michigan, and Newark, New Jersey. Thurgood Marshall was the first black named to the Supreme Court. Carl Stokes was elected mayor of Cleveland and Richard J. Hatcher became mayor of Gary, Indiana. They were the first blacks to hold such roles in major cities in the United States.

In 1968 King was assassinated by James Earl Ray in Memphis, Tennessee. The Poor People's March on Washington, planned by King, went on. The Urban League finally had a chapter in Knoxville, Tennessee. Howard University students seized the administration building and demanded a black-oriented curriculum.

In 1969, seventeen states still banned interracial marriage. President Richard Nixon initiated the "Philadelphia Order," targeting unfair hiring practices in craft unions and the construction industry. Philadelphia was the test case. Quotas were not imposed, but a definite timetable for goals was set.

The 1970s showed an overall trend toward greater systemic equality. Cases involving busing of schoolchildren in the North, in areas with de facto segregation, were common. In 1970, the Louisiana State legislature ruled that any person with 1/32 or more black blood is black. In 1973, Maynard Jackson was elected mayor of Atlanta, the first time a major southern city had a black in such an office. The year 1975 saw the voting rights act extended, and in 1977 Clifford Alexander, Jr., became the first black secretary of the army.

On June 28, 1978, *Regents of the University of California v. Bakke* limited affirmative action so that it did not come at the expense of more qualified candidates. Allan Bakke had been rejected by the University of California, Davis, Medical School twice because of the school's quota of sixteen places, out of 100, that were allocated to minorities and economically disadvantaged students. This quota allegedly violated the Equal Protection Clause of the Fourteenth Amendment.

The proportion of black males moving up from lower class to middle class rose from one-fifth to one-third; 48 percent of the next generation of black families followed; this was less dramatic than the 67 percent of whites that moved up, but it was still a marked increase.

In 1979, a shoot-out in Greensboro, North Carolina, killed five anti-Klan protesters and left a dozen Klansmen charged with the murders.

The 1980s overall were a time of relative prosperity for America and a time for debating what was and was not fair. Affirmative action decisions, both pro and con, marked the decade. In 1980, the census showed that seven states had a black population of over 20 percent. On July 2, 1980, *Fullilove v. Klutznick* decided that though *Bakke* had struck down strict quotas, modest ones with a narrow focus were constitutional. A law requiring 15 percent of public funds to be set aside for qualified minority contractors was upheld. In 1983, Martin Luther King, Jr., Day became a federal holiday to be observed on the third Monday in January. In 1984, the *Philadelphia Tribune,* the nation's oldest African American periodical, celebrated its centennial, and the Birmingham, Alabama, Rotary admitted its first black member.

On May 19, 1986, *Wygant v. Jackson Board of Education* decided that a school board policy of laying off employees based on minority status rather than seniority was not constitutional, as minority benefits were outweighed by injury to nonminorities losing jobs. Racial hiring factors were found less injurious, as jobs could be found in many places, and were allowed.

On February 25, 1987, *United States v. Paradise* upheld strict racial quotas for the State of Alabama Department of Public Safety, where one black trooper had been hired in thirty-seven years. Federal courts had ordered changes in 1970, but a fair hiring system had not been implemented nor had promotions beyond entry level occurred. To combat systemic racism, quotas were upheld so that 25 percent of all new hires and promotions would have to be black.

In 1988, Congress passed the Civil Rights Restoration Act over President Ronald Reagan's veto. In 1989, Army General Colin Powell became the first black to serve as chairman of the Joint Chiefs of Staff; the first black elected governor of Virginia was L. Douglas Wilder.

On January 23, 1989, *City of Richmond v. Croson* upheld a challenge to a 30 percent quota on city construction funds allocated for black-owned businesses. The court ruled that strict racial quotas could not be used unless racial discrimination could be proven to be widespread in a particular industry. This was the first time that affirmative action was judged as suspect.

The 1990s were a time of refinement and determination of necessity. In 1990, President George H. W. Bush vetoed a civil rights bill that imposed employer quotas. A weaker bill passed in 1991. A Civil Rights Museum opened at the Memphis, Tennessee, site where King was assassinated. In 1994, Byron De La Beckwith was finally convicted of the 1963 assassination of Medgar Evers.

On June 12, 1995, in *Adarand Constructors, Inc. v. Peña,* the Supreme Court decided that strict scrutiny was called for in federal programs to determine that discrimination existed before implementing programs of affirmative action. Such programs were to be situation-specific, narrowly tailored, and requiring compelling government interest to exist. Justices Antonin Scalia and Clarence Thomas felt that affirmative action should be completely banned. The remaining justices still saw a need for it when both practice and effect of racial discrimination continued.

On July 19, 1995, President Bill Clinton made a speech on affirmative action and the need for it, as the *Adarand* decision showed that systematic discrimination still existed. He proposed White House guidelines on affirmative action, calling for the elimination of programs that created quotas, preferred less-qualified candidates, created reverse discrimination, or continued beyond achievement of set goals.

In 1996, the Supreme Court ruled that creation of congressional districts along specifically racial lines was unconstitutional. On March 18, in *Hopwood v. University of Texas Law School,* four University of Texas white applicants challenged the school's affirmative action program, citing unfair preference for those less qualified. The decision ruled that racial diversity was not recognized as a compelling state interest.

On November 3, 1997, controversial Proposition 209 was enacted in California, barring all forms of affirmative action. On December 3, 1998, the similar Initiative 200 was passed in Washington State.

On February 22, 2000, the Florida legislature approved the education component of Governor Jeb Bush's One Florida initiative, meant to end affirmative action in the state. This banned it as a factor in college admissions. On December 13, 2000, *Gratz v. Bollinger* upheld the University of Michigan's undergraduate affirmative action policy, finding that a compelling interest was served through student diversity.

On March 27, 2001, the University of Michigan Law School's affirmative action policy was struck down in *Grutter v. Bollinger,* where intellectual and racial diversity were not found to be the same thing. On May 14, 2002, this decision would be reversed.

On June 23, 2003, the Supreme Court upheld affirmative action in university admissions. The University of Michigan Law School could include race as one of many factors, though the undergraduate point system would have to be modified, as it was not individualized enough. This was an important decision, citing compelling interest in diverse student composition.

Although instances of racism still occur, the nation has taken great strides to purge itself of such practices from the federal level down. The United States is a very different place from the one it was at the time of the 1963 march, itself a major turning point in the ongoing struggle to create a fairer and more just society. Injustices once seen as the norm are now decried on national news. Hate crimes are federally prosecuted. King may not be here to see it, yet the dream has not died.

ALTERNATE HISTORY

On August 28, 1963, the March for Jobs and Freedom could have ended in tragedy, violence, and further restrictions for African Americans. The temper of the time could have taken its toll and climaxed with the march. Bowing to political pressure from southern congressmen, Kennedy could have warned that the demonstration would not be allowed to proceed, and as approximately a quarter million people began to make their way toward the Lincoln Memorial, they could have been met by force.

Federal reserve and National Guard troops would have first tear-gassed the crowd of protesters to disperse them, but once threatened, some of the militia could have opened fire. Television tapes would have shown that the demonstration was completely nonviolent until the first row of marchers, refusing or unable to stop due to the press behind them, was met by gunfire. Mass panic would have ensued, and many more would have been trampled. Others would have stood their ground, linked hands, and sung "We Shall Overcome." Thousands of protesters been arrested and held for days across Washington, D.C., or would have been marched to a nearby field and imprisoned behind chain link fencing.

Early figures could have shown 200 dead, and more than a 1,000 wounded, though debates would have continued for decades as to the exact numbers. King most probably would not have been injured but would have been held incommunicado for nearly three months, a further disaster to the nonviolent portion of the movement, many would have believed.

By nightfall, reports of the violence would have spread around the globe, and riots would have ripped through New York; Washington, D.C.; Los Angeles; and across cities in the South. Cars would have been smashed and set alight; businesses, stores, and homes would have been looted and burned. Both black and white neighborhoods would have been in flames.

By the morning of August 29, the National Guard would have been called out, and hundreds more would have died, especially across the South. Martial law would have been declared in some cities, and a 4 P.M. curfew would have been broken by angry mobs.

By August 30, the situation would have worsened. More troops would have been called in, but it would not have been until mid-September that the rioting would have been brought under control. By today's figures, some $50 billion in damage could have been done. Shocked by the level of violence, those formerly sympathetic to the cause of civil rights would have split into two camps: those blaming the troops and government, and thus more supportive of equal rights legislation than ever, and those who lost sympathy and agreed with anti–civil rights proponents who condemned the marchers and the movement as a whole, insisting that blacks would only revolt further if more concessions were made and that white America should protect itself now.

The fear tactics would have been all too effective. Kennedy, noting that the popular support for civil rights legislation would have been eroding, could have been pressured to give in to demands that would limit rights already given—something he would have later profoundly regretted. Efforts at integration would have been almost wholly curtailed and penalties completely forgone as the South yet again would have instituted widespread policies of segregation.

Citing an overwhelming threat to national security, the army would have reinstituted segregated units, striking down Truman's Executive Order 9981 and further eroding court rulings.

At this point in the alternate history, and in this acrimonious atmosphere, Kennedy's assassination on November 22, 1963, would have caused a darker scenario than occurred in actual history. As Vice President Johnson in this time line would have become president, he could have entered the presidency under the influence of a reactionary Congress, demanding forceful action to stop the race riots in the United States.

Thus, several hundred thousand primarily adult male African Americans would have been subsequently rounded up on suspicion of sedition, treason, incitement, and other charges and would have been taken by train to a military base in the Nevada desert, where they would have been held without access to counsel, telephones, or postal services under harsh and demeaning conditions while awaiting trial. These citizens would have been denied rights that included, but were not limited to, the right to a speedy trial, the right to face one's accusers, and the right to counsel.

With Johnson occupied by the Vietnam War, it is conceivable that the racial social problems in the United States would have remained unresolved during the mid-1960s, despite ongoing protests and demonstrations and notable speeches by the surviving Martin Luther King, Jr. (It is interesting to consider what would have happened in 1968 if presidential candidate George Wallace, governor of Alabama, had succeeded in gaining the presidency in an increasingly divided America. His election could have begun one of the more shameful episodes in U.S. history. Acts might have been passed that could have included a complete moratorium on all nonwhite immigration, mass deportations, severe job quotas and job field restrictions, complete racial restrictions on gun ownership and handling of hazardous materials, quotas for marriage licenses and size of family for all nonwhite Americans, and a complete ban on all interracial relationships nationwide.)

As in actual history, this alternate history follows the election of Richard Nixon in 1968. Marches would have continued to occur, as would other protests, over the next years, but they would have been smaller and more reserved. Due to the Vietnam War and the need for troops, desegregation would have again been attempted in the military. Anti-war demonstrations would have mixed with the movement for racial equality, as in actual history.

Almost universal continuing nonviolence at the behest of King would have eventually gained the upper hand, allaying many fears and winning back much sympathy among the white population. Majority public opinion would have slowly become more amenable to the rights movement, as inequality and its unfairness would have became more and more obvious. It would have taken, however, nearly another decade before significant change again occurred.

President Jimmy Carter would take office in 1977. Almost from the outset, though not entirely expected from a Democratic leader from the South, Carter would have begun to take measures to pass legislation once and for all ensuring African American rights. Thus the provisions of the 1965 Johnson civil rights act would not have come into being until the mid-1970s under Carter.

Full integration would have been again attempted in the South. At last, after a stirring broadcast speech, and even more stirring speeches by King, Carter would have pushed through a civil rights act that not only guaranteed equality in hiring, public accommodations and facilities, schools, and voting rights, with expanded abilities for the justice department to sue on behalf of individuals for all races, but equality for both sexes. Women, always strong in the civil rights movement, though less visible a decade and a half earlier, would have finally found a place in the spotlight as well.

But not until the second Gulf War conflict would women have achieved complete official equality in the military, and nearly two more generations beyond that for blacks to achieve full economic equality with their white counterparts on a statistically even basis. Families would have worked their way out of poverty, and more and more individuals would have equally sought baccalaureate and more advanced degrees; and with affirmative action programs and a fairer climate, many would have sought and obtained better jobs.

Elizabeth A. Kramer

Discussion Questions

1. In the 1940s and 1950s, the NAACP supported the use of courts to achieve integration of schools and to work for other civil rights. Why do you think that Martin Luther King, Jr., and other civil rights leaders of the 1960s adopted other tactics, such as sit-ins and marches, rather than continuing to rely on the courts to achieve recognition of rights?

2. In the 1960s, in actual history, numerous African American leaders, including Malcolm X and Stokely Carmichael, became impatient with the methods employed by both the NAACP and by the followers of Martin Luther King, Jr. Why do you think they felt those methods were not useful or appropriate?

3. Why do you think that certain white politicians, like John Kennedy and Lyndon Johnson, supported civil rights legislation? What did they stand to win? What did they stand to lose?

4. What factors in actual history, and in the alternate history presented in this chapter, led to a white backlash against civil rights gains by African Americans?

5. Despite the gains of the civil rights movement, social inequality in the United States still prevails in poverty rates, in mortality among African American youth, and in employment. What factors account for the continuing inequality? What measures can be adopted in the twenty-first century to deal with the persistence of social injustice?

Bibliography and Further Reading

"African American Odyssey, the Civil Rights Era," rs6.loc.gov/ammem/aaohtml/exhibit/aopart9b.html (accessed February, 2006).

Barker, Lucius J., and W. Twiley, Jr. *Civil Liberties and the Constitution, Cases and Commentaries.* Upper Saddle River, NJ: Prentice Hall, 1978.

Bass, Patrick Henry. *Like a Mighty Stream, the March on Washington August 28, 1963.* Philadelphia: Running Press, 2002.

Broyan, Hugh. *The Penguin History of the USA,* new ed. New York: Penguin Books, 2001.

Carrier, Jim, with Foreword by John Lewis. *A Traveler's Guide to the Civil Rights Movement.* New York: Harcourt, 2004.

Corbin, Raymond M. *1999 Facts about Blacks, a Sourcebook of African American Accomplishments.* Silver Spring, MD: Beckham House, 1986.

DeGregorio, William A. *The Complete Book of US Presidents.* Fort Lee, NJ: Barricade Books, 2005.

Eskown, Dennis. *Lyndon Baines Johnson.* New York: Franklin Watts, 1993.

Geselbracht, Raymond H. *The Truman Administration and the Desegregation of the Armed Forces, a Chronology,* www.trumanlibrary.org/deseg1.htm (accesssed February 2006).

Gillert, Douglas J. *Truman's Order Begins Long Process of Desegregation,* www.defenselink.mil/news/Jul1998/n07171998_9807163.html (accesssed February 2006).

King, Martin Luther, Jr. "Douglass Archives of American Public Address," http://douglass.speech.nwu.edu, prepared by D. Oetting http://nonce.com/oetting (accessed March 2006).

Klarman, Michael, J. *From Jim Crow to Civil Rights, the Supreme Court and the Struggle for Racial Equality.* New York: Oxford University Press, 2004.

Lynn, Mary C., and Benjamin D. Berry, eds. *The Black Middle Class.* Saratoga Springs, NY: Skidmore College, 1980.

Mayer, Robert H. *At Issue in History, the Civil Rights Act of 1964.* Farmington Hills, MI: Greenhaven Press, 2004.

Olson, Lynne. *Freedom's Daughters, the Unsung Heroines of the Civil Rights Movement from 1830 to 1970.* New York: Scribner, 2001.

United States Department of Justice. *Introduction to Federal Voting Rights Laws,* www.usdoj.gov/crt/voting/intro/intro.htm (accessed February 2006).

"We Shall Overcome, Historic Places of the Civil Rights Movement, Lincoln Memorial," www.cr.nps.gov/nr/travel/civilrights/dc1.htm (accessed February 2006).

Zinn, Howard, ed. *A People's History of the United States, 1492–Present.* New York: HarperCollins, 2003.

(TURNING POINT

The Pill, a contraceptive drug, helped launch the "second wave" of the women's movement. What if the Pill had not been introduced?

INTRODUCTION

Most Americans associate the women's rights movement with the 1960s and 1970s. However, American women first sought basic civil rights over a century earlier. In July 1848, Elizabeth Cady Stanton and Lucretia Mott organized the Seneca Falls Conference in New York. At this conference, the attendees drafted and signed a Declaration of Sentiments, based on the Declaration of Independence. The document called for new rights for American women. It was signed by sixty-eight women and thirty-two men.

What rights were women seeking? In 1848, U.S. women did not have the right to vote. In many states, they did not have the right to own or inherit property. In other states, any property they had became their husband's when they married. Women were paid far less than men for their work, and almost all colleges and universities refused to admit them. The Declaration of Sentiments called for women to gain the right to vote, or suffrage; property rights; college and university admission; and the right to equal pay for equal work. Pursuit of these rights would take the fledgling women's movement over a century.

Who were the majority of people in this early women's movement? Many of the women met at meetings of the abolitionist movement. Abolitionists began the fight to abolish slavery in the earliest days of the country. In working toward an end to slavery, women learned to make arguments that women should also be given rights equal to those of white male citizens. (This connection between the goals of women and ethnic minorities emerged again in the 1960s during the civil rights movement.) After the Civil War, the Fifteenth Amendment passed. It gave African American males the right to vote. African American women, though, were left as disenfranchised as white women.

Other people who joined the fight for women's suffrage came from the temperance movement, which fought to outlaw alcohol in the United States. Temperance workers assumed that outlawing alcohol would lower crime rates and reduce poverty. By putting the vote in the hands of women, they hoped to create voters who would join their battle to make alcohol illegal. Ironically, Prohibition began just before women received the vote, with the passage of the Eighteenth Amendment in January 1920. The Eighteenth Amendment was repealed in 1933. By then, women had succeeded in winning the vote, but Prohibition was proved a failure.

Others who participated in the struggle for women's suffrage belonged to one of many workers' unions. The National Women's Trade Union League (NWTUL) formed in 1903. The NWTUL fought for higher wages and improved working conditions for women. Generally, unions fought for women's suffrage because they wanted female union members to be able to vote. Female union members were more likely to be politically active. Their participation in women's suffrage activities proved a natural outgrowth of their union membership. Issues of equal pay and access to education affected these workers most.

Women's rights crusaders first succeeded in the area of education. The first female medical doctor, Elizabeth Blackwell, graduated from the Medical College of Geneva in 1849. Twenty years later, Ada H. Kepley became the first U.S. woman to graduate from law school. After the Civil War ended, women's colleges began to spring up across the country. New opportunities opened to women to pursue careers beyond teaching and motherhood. By 1910, the availability and quality of women's higher education had greatly improved. Victorian-era standards suggested that women were too physically delicate to pursue rigorous higher education and not intellectual enough to benefit from training other than in household duties. After the Civil War, though, medical advances demonstrated the strength of the female body. Women's own successes demonstrated their intellectual capabilities.

New rights to own and inherit property were also successes of this early women's movement. By 1900, married women were granted at least partial control over their own property and wage earnings in all U.S. states.

Perhaps the greatest success of the women who worked in that early movement was gaining the right to vote. State by state, women worked for suffrage, succeeding first in the territory of Wyoming in 1869. Colorado was the first state to give women the vote, in 1893. The seventy-two-year campaign to win the vote for women took the long, hard efforts of thousands of men and women across the country. Organizations such as the Equal Rights Association, founded by Susan B. Anthony, circulated petitions, staged protests, and got women's suffrage onto state legislative agendas. By 1920, when the Nineteenth Amendment gave women the right to vote at the federal

Elizabeth Cady Stanton (seated) and Susan B. Anthony were early leaders of the women's rights movement. (Library of Congress)

level, most of the women of Seneca Falls were dead. The legacy of this "first wave" of the women's movement was to give women the political tools they would need to create social change.

As for women gaining equal pay for equal work? That right would take another forty years to put into law. In 1938, when the Fair Labor Standards Act passed in Congress, the law was made without mention of sex. This meant that women were guaranteed the same minimum wage as male workers, which increased many incomes sharply. It would take until 1963 for an Equal Pay Law to pass successfully through Congress. In 1964, it became illegal to pay women less than men for substantially equal work.

Another area of concern for many women involved birth control. Access to contraception was too controversial for the women of Seneca Falls to include in their Declaration of Sentiments. Eventually, a number of women began to recognize the importance of controlling their reproductive systems to limit the size of their families. In 1873, information regarding birth control was declared obscene, and its distribution in the United States was outlawed. Margaret Sanger was a pioneer in the struggle to make birth control legal and available to married couples in the United States. Born in 1879, she was a nurse whose work with the poor taught her the importance of birth control to women's health and women's lives. She founded an organization that became Planned Parenthood. Sanger was jailed several times for her activism in making contraceptives available in states where they were outlawed. In 1936, the Supreme Court ruled that the distribution of birth control information was not obscene. However, not until 1965 was the sale or distribution of contraceptives made legal in all U.S. states.

During World War II, because of the number of men drafted and serving overseas, it became critical for women to work outside the home to support the war effort. Over 6 million women joined the workforce, serving in fields from factory work to journalism to civil service, from 1941 to 1945. When the war ended, the servicemen returned, and many women lost their jobs to men or were fired or laid off from their wartime employment. Although most of these women returned home to care for their families, the number of women in the labor force has steadily increased ever since. Women's employment during World War II demonstrated that women were competent and capable of performing many jobs they had been banned from in the past.

During the war effort, the federal government created child care centers so that more mothers could enter the workforce and help with the war effort. Nationwide, over 3,100 child care centers provided high-quality care for almost a million children. These centers closed at the end of the war in every state but California. During those war years, however, the success of the centers demonstrated that if mothers had access to good care for their children, they could make significant contributions to the American economy.

The decade of the 1950s is often considered the low point of the twentieth century for women's rights. The vast majority of women during this time were housewives and stay-at-home mothers whose work was not paid. The "baby boom" began in this decade, as soldiers returning from war began to have families. Less than a third of women worked outside the home by 1950, and those women primarily worked in clerical, nursing, and teaching jobs. Women at work often faced both sexual harassment and wage discrimination. The average age of marriage for women was just over twenty years; the average age for males was twenty-three. The divorce rate was about half the current rate, due largely to restrictive laws governing divorce in many states. Contraception was still illegal in many U.S. states.

These various social restrictions set the stage for the legal and political advances in women's rights during the 1960s and 1970s. As the civil rights movement began in the mid-1950s, African Americans began to organize to demand an end to public segregation and discrimination, and to gain voting protections. Many women's groups realized they had serious issues in common with those of the civil rights movement and began to work for social change. Although there were few female leaders in the civil rights movement, the gains of that movement did much to benefit U.S. women as well.

In 1961, President John F. Kennedy convened the President's Committee on the Status of Women and appointed Eleanor Roosevelt to lead it. In 1962, that committee published the *Peterson Report,* the first federal investigation of discrimination against women in the workplace. The report illustrated the importance of enabling women to contribute to the U.S. economy through work outside the home. It called for increased education and job training for women and pointed to the extra burdens carried by women of color and single mothers in caring for their families.

One of the most interesting recommendations of the committee concerned increasing "continuing education for mature women," meaning women of forty and older who could rejoin the workforce after bearing children. The committee also called for more flexible types of child care, not only for full-time working mothers but also for "after school or intermittent care." It also recommended an increase in tax deductions for working parents to cover child care expenses. In studying women's employment, the committee found that discrimination based on sex was common and that women were underpaid when compared to men performing the same jobs. This report led directly to important legislation, including the Equal Pay Act of 1963. In 1963, according to the Bureau of Labor Statistics, women earned 53 cents for every dollar men earned in comparable jobs. In 2002, that figure had increased, but only to 76 cents for a woman per one dollar for a male. Scholars in fields such as economics and sociology continue to study why this wage gap still exists.

Former First Lady Eleanor Roosevelt led the President's Committee on the Status of Women in the early 1960s. (Library of Congress)

In 1959, Searle Pharmaceuticals applied to the Food and Drug Administration (FDA) for approval to sell "the Pill" as a contraceptive. In

1965, in *Griswold v. Connecticut,* the Supreme
Court struck down the last state law outlawing
contraception. By the mid-1960s, millions of
women nationwide had access to relatively
inexpensive, reliable means for controlling their
pregnancies. This increased reproductive freedom was a major contributing factor to two
social movements: the "second wave" of U.S.
feminism, and the sexual revolution.

The second wave of feminism brought long-
awaited social and political changes to the
country. In 1963, Betty Friedan's book *The
Feminine Mystique* hit the best-seller lists,
spreading the idea that housework and motherhood were not fulfilling goals for modern
women. The book argued that as middle-class
women grew more educated, the traditional
models of domesticity were failing to fit their
goals and their economic realities. African
Americans celebrated the passage of the Civil
Rights Act of 1964, and women looked to the
civil rights movement as a model of organiza-

The women's movement questioned whether
motherhood and housework were fulfilling goals
for women. (Library of Congress)

tion for social change. The 1964 Act included a section, Title VII, which
outlawed employment discrimination on the basis of race or sex. The act
also established the Equal Employment Opportunity Commission
(EEOC) to investigate employment discrimination and administer penalties to businesses. In 1966, Friedan and others founded the National
Organization for Women (NOW), with the goals of ending sexual discrimination in employment and passing an equal rights amendment.
NOW and other women's groups borrowed tactics from the civil rights
movement, including petitions, protests, and political lobbying.

The changes in society were not only political but personal. While
large political groups were forming to begin the struggle for women's
political rights, smaller groups of women were organizing in homes across
the country. These "consciousness-raising," or CR, groups were formed of
five to ten women who met to discuss their experiences as women. First
formed by women who were involved in the civil rights movement, by the
late 1960s they had spread through cities and suburbs. These groups generally had no leader or formal structure. They were meant to be safe
spaces where women could discuss and analyze their experiences with
each other. The idea behind such groups was to become self-aware and
fight daily sex discrimination at the local level in marriages, in homes, and
at work.

While women in their thirties and forties raised their consciousness of
sexism, social morality was challenged and tested by the children of the
baby boom as they reached adolescence. Because sex outside of marriage
no longer carried the risk of unwanted pregnancy, adolescent and young
adult sexuality took on a new focus. Sexual experimentation became more
pervasive before marriage, with both positive and negative consequences.
According to the Centers for Disease Control and Prevention (CDC), the
number of teenagers who admitted to participating in premarital sex rose

IN CONTEXT   The Myth of "Bra-Burning" Feminists

In 1968, feminist demonstrators outside the Miss America Pageant held a protest in Atlantic City. The New York Radical Women wanted to put an end to the Miss America Pageant, saying that the event encouraged spectators to judge women like cattle, based on their appearance. They accused the pageant of racism, reminding Americans that no woman of color had ever been a Miss America finalist. They also accused the pageant of teaching young girls that their appearance was all that made them valuable, and of providing a false standard of beauty to women. Several of the protesters managed to sneak inside and display a large banner reading "Women's Liberation."

Meanwhile, protesters outside threw items of women's clothing into a "Freedom Trash Can," including girdles, garter belts, high-heeled shoes, curlers, and bras. The protesters planned to burn the items in the trash can but stopped when police told them it would be hazardous to Atlantic City's famous wooden boardwalk. However, when the story was picked up by national news media, the protesters became "bra-burning" feminists, and the bra quickly became a symbol of women's oppression. Although the media coined this term as a putdown for radical feminists, the myth of bra-burning still exists today.

from 30 percent to over 50 percent over the decade of the 1970s. Changes in sexual morality, the availability of the Pill, and the decreased use of condoms led to an increase in sexually transmitted diseases (STDs). For example, according to *Morbidity and Mortality Weekly Report,* gonorrhea became much more widespread in the late 1960s, but rates of infection stabilized by the mid-1970s. By 1976, chlamydia appeared in the United States. It was an STD with potentially serious consequences for women; if left untreated, it could cause pelvic inflammatory disease (PID) and even permanent infertility. However, the primary STDs of the 1960s and 1970s could be cured with the administration of antibiotics. With the advent of the Pill and various medical improvements, sexual activity was no longer associated automatically with disease and pregnancy, and social attitudes toward sex outside of marriage began to shift.

Literature and film also indicated a new permissiveness, as sex became a topic of national conversation. Books such as D. H. Lawrence's *Lady Chatterley's Lover* and Henry Miller's *Tropic of Cancer* described sexual activities in graphic terms. They were banned from publication in the United States until a series of landmark court cases defined obscenity in specific terms. In 1973, *Miller v. California* defined "obscene" materials as those that appeal to the prurient interest, describe sexual conduct in a patently offensive way specific to each state's laws, and lack "serious literary, artistic, political, or scientific value." This court case had the effect of legalizing many types of sexually explicit materials because they did not meet all three conditions that the *Miller* test specified. The publication of nonfiction books such as *Sex and the Single Girl* (1962), *Our Bodies, Ourselves* (1970), and *The Joy of Sex* (1972) made factual and educational sex materials widely available to the general public.

TURNING POINT

With the FDA approval of the Pill as a contraceptive in 1960 and the eventual overturning of all state laws regarding contraception by 1965, new worlds of opportunity opened to American women. The ability to control their pregnancies meant that women could participate more freely in sexual activities without fear of lifelong consequences. With the Pill, women could continue to work after marriage, gaining seniority and breaking into new career fields. They could also "plan" their children so that they would have fewer unwanted pregnancies and be able to provide economic support for their wanted children. While an accurate social history also includes the negative outcomes of widely available contraception, there is no doubt that significant opportunities for women resulted from the introduction of reliable birth control.

Before the 1960s, it was difficult for married women to control the frequency and spacing of their pregnancies because the birth control methods available were not highly reliable. In numerous states, contraception was outlawed until the early 1960s, so many women did not even have legal access to the birth control methods that were available: condoms, various intrauterine devices, and male withdrawal. Even when they did work, two of these three methods depended on men to take responsibility for birth control. Many men found condoms and withdrawal unpleasant and unsatisfying methods. Thus, women had difficulty in planning their families because they had little control over the consequences of sexual intercourse.

With the introduction of the Pill and the legalization of birth control nationwide, women could take responsibility for their fertility for the first time in history. The Pill had numerous advantages for women. It was reliable, with effectiveness rates of approximately 92 percent according to studies by the Mayo Clinic. It could be taken orally, and it did not require regular visits to a physician to be administered. The Pill did require a doctor's prescription, though, and its costs varied. Planned Parenthood clinics quickly made the Pill available for a fee based on a woman's income so that low-income women could have access to birth control.

With a few changes in personnel at the federal level, the Pill might never have become legal. FDA approval was critical to the success of this form of birth control. Without that approval, it would never have been made widely available to American women. A second critical component of the Pill's success was the Supreme Court case *Griswold v. Connecticut.* That case overturned the last state law keeping contraception illegal. If that ruling had had a different outcome, it would have been difficult if not impossible to distribute the Pill in many U.S. states. Without such a widely available, relatively inexpensive form of contraception for which women could take charge, it is likely that the sexual revolution would have been quite different. Impacts on the women's rights movement would also have been significant.

KEY CONCEPT Sex, Gender, and the "Nature versus Nurture" Debate

It may seem obvious, but what makes a person either a woman or a man? As the women's movement moves into the twenty-first century, scientists and theorists are examining this question in new ways. Put most simply, a person's sex is biological. Males are born with one X chromosome and one Y chromosome, while females have two X chromosomes. The male parent's sperm determines the sex of a baby. Sperm may contain either X or Y chromosomes, while all eggs contain X chromosomes.

A person's gender, by contrast, is determined to some extent by his or her social environment. Gender is understood as the display of a spectrum of behaviors. For example, a woman may be very feminine, somewhat feminine, somewhat masculine, or very masculine in her behavior. Men, likewise, may behave in traditionally feminine or masculine ways. Exactly how gender works is a matter of great debate. It is hard to construct scientific studies to determine which characteristics of gender behaviors might be due to biology (or "nature"), and which are due to social environment ("nurture"). Controlling people's social environ-

ments to the degree necessary for scientific study would be unethical, if not impossible. Rather than controlling people to study the results, social scientists use methods like surveys, tests, and "case study" observations to find answers to gender questions. Some questions currently under study:

* Is maternal (mothering) behavior "natural" for females, or is it culturally taught?
* Do male hormones like testosterone make boys "naturally" more aggressive than girls? Or do other conditions make boys more likely than girls to display aggressive behaviors?
* Why are the people in certain careers more likely to be male (engineering and plumbing), while others are more likely to be female (nursing and elementary education)?

Increasingly, scientists believe that gender is based on a combination of biology and social influences. The "nature versus nurture" debate will continue until we have a better understanding of the interaction between human genetics, social conditions, and individual choices.

ACTUAL HISTORY

In the 1970s, legal breakthroughs gave the second wave of feminism major advances in women's rights on four fronts. In 1973, the Supreme Court heard *Roe v. Wade*. The justices' decision made abortion legal in all U.S. states during the first trimester of pregnancy, although with restrictions that varied from state to state. Reproductive rights remain a primary focus of the women's movement up to the present day, given various restrictions on the availability of contraception and emergency contraception, insurance coverage for birth control, and abortion.

Women won sexual harassment protections at work, as the EEOC began investigating complaints and administering penalties. For the first time in American history, women could use the legal system to prosecute if they were harassed or discriminated against in the workplace. The impacts of Title VII on American workplaces were rapid and significant. In the first year after Title VII, one-third of the complaints filed with the EEOC were related to sexual discrimination. Women used Title VII to challenge in the courts, and to win, access to jobs that had previously been closed to them. They overturned protective legislation in several states. These laws were supposedly put in place to protect women but actually banned them from certain types of employment. After Title VII, women were no longer banned from applying to jobs where heavy lifting was involved and no longer had to meet height and weight requirements for Georgia state trooper positions. In 1973, an EEOC investigation of General Electric resulted in class-action settlements in which women and minority employees received over $29 million in back pay and benefits they had been denied because of discrimination. Investigations of other major American companies and industries followed, and similar penalties made companies realize the price of discrimination was too high to pay.

Women won protections for themselves as mothers. In 1971, the Supreme Court ruled in *Phillips v. Martin Marietta Corp.* that corporations could not refuse to hire women with preschool-age children unless they also refused to hire men with preschool-age children. The Pregnancy Discrimination Act of 1978 made it illegal to discriminate against women in hiring or on the job due to potential or actual pregnancy.

New educational opportunities also emerged because of Title IX of the Civil Rights Act. Most people who have heard of Title IX today think it specifically protects opportunities for women to participate in sports, but the law actually does much more. It gave females equal access to all educational programs receiving federal financial assistance. As recently as the 1960s, girls were not allowed to take math and science classes in many public schools, and women were still excluded from many public universities. Pregnant teenagers were often suspended or expelled, and married women were not admitted to many colleges and trade schools. Title IX made all these forms of sex discrimination illegal and opened unprecedented educational opportunities to women of all ages.

The final legal protection that women sought, though, remained elusive. The idea of an Equal Rights Amendment (ERA) to the Constitution has existed since 1923, when Alice Paul first drafted one that was introduced in Congress but failed in committee. The ERA did not even get a full hearing in Congress until 1946. An ERA was meant to ensure that all the protections of the Constitution would apply to women as well as men. A version of the ERA finally passed in Congress in 1972, but a two-thirds majority of the states was required to ratify the amendment. By 1982, the ERA was dead. Women's groups could not win ratification in the required number of states, falling three short of the required number.

The 1970s also marked the peak of the sexual revolution. Teenagers and young adults questioned the strict morality, religious beliefs, and stereotypical sex roles of their parents' generation. The number of churchgoing Americans dropped to a new low, as these youth left Judeo-Christian religious values behind. The easy availability of

Alice Paul drafted the first Equal Rights Amendment in 1923, but it failed in Congressional committee. (Library of Congress)

birth control freed a generation from the stigma of teen pregnancy, but it raised serious questions about the meaning of sex outside of marriage. Pornographic magazines, films showing nudity and sexual acts, and literary erotica became more easily available after they were legalized by *Miller v. California*. The visual arts became more concerned with issues of gender and sex. The women's art movement of the 1970s helped female artists to break through the sexism of visual-art galleries and museums. As the Vietnam era began, more people were attending colleges and universities than ever before. Campuses became hotbeds of social activism and sexual experimentation, as women fought to put an end to the double standards of previous decades.

The hippie movement, which began in California in the mid-1960s, encouraged free love and communal living, environmental awareness, and peace activism. Some of these hippies tried experiments with different types of living arrangements instead of the nuclear family (mother, father, and children). The peak years of the commune movement in the United States were roughly from 1960 to 1975. Communes were groups of people who lived together, leaving behind traditional structures of marriage and family, and sharing their incomes. While the actual numbers of people involved in these social experiments were small, their impact on the larger society was not.

The model commune was a collective society resembling an idealized tribal village. All adults would take on parenting, housework, and job responsibilities, and this division of labor was supposed to free people from the burdens of modern living. In practice, though, few communes held together for longer than a few years. Drug use and multiple sexual relationships within a mixed-gender commune commonly led to problems, as women complained of sexual abuse and sexist behaviors in general. The foundation of single-gender communes during this time led to other tests of feminist ideals.

The rise of a lesbian feminist movement in the 1970s suggested that sexism was the problem and excluding men from female lives was the answer. One example group was the Lesbian Separatist Society, which formed in Seattle, Washington, in the early 1970s. All-female communes were supposed to put an end to oppression by males, but they overwhelmingly failed in practice. Lesbian feminism, as a philosophy, was criticized by other feminists and by society for several reasons. It essentialized both genders, or created rigid definitions about sex roles based on broad general statements. It was a white, middle-class movement that ignored the issues of women of color and working-class women. It made raising sons nearly impossible for its members who were mothers. Although ultimately this subsection of the women's movement was discredited, it did bring a few critical issues into national discussion. The lesbian feminist movement provided opportunities for women to discuss their sexual feelings toward one another and to explore their own sexuality. Members published gay erotic writing, founded crisis centers for homosexual teens, and worked to provide safe spaces for gays and lesbians. In these ways, the lesbian feminist movement laid the groundwork for gay rights activists of later decades.

The 1980s brought political conservatism to the country and a backlash against the women's movement. The ERA failed to win ratification.

ANOTHER VIEW   What about a Men's Movement?

By the 1980s, U.S. men began to examine their own preconceptions about what it meant to be male. While no nationwide "men's movement" created declarations or pursued a clear set of goals, a few significant groups formed to work toward specific aims. In 1981, the National Congress for Men formed, with the goal of securing rights for fathers. These men pointed out the discrimination inherent in giving women custody of children after divorce. They fought for improved custody and visitation rights. (This organization still exists, and it is now called the National Congress for Fathers and Children.) Other groups formed to support feminist women in their political and social struggles, such as the Men's Awareness Network (MAN), which worked toward passage of the Equal Rights Amendment. Anti-feminism among men was also common, but it was often tied to larger political and religious movements instead of being a specific focus.

Also in the early 1990s, the book *Iron John* by Robert Bly spawned mythopoetic men's groups.

These small local groups of men studied mythology and fairy tales, read and wrote poetry, and created drum circles in a search for personal insight and emotional health. One of the largest men's organizations still in existence is the Promise Keepers. Founded in 1994, the Promise Keepers is an evangelical Christian group aiming to explore how men can live the Christian faith in modern society. Promise Keepers created a good deal of controversy among the feminist community for their reinforcement of traditional men's roles as husbands, fathers, and heads of household.

These men's groups influenced the lives of their members, but most have left little impact on American history to date. Recent social theories focus on the problems with automatically assigning characteristics, behaviors, and expectations based on sex. Neither men nor women automatically form a group on any social or political issue. Many factors make up a person's identity, including sex, race, economic class, profession, and the region where the individual lives.

The first woman nominated to be vice president of the United States, Geraldine Ferraro, ran on the Democratic ticket with presidential candidate Walter Mondale. Mondale and Ferraro lost in a landslide victory for Ronald Reagan and George H. W. Bush in 1984. Anti-feminist women from a variety of backgrounds began publishing books and appearing on radio and television shows. Some were religious conservatives who based their opposition on Judeo-Christian religious traditions. Others were politically conservative and feared the social effects of women's increased economic and political power. The anti-feminists challenged women's ability to "have it all" and called for a return to traditional family roles. Anti-feminists blamed the women's movement for many social ills, from divorce to adolescent anorexia to increased assaults on women to the destruction of the family. Most of their attacks failed, although they attracted a lot of media attention. (For example, there was a sharp increase in the number of sexual harassment incidents reported from 1964 to 1973, according to Susan Faludi in *Backlash: The Undeclared War against American Women*. Yet sexual harassment did not suddenly occur because of the women's movement. More incidents were reported after government agencies were required by law to record and investigate them.)

Yet women still advanced, playing new roles in the judicial system, science, politics, and the media. Sandra Day O'Connor, the first female

In 1981, Sandra Day O'Connor began service as the first female Supreme Court justice. (Library of Congress)

Supreme Court justice, began service in 1981. In 1983, Sally Ride became the first U.S. female astronaut to go into space; 1983 was also the year that the last all-male Ivy League university, Columbia, opened its doors to women. In 1985, EMILY's List was founded. EMILY is an acronym for "Early Money Is Like Yeast," and the core idea was to provide seed money for Democratic pro-choice women who ran for public office. Because of the effort and financial support of groups like EMILY's List, a significant number of women were elected as governors, senators, and representatives in the rest of the decade. The work of the women's art movement continued with the foundation of the Guerilla Girls in 1985. The Guerrilla Girls are a group of female artists who remain anonymous and continue their work to the present day. They put up posters and stickers in public museums, place print ads in magazines, and perform at outside events such as the Tony Awards and Academy Awards ceremonies to call attention to sexism and racism in the arts. They use humor to win the attention of their audiences and maintain their anonymity by appearing in public wearing gorilla masks.

By the late 1980s, the women's movement had spawned women's studies departments in most major universities. Academics in these departments began to chronicle the pressures on women to succeed in a high-powered workplace while still fulfilling the duties of mother, wife, and homemaker. The women's movement during this time splintered into many movements and lost a lot of its political power and focus in battles over identity politics. Some of these splits were philosophical. For example, radical feminists believed in emphasizing women's differences from men and forming all-female groups to transform society. Socialist feminists believed that capitalism was the root of sexism in society, and they wanted to put an end to class and gender. Liberal feminists believed that sexism could be overcome by working through existing governmental and social structures. These three groups were at odds for obvious reasons. They saw fundamentally different problems and fundamentally different means to solve them.

Working-class women, women of color, and lesbians criticized the women's movement for being racist, classist, and heterosexist. African Americans began the "womanist" movement to work for change on issues of importance to African American women. The first African American woman in Congress, Shirley Chisholm, took office in 1969. The Latina feminist movement also spurred social and political changes for Hispanic women. The first Hispanic woman to be elected to Congress was Ileana Ros-Lehtinen of Florida, who took office in 1989. Lesbianism had been present, and the source of argument, in the women's movement from the beginning of the second wave of feminism in the late 1960s. It would take another generation before the issues surrounding sexual preference and civil rights for nonheterosexuals would move into the political spotlight.

The unified women's movement of the 1970s largely fell apart in the 1980s, in part because of divisions based on ethnic or philosophical differences. However, the deepest divide in the women's movement came between women who identified as pro-choice and those who identified as pro-life. Debates over the abortion issue absorbed women's groups to the exclusion of work on other important social and political issues. Fragmentation of the movement made it hard to gain sufficient political momentum to achieve any group's specific goals.

The introduction of the human immunodeficiency virus (HIV) into the American population began in the mid-1980s, bringing the era of sexual revolution to an end. Infection with HIV eventually leads to acquired immune deficiency syndrome (AIDS), an STD that kills millions of people worldwide each year. Condoms had dropped sharply in popularity as a birth control method with the introduction of the Pill, but resurfaced as a popular method of preventing the transmission of sexual diseases such as AIDS. At first, it was believed that HIV was transmitted only through homosexual activity, but rates of transmission among the heterosexual population also rose over time. HIV attacks the human immune system, rapidly rendering it ineffective so that carriers die of other infections, such as pneumonia or cancer. By the late 1990s, a combination of drugs and careful medical monitoring made it possible for people infected with HIV to live for decades after their initial infections, but no cure has yet been found.

By the 1990s, the face of feminism had changed significantly. Books such as Naomi Wolf's *The Beauty Myth* and Susan Faludi's *Backlash* chronicled the struggles of white middle-class American women in the 1980s. Women's studies classes became part of the core curriculum in colleges nationwide. Most adolescents and young adults were the product of two working parents, and women's rights in the workplace and on the athletic field were increasingly taken for granted. At the end of the decade, new women's groups defining themselves as "third wave" began to emerge. These young women, primarily associated with Generation X (those born roughly from 1965 to 1980), brought a new awareness of women's rights worldwide into the public spotlight.

Third-wave feminists criticized the second wave, arguing that it failed in part because of its focus on rigid gender definitions and white middle-class women's issues. By contrast, the third wave of feminism focused on inclusion across racial, economic, and national lines, and on free expression of gender for both sexes. Third-wave feminists used nontraditional media forms like print "zines," punk rock, and some of the first blogs to get their message to the public. They also published books full of essays and theories, such as *Manifesta: Young Women, Feminism, and the Future.* Gay rights became a feminist issue, as third-wavers encouraged exploration of all dimensions of human sexuality and studied discrimination against homosexuals.

New victories were won on the political front, such as the passage of the Family Medical Leave Act (FMLA) in 1997. The FMLA guaranteed men and women twelve weeks of unpaid absence from their jobs after the birth or adoption of a child. The FMLA brought national parental leave policies closer in line to those of other first-world countries, although the United States still lags behind in worker protections for parents compared to other industrialized countries.

In the twenty-first century, what rights are American women still seeking? As the third wave of feminism continues, many women are working for employment policies that will create a better work/life balance for men and women. New work arrangements have made working from home not only possible but a realistic choice for certain careers. Flextime, job sharing, and telecommuting are three examples of work arrangements that make it possible for people to balance their careers with their own and their families' needs. These workplace policies are not available to everyone, though, and many families still struggle with getting the right balance.

As female enrollment and retention rates increase, some evidence suggests that boys are disconnecting from educational opportunities and dropping out of school at higher rates than before the women's movement, according to Michael A. Fletcher, in "Degrees of Separation: Gender Gap Has Educators Wondering Where the Men Are," in the *Washington Post*. Education reform continues to be a feminist issue, with the goal of equal educational opportunity for both sexes and all races. Increasing numbers of women are caring both for their children and for their aging parents, making the pressures of elder care a third critical U.S. feminist issue.

Women's groups also continue to work in areas where rights have been won but might be taken away, such as reproductive rights and worker protections. Groups such as EMILY's List raise money and continue to lobby for women to win political offices; as yet, there has not been a female U.S. president. American women are also doing important work to aid women in other countries where their rights are sharply restricted. At the beginning of the twenty-first century, U.S. women realize they have gained many rights in a short time, and they continue to work toward full equality and participation in a democratic society.

ALTERNATE HISTORY

The second-wave feminist movement of the 1960s and 1970s based its success on a combination of social conditions. Battles for civil rights for minorities played a role in raising women's consciousness, as did literary and political developments that brought topics like sex and birth control into public conversation. The United States was also fighting an unpopular and ultimately unsuccessful war in Vietnam. Vietnam protests and civil unrest contributed ideas and tactics to the women's movement. Perhaps no single social contribution was more responsible for the rise of the second wave than the introduction of the Pill.

If the FDA had refused to approve the Pill in 1960 or the Supreme Court had decided *Griswold v. Connecticut* differently, the women's movement might have taken a different shape. The sexual revolution might not have occurred at all, because pregnancy would have remained a likely consequence of sexual activity. Women burdened with significant and unwanted family responsibilities would have had less time for social and political activism. What might the United

States look like today if women still did not have access to reliable birth control?

Birth rates in the United States prior to the introduction of the Pill were much higher than they are today. According to the National Center for Health Statistics, in 1960, there were 23.7 births for every 1,000 women. By 1999, that rate had fallen to 14.5 births per 1,000 women. The average age of motherhood has increased over the past four decades, and the rate of teen pregnancies has declined. While the Pill is not the only contributor to these changes in birth rates, it does play an important role. Reviewing data for the years before 1960, then comparing them to the decades after 1960, shows that women without reliable birth control had more children. Obviously, women took advantage of the Pill to reduce their chances of pregnancy. The CDC reported in 2002 that 98 percent of American women had tried at least one form of birth control at some time from the ages of fifteen to forty-four. Of those women, roughly 82 percent tried the Pill.

If the Pill had not been legalized, birth rates in the United States would have remained higher for years, if not decades. Average family size would be larger, and more women would be responsible for raising children. Women would also be likely to become parents at younger ages, since teen sex would be more likely to lead to pregnancy. Teen pregnancy greatly decreases a young woman's chance of completing a high school education, and it is a major risk factor for poverty later in life. Without reliable birth control, women would have less time to pursue education and career. Each child born means more years spent on child care duties, possibly without the ability to take on work outside the home.

Increasing numbers of educational opportunities for women contributed to their winning legal and social rights in the 1960s and 1970s. Would women have been as likely to take advantage of these opportunities without the Pill? This may seem a strange question at first, as women's achievement of educational goals seems disconnected from whether they participate in sexual activity. However, the likelihood that a woman would complete a college-level education increased sharply after 1960 when the Pill was made legal. (According to the U.S. Census Bureau, in 1960, less than 7 percent of U.S. women had completed a college education. By 2004, 26 percent of all U.S. women held at least a bachelor's degree. Women have slightly outnumbered men in college enrollment since the late 1970s, accounting for roughly 55 percent of all students at U.S. colleges and universities in 2005.)

In actual history, the average age for marriage began creeping upward after 1960. In part because sexual activity before marriage without pregnancy was possible, women began to postpone marriage until later in life, pursuing educational and career opportunities first. The average age of marriage for U.S. women rose from 20.3 in 1960 to 25.8 by 2004. Education also made a huge difference in social attitudes toward women in the workforce, as a recent Harvard Economics study demonstrates. In surveys of college freshmen taken in 1967, 41 percent thought it would be improper for a married woman to work. By 1973, only 17 percent thought the same.

The successes of the first wave of feminist activism indicate that reliable birth control was not essential for women to win political victories. Women won property rights and the right to vote while raising children and lacking access to higher education. However, the advent of the Pill did free many women from the burdens of caring for unwanted children. The second wave of feminism might have taken a different shape and fought for different goals without reliable contraception. How might it have been different?

Imagine the United States with a workforce that still resembled the workforce of the early 1960s. That workforce would be primarily white, male, and supporting a family on a single income. Less than 10 percent of women would have college degrees, and the percentage of female doctors, dentists, lawyers, and college professors would be very small. The primary career options for women would still be nursing and elementary teaching, and the average family would have almost twice as many children as today. And in 1960, according to the U.S. Census Bureau, over 25 percent of U.S. citizens lived in poverty. (In 2004, that number was 17.8 percent.)

Without reliable birth control, the U.S. economy would have suffered over the past forty years. Fewer women would have entered the workforce, and even fewer would have sustained careers due to the burden of additional parenting responsibilities. Without the additional wage-earning power that women represent, the U.S. economy would have grown more slowly over time. If fewer women worked outside the home, the number of America's poor would be larger. Without the advances won by the educated women of the second wave of U.S. feminism, the majority of working women would hold low-paying jobs without legal help to protect them from discrimination. Married women and women with children would have a difficult time finding positions at all. Without the education and experience to hold jobs that pay well above minimum wage, women would still be trapped, intellectually and economically, in the 1950s. Although increasing numbers of women postponed marriage to seek education beginning in the 1960s, without birth control, they would have also had to postpone sexual activity to succeed.

Potentially, one outcome of a women's movement without the Pill could have been a sexual abstinence movement. This seems ironic, given the sexual revolution's close connections with second-wave feminism. In the 1960s and 1970s, feminists encouraged sexual exploration with multiple partners and claimed sexual pleasure as a woman's right. In the present, third-wave feminists angrily criticize current abstinence-only sex education programs for their failure to address the realities of teenagers and sexual behavior. Yet if women did not have access to reliable contraception, the only way they could be sure to achieve their educational and career goals would be to abstain from sexual intercourse.

What might a feminist abstinence program look like? It would encourage young feminists to abstain from sex in their teenage years, in order to pursue other important goals first. It would refuse to make human sexuality "bad" or "dirty" and would focus on the real pleasures and dangers of sexual relationships. Unlike abstinence-only programs that are based in a specific religion or morality, a feminist abstinence movement would be rooted in practical reasoning. It would urge young women not to let early sexual activity keep them from completing their other life goals. It would teach young women, and young men, accurate information about their biological systems and about how to deal with sexual feelings. It would provide information on the forms of contraception that are available and explain how they work and what their failure rates are. A feminist abstinence program would encourage other forms of sexual intimacy besides intercourse. It would also encourage both men and women to take responsibility for their individual sexual behavior and to treat each other with respect.

If an abstinence movement had been successful, the women's movement might have eventually been able to achieve the same successes, or perhaps even greater ones. However, it would have taken more time. Without a simultaneous sexual revolution, the women's movement might have fallen apart before it could achieve meaningful results. The sexual revolution enabled a generation of young women to postpone marriage and the start of a family. Freedom from early pregnancy gave women the chance to participate in higher education, move away from home, and enter careers that gave them economic power. Without the 1960s generation of empowered young women, there might never have been a political movement to fight for workers' rights and family benefits. The women's movement would have had to find another effective way of helping young women deal with the possibility of pregnancy if the Pill had not been legalized. Otherwise, it would not have had the sheer numbers of women needed to bring about social and political change.

Heather A. Beasley

Discussion Questions

1. Do you think the reduction in unwanted births through the use of the Pill has had beneficial or detrimental social effects?

2. If the Pill had not been legally introduced in the United States, what effect do you think that would have had on the rates of abortion in the United States in the 1970s and later?

3. What factors would limit the success of a sexual abstinence movement in the United States? What factors would help such a movement?

4. What effect do you think the introduction of the Pill had upon the effort of women to achieve equal employment and work compensation? What factors continue to make it difficult for women to achieve equality in the workplace?

5. What effect do you think that equal funding for girls' athletics in schools has had upon gender roles and gender stereotyping?

Bibliography and Further Reading

Baumgartner, Jennifer, and Amy Richards, eds. *Manifesta: Young Women, Feminism, and the Future.* New York: Farrar, Straus and Giroux, 2000.

Boston Women's Health Book Collective. *Our Bodies, Ourselves: A New Edition for a New Era.* New York: Touchstone, 2005.

De Beauvoir, Simone. *The Second Sex.* New York: Knopf, 1953.

Faludi, Susan. *Backlash: The Undeclared War against American Women.* New York: Crown, 1991.

Fletcher, Michael A. "Degrees of Separation: Gender Gap Has Educators Wondering Where the Men Are." *Washington Post,* June 25, 2002, p. A1.

Friedan, Betty. *The Feminine Mystique.* New York: W.W. Norton, 1997.

Goldin, Claudia, Ilyana Kuziemko, and Lawrence F. Katz. "The Homecoming of American College Women: The Reversal of the College Gender Gap." Published online September 20, 2005. Harvard University Department of Economics. http://post.economics.harvard.edu/faculty/katz/papers/Homecoming.pdf (accessed March 2006).

Guerrilla Girls. *Confessions of the Guerrilla Girls.* New York: Perennial, 1995.

Howard, Angela, and Sasha Ranae Adams-Tarrant, eds. *Reactions to the Modern Women's Movement, 1963 to the Present.* New York: Garland, 1997.

Mascola, Laurene, et al. "Gonorrhea and Salpingitis among American Teenagers, 1960–1981." *Morbidity and Mortality Weekly Report,* August 1, 1983, p. 32.

Messer-Davidow, Ellen. *Disciplining Feminism: From Social Activism to Academic Discourse.* Durham, NC: Duke University Press, 2002.

Miller, Timothy. *The Sixties Communes: Hippies and Beyond.* Syracuse, NY: Syracuse University Press, 1999.

Mosher, William D., et al. "Use of Contraception and Use of Family Planning Services in the United States: 1982–2002." *Advance Data from Vital and Health Statistics* 350: December 10, 2004. Centers for Disease Control and Prevention. www.cdc.gov/nchs/data/ad/ad350.pdf (accessed March 2006).

Nicholson, Linda, ed. *The Second Wave: A Reader in Feminist Theory.* London: Routledge, 1997.

U.S. Centers for Disease Control and Prevention. "Table 1. Live births, birth rates, and fertility rates, by race: United States, specified years 1940–1955 and each year, 1960–1999." *National Vital Statistics Report* 49.1: April 17, 2001. www.cdc.gov/nchs/data/natality/nvs49_1t1.pdf (accessed March 2006).

U.S. Census Bureau. "Average Population per Household and Family: 1940 to the Present." Table HH-6, "Families and Living Arrangements" webpage. www.census.gov/population/socdemo/hh-fam/hh6.pdf (accessed March 2006).

U.S. Census Bureau. "Estimated Median Age at first Marriage, by Sex: 1890 to the Present." Table MS-2, "Families and Living Arrangements" webpage. http://www.census.gov/population/socdemo/hh-fam/ms2.pdf (accessed March 2006).

Wolf, Naomi. *The Beauty Myth: How Images of Beauty Are Used against Women.* New York: Morrow, 1991.

TURNING POINT

What if an AIDS-like sexually transmitted disease had spread in the 1960s, bringing a halt to the counterculture movement?

INTRODUCTION

Counterculture, often described as "rebelling against the establishment," is a term used to describe a movement that swept the United States in the 1960s and early 1970s. It was a phenomenon that challenged the national imagination: the transformation of the promising middle-class youth with many material advantages into what was popularly known as "the hippie." The movement members were typically characterized by long hair, brightly colored clothes, communal living, promiscuous sex, and heavy drug use. Members of the movement questioned America's materialism and commercialism, as well as its cultural and political institutions. They sought to change the norms that had defined the prior decades as various groups came together. As Keith Melville wrote of the time in *Communes in the Counter Culture: Origins, Theories, Styles of Life,* "It was easy enough in the early sixties to distinguish activists and hippies, to distinguish political from personal goals. But many of the most significant developments in the counterculture have resulted from a blending of styles. Both the rhetoric and the logic of radical activism have changed, and the hippies and activists have converged under the banner of the cultural revolution."

Rather than remain a subculture, the counterculture members hoped to transform the values and morals of the dominant culture. The movement's underlying values helped to invoke thinking beyond the individual while also promoting the need to examine each person's role and experience in society, such as through the consciousness-raising groups that are often associated with the second wave of the women's movement. Members of the counterculture were often viewed with suspicion by the "establishment"—the white middle and upper classes. As *Time* magazine reported, "For all the hippies' good works and gentle ways, many Americans found them profoundly unsettling."

The questioning of authority was based on numerous political decisions. After the end of World War II, soldiers returned to the United States and women, who had taken over their jobs during wartime, returned to

The ubiquitous and decorated Volkswagen bus was the preferred mode of transportation for hippies. (Shutterstock)

the home. Many of the soldiers went to college on the G.I. Bill, a federal education program. Families began to migrate to the suburbs, and the baby boom began.

Politically, there was a rapid rise in conflict between the United States and the Soviet Union, known as the Cold War. Rather than an armed conflict, this was waged by means of economic pressures, diplomatic maneuvering, intimidation, and propaganda. There was also a large nuclear arms race, which led to widespread fears of a potential nuclear war.

The American educational system was undergoing dramatic changes. Until the early 1950s, the policy of "separate but equal" educational opportunities for African American students was widely followed. In 1954, the Supreme Court ruled in *Brown v. the Board of Education of Topeka, Kansas* that separate facilities for African American students did not make those facilities equal according to the Constitution. The result of the case was integration in public schools across the nation—although it was not a smooth process in many states. For example, the first African American teenager entered the all-white Little Rock Central High School in Little Rock, Arkansas, in 1957. The resulting confrontation showed that public opinion on the issue of integration was divided. A precursor to the counterculture movement was what was called the "Beat Generation," which began in the early 1950s with a small group of young writers who advocated a carefree, often reckless, and unique approach to literature and a demonstrative social stance toward authority, or "the establishment." The label *Beat Generation* was coined by Jack Kerouac in

KEY CONCEPT   *The Feminine Mystique*

Betty Friedan was a highly educated housewife with a background in journalism when she began work on the book that would make her famous and contribute to major social change in the United States: *The Feminine Mystique*. First published in 1963, by 2000 the book had sold more than 3 million copies. Friedan's 2006 *New York Times* obituary noted that "rarely has a single book been responsible for such sweeping, tumultuous and continuing social transformation."

Friedan was a freelancer writing for women's magazines when the concept of the book was developed. It started with a survey she conducted in 1957 for her fifteenth class reunion from Smith College. What she discovered among her female classmates was a "nameless, aching dissatisfaction" that she termed "the problem that has no name" in her book. She repeated her study with graduates from other universities and found similar results.

A study of mass media images reinforced the message that middle-class women's roles were limited to that of wife and mother. Their fulfillment was to be found in clean houses and well-behaved children or what Friedan referred to as the "feminine mystique." She questioned whether the post–World War II suburban utopia was really enough to satisfy educated women.

In the preface to her book, she wrote: "Gradually, without seeing it clearly for quite a while, I came to realize that something is very wrong with the way American women are trying to live their lives today. I sensed it first as a question mark in my own life, as a wife and mother of three small children, half-guiltily, and therefore half-heartedly, almost in spite of myself, using my abilities and education in work that took me away from home."

The book united suburban housewives to question women's roles in society and paralleled questioning of traditional beliefs by women in the counterculture movement. The questioning helped to create the foundation of the women's liberation movement, which led to sweeping changes in American society by the 1970s.

the late 1940s but became more widely used as his contemporaries, such as writers Allen Ginsberg and Lawrence Ferlinghetti, were beginning to be noticed. Kerouac's *On The Road*, published in 1957, marked the beginning of Beat popularity. By the time the Beat Generation was recognized by most of society, many of the Beat writers were addicted to drugs and no longer very active. City Lights Bookstore in San Francisco, founded in 1953 by Ferlinghetti and Peter Martin, became a symbol of the anti-establishment viewpoint of the writers. These counterculture writers of the 1950s reflected the new consciousness, which became the groundwork for the social and cultural revolution of the 1960s.

The effect of suppressing numerous social problems in the 1950s had a significant impact on the rest of the twentieth century, leading to numerous changes in the 1960s in America. Following years of conservative social practices that oppressed women and minorities, the foundation for the counterculture movement was spawned. In 1963, Martin Luther King, Jr., delivered his "I Have a Dream" speech, and numerous steps were taken to eliminate segregation. Also that year, Betty Friedan's book *The Feminine Mystique* was published. The book, often viewed as the beginning of the second wave of the women's movement, spoke to many of those educated wives who felt trapped in their suburban homes. The following year the Civil Rights Act of 1964 was passed, which prohibited discrimination in public accommodations and workplaces.

IN CONTEXT The Port Huron Statement

The Port Huron Statement is the manifesto of the Students for a Democratic Society (SDS), written primarily by Tom Hayden and completed on June 15, 1962, at an SDS convention in Port Huron, Michigan.

From the Introduction: Agenda for a Generation:

"We are people of this generation, bred in at least modest comfort, housed now in universities, looking uncomfortably to the world we inherit.

"When we were kids the United States was the wealthiest and strongest country in the world: the only one with the atom bomb, the least scarred by modern war, an initiator of the United Nations that we thought would distribute Western influence throughout the world. Freedom and equality for each individual, government of, by, and for the people—these American values we found good, principles by which we could live as men. Many of us began maturing in complacency.

"As we grew, however, our comfort was penetrated by events too troubling to dismiss. First, the permeating and victimizing fact of human degradation, symbolized by the Southern struggle

against racial bigotry, compelled most of us from silence to activism. Second, the enclosing fact of the Cold War, symbolized by the presence of the Bomb, brought awareness that we ourselves, and our friends, and millions of abstract 'others' we knew more directly because of our common peril, might die at any time. We might deliberately ignore, or avoid, or fail to feel all other human problems, but not these two, for these were too immediate and crushing in their impact, too challenging in the demand that we as individuals take the responsibility for encounter and resolution.

"While these and other problems either directly oppressed us or rankled our consciences and became our own subjective concerns, we began to see complicated and disturbing paradoxes in our surrounding America. The declaration all men are created equal … rang hollow before the facts of Negro life in the South and the big cities of the North. The proclaimed peaceful intentions of the United States contradicted its economic and military investments …" (Courtesy Office of Senator Tom Hayden.)

Objection to the American involvement in the Vietnam War played a large part in the origins of the counterculture. The war was based on a conflict between the Democratic Republic of Vietnam, or North Vietnam, which was allied with communist countries, including the Soviet Union and China, against the Republic of Vietnam, or South Vietnam, along with its allies, which primarily included the United States. The American combat troops were part of the war from 1965 until their official withdrawal in 1973.

Opposition to the Vietnam War began in 1964 on college campuses across the country. Formal protests against the draft began in October 1965, when the college student–run National Coordinating Committee to End the War in Vietnam publicly burned a draft card. Potential abuses in the Selective Service System were part of the reason for the protest because local draft boards had wide discretion in deciding who should be drafted into the military and who should be granted deferments, which usually meant escaping service. Some men joined the National Guard or the Peace Corps to avoid being drafted. There was concern about the fairness of who was drafted, as often those without political connections were selected.

The first draft lottery since World War II in the United States was held in December 1969, based on a potential draftee's date of birth. This meant that young men had an increased chance of being drafted. Many critics of the war argued that the government of South Vietnam lacked political legitimacy and thus support for the war was immoral. The anti-war protests alarmed the United States government. On August 16, 1966, the House Un-American Activities Committee began investigations of Americans who were suspected of aiding the communist Vietnamese cause. Anti-war demonstrators disrupted the meeting, and fifty people were arrested. Thousands of young American men chose to move to Canada or Sweden rather than risk being drafted.

Perhaps no campus was more symbolic of the beginnings of the counterculture movement than the University of California, Berkeley. In 1964, student activists, who had taken part in civil rights protests in the South, confronted administration officials over their right to use campus facilities for their political campaigns. The conflict, under the informal leadership of student Mario Savio and others, marked the beginning of a new wave of student protests as students used the skills honed in the civil rights battle to promote the anti-war movement. The situation boiled over in December 1964 when hundreds of students were arrested for occupying the campus's administration building; it was the largest mass arrest of students in U.S. history and caught the nation's attention. The movement led to questions of students' free speech and academic freedom.

Alternative publications, many of which had started in the 1950s, such as the *Village Voice*, helped to spread the movement. One of the first underground newspapers of the counterculture movement was the *Los Angeles Free Press*. In 1967, a cooperative process, known as the Underground Press Syndicate (UPS), was formed to allow member papers to reprint articles from any of the other member papers at no cost. Most college campuses included numerous alternative newspapers and magazines.

The most visible symbols of the counterculture movement were the hippies, or those who rejected mainstream images and behaviors. The term, sometimes spelled "hippy," was made popular by *San Francisco Chronicle* columnist Herb Caen, according to some historians. He was well connected within the San Francisco counterculture community. Others feel the 1960s hippie culture was a result of the Beat culture in New York City. They claim that the first use of the word *hippie* was on channel WNBC in New York City at the opening of the New York World's Fair on April 22, 1964. It was used in a story about anti-war protesters who staged a sit-in and were called "hippies" by New York Police Department officers and reporters. The police attempted to chase them off but the protestors fought back and were arrested. Before that date, they claim this group was described as "beatniks." There were groups in New York's Greenwich Village coffee shops that were known as "hips," which represented being "in the know." Many of the New York hippies later relocated to San Francisco.

The hippies typically had a recognizable appearance. It included bell-bottom pants, tie-dyed shirts, and peasant blouses. They also wore sandals, head scarves, and beaded necklaces. Their clothes were often handmade as a form of protest against the consumer culture. Men sported full beards. Hippies often traveled in Volkswagen buses or vans, which featured peace symbols and other graffiti.

Some hippies began to live in communes and exercise various forms of nonconformity. Practices such as meditation and yoga as well as taking psychedelic drugs were often used to expand the consciousness. The movement challenged governmental authority and attitudes about traditional gender roles. It encouraged greater social tolerance and environmental awareness. "Flower power" became a symbol of the movement. Some followed the mantra of psychedelic guru Timothy Leary to "tune in, turn on and drop out," meaning tune into the movement, turn on to the philosophy, and drop out of the mainstream culture. These believers built new lives away from the suburban conformity and created communities that were based on organic farming and community service.

Women were a large part of the movement but often lacked a powerful position. In Todd Gitlin's book on this period, *The Whole World Is Watching,* he points out that the voices and work of women were often overlooked. Gitlin cited a cartoon of a woman holding a screaming baby, while washing a pile of dishes, saying into the telephone, "He's not here, he's out helping the struggle of oppressed people."

The Diggers were another well known community-action group, including local actors, operating out of the Haight-Ashbury neighborhood of San Francisco, beginning in 1966. Their publications, particularly the *Digger Papers,* were the origin of movement phrases such as "Do your own thing" and "Today is the first day of the rest of your life." They have been described as left-wing, but others considered them community anarchists who combined a desire for freedom with a consciousness of their community. The Diggers were social justice advocates and provided a free food service each afternoon, feeding more than 200 needy people. The Diggers also provided whole-wheat bread, known as Digger Bread, baked in coffee cans at the Free Bakery. They opened several Free Stores in the neighborhood, offering free items that had been discarded but were still in usable condition. They also opened a free medical clinic. By the end of 1968, the Diggers had disintegrated for several reasons, including allegations of heavy drug use and growing violence, rather than peace, in the area.

The Diggers inspired later groups like the Youth International Party, or the Yippies. They were an offshoot of the free speech and anti-war movements. They employed media-savvy measures to challenge the social status quo. For example, they nominated a pig ("Pigasus the Immortal") as a presidential candidate in 1968. Like other counterculture groups, the Yippies had no formal membership or officers, although reported members included Abbie Hoffman, Anita Hoffman, Paul Krassner, and Jerry Rubin.

Prior to his time as a Yippie, Abbie Hoffman was a member of the Student Nonviolent Coordinating Committee (SNCC), which supported the civil rights movement and opposed the Vietnam War. He led many memorable mass demonstrations, including one in which more than 50,000 people attempted to levitate the Pentagon, using psychic energy, and another in which he led a group of protesters to the gallery of the New York Stock Exchange (NYSE) and threw fake dollar bills down to the traders below. Hoffman also had several confrontations with law enforcement. He was arrested for conspiracy and inciting to riot as a result of his role in protests that led to violent confrontations with police during the 1968 Democratic National Convention in Chicago, Illinois. He was among the group that came to be known as the Chicago Seven, which also included fellow Yippie Jerry Rubin, Black Panther Party cofounder Bobby

IN CONTEXT   Founding Statement

Student Nonviolent Coordinating Committee Founding Statement:

"We affirm the philosophical or religious ideal of nonviolence as the foundation of our purpose, the presupposition of our belief, and the manner of our action.

"Nonviolence, as it grows from the Judeo-Christian tradition, seeks a social order of justice permeated by love. Integration of human endeavor represents the crucial first step towards such a society.

"Through nonviolence, courage displaces fear. Love transcends hate. Acceptance dissipates prejudice; hope ends despair. Faith reconciles doubt. Peace dominates war. Mutual regard cancel

enmity. Justice for all overthrows injustice. The redemptive community supersedes immoral social systems.

"By appealing to conscience and standing on the moral nature of human existence, nonviolence nurtures the atmosphere in which reconciliation and justice become actual possibilities.

"Although each local group in this movement must diligently work out the clear meaning of this statement of purpose, each act or phase of our corporate effort must reflect a genuine spirit of love 'and good-will." (Source: Institute of Advanced Technology in the Humanities at the University of Virginia, Charlottesville)

Seale, and several other activists. Hoffman was arrested in 1973 on drug charges and later dropped out of sight for many years. He wrote *Steal This Book*, a guide to surviving outside of the established capitalist system.

The two best-known events of the counterculture movement were the Summer of Love and Woodstock. At an event called a "human be-in," thousands of people gathered at the Golden Gate Park in San Francisco in the summer of 1967 to promote peace and love. The celebration included musical performances, poetry readings, speeches, and theater-style productions.

Music was an integral part of the counterculture movement. There were certain styles of music that are connected to the movement. Varieties included psychedelic rock from artists such as Jimi Hendrix and Jefferson Airplane, blues music by singers such as Janis Joplin, folk music from Bob Dylan, and bands like the Grateful Dead. Music was used as a way to distinguish an alternative lifestyle and to protest against war and oppression. There were numerous outdoor music festivals across the United States, and the best known of the concerts was Woodstock. It took place from August 15 to 17, 1969, on a thousand-acre farm in upstate New York. About 50,000 were expected but more than 500,000 attended. There were many traffic jams, and food and water were scarce, but the message of peace and love persisted. Musicians at the event included Jimi Hendrix, Joan Baez, and Janis Joplin. Woodstock remains the most lasting symbol of the peace movement.

A popular saying among ex-hippies today is, "If you remember the 1960s, you weren't there." The lack of memory in large part is due to drug use. Known as the "psychedelics guru," Harvard professor Timothy Leary advocated the use of drugs as a form of mind expansion. Many hippies participated in recreational drug use, particularly hallucinogens such as LSD. The use of marijuana had been established by the Beats, and the drug appeared in Kerouac's *On the Road*, which was widely read among

This marker commemorates the original site of the Woodstock Music Festival, held in Bethel, New York, 1969. (Shutterstock)

soon-to-be hippies. The use of drugs was seen as a way to express disaffection with societal conventions.

Another prominent drug-related figure in the counterculture movement was Ken Kesey. He led a group of psychedelic sympathizers around the country in a painted schoolbus, labeled "Further," and encouraged LSD-induced "acid tests" throughout the trip. Kesey was initially known as the author of *One Flew over the Cuckoo's Nest*, which he wrote while a student at Stanford. He soon became the leader of a group of friends, known as the Merry Pranksters. The first acid test was held in California in November 1965. (It is important to remember that LSD was legal in the United States until laws were changed in 1966.) The young psychedelic music band the Grateful Dead performed music during these events and garnered a dedicated following for decades.

 **TURNING POINT**

The counterculture movement reached its height in the late 1960s. By 1972, many of its ideas and styles had, more or less, been accepted by most of society. One of the counterculture's mantras was "don't trust anyone over thirty." Yet, as the years passed, many of those in the movement were approaching that age. Some moved through the movement as if it were a phase. They shaved their beards, donned suits, and joined the corporate community. Major trends initiated by the counterculture continued into the 1970s. These included a growing suspicion of governmental officials, advances in civil rights, an expansion of women's roles, an increased concern about the environment, an exploration of alternative communication forms, and a drive to eliminate drug abuse.

The drug abuse and resulting violence aided the demise of the movement. The Haight-Ashbury neighborhood of San Francisco was one of the best known of the gathering places for counterculture events. Most of the gatherings were peaceful, but by the end of 1967, the increased use of drugs and the resulting crime signaled a shift in the movement. As it began to change, some hippies announced their own death in the fall of 1967, with the "Death of Hip" ceremony. They burned a coffin labeled the "Summer of Love." It was a sign that the counterculture had shifted from the innocence of "flower power" to a mature movement with problems.

As the years passed, mainstream culture embraced what was once counter to the culture. The fashion and music of the time became less alternative and instead, widely accepted. Tie-dyed clothing was manufactured by and sold in corporate-owned businesses. Those outside the movement began wearing the clothes made popular by the hippies, thus bringing them into the mainstream. Politics changed, too. Young people, including Vietnam veterans and anti-war activists, were elected to local and national offices. Their priorities were reflected in their political agendas as legislation was passed to address counterculture priorities such as discriminatory practices in the workplace and environmental protections. Thus, the turning point was the 1967 Summer of Love; had the demise of the counterculture been more forceful due to a new disease, future events might have turned out quite differently.

ACTUAL HISTORY

The assassinations of leaders John F. Kennedy, Robert F. Kennedy, and Martin Luther King, Jr., turned the political landscape into turmoil. The suspicion of established authority that came out of the 1960s was validated by governmental actions in the 1970s. In 1972, Richard Nixon won reelection against Democratic candidate George McGovern. During the election campaign, there was a burglary at the Democratic Party headquarters at the Watergate building in Washington, D.C., that prompted the problems to come. *Washington Post* reporters Bob Woodward and Carl Bernstein began writing about the burglary and began to connect several members of the Nixon administration to the Watergate break-in. Nixon publicly denied any connection to the case, yet in April 1973, two of Nixon's top advisors, H. R. Haldeman and John Ehrlichman, resigned. A third advisor, John Dean, was fired. Vice President Spiro T. Agnew resigned after being charged with income tax evasion. He was replaced by Gerald Ford; it was the first time that the Twenty-Fifth Amendment, which clarified the succession to the presidency, was applied.

IN CONTEXT Black Panther Party's Ten Point Program

On October 15, 1966, the Black Panther party leaders wrote the party's Ten Point Program. The program represented a combination of ideas ranging from contemporary concepts of national self-determination as practiced against colonial regimes around the world to ordinary social goals such as employment and decent housing. The program also included ideas derived from Marxism as well as from the American Constitution and Declaration of Independence. Expressed as goals that were wanted, backed by a statement of the beliefs that justified the desired goal, the statement voiced a wide range of concerns that had not been addressed by the movement for desegregation and voting rights that had characterized the 1950s and early 1960s. The following extracts from the program reflect the tone of the Panther movement:

1) We Want Freedom. We Want Power To Determine The Destiny Of Our Black Community. We believe that Black people will not be free until we are able to determine our destiny.

2) We Want Full Employment For Our People. We believe that the federal government is responsible and obligated to give every man employment or a guaranteed income....

3) We Want An End To The Robbery By The Capitalists Of Our Black Community. We believe that this racist government has robbed us, and now we are demanding the overdue debt.... We will accept the payment in currency which will be distributed to our many communities. ...

4) We Want Decent Housing Fit For The Shelter Of Human Beings....

5) We Want Education For Our People That Exposes The True Nature Of This Decadent American Society. We Want Education That Teaches Us Our True History And Our Role In The Present-Day Society.

6) We Want All Black Men To Be Exempt From Military Service. We believe that Black people should not be forced to fight in the military service to defend a racist government....

In June 1973, testimony before the Senate committee investigating Watergate reported that Nixon was a part of the cover-up and that he probably had tape recordings of meetings about the break-in. The special prosecutor called for access to the tapes, and the Supreme Court reinforced the request. The content of the tapes revealed that Nixon was involved in the cover-up. Several senators called for Nixon's impeachment. On August 9, 1974, Nixon resigned the presidency. Ford then became president, and he granted Nixon a full pardon. The political cynicism in the country was palpable.

Civil rights were a continuing cause resulting from the counterculture movement. An important landmark in the battle for civil rights for African American citizens came in 1964 when President Lyndon Johnson signed into law a comprehensive civil rights act. It prohibited discrimination in education, voting, and the use of public facilities. The Supreme Court had ruled on segregation in public schools in 1954, but the federal government now had a means of enforcing desegregation as Title VI of the act barred the use of federal funds in segregated programs and schools. The problem of segregated housing was addressed in the Civil Rights Act of 1968; it contained a clause barring racial discrimination in housing sales and rentals.

The Voting Rights Act was passed in 1968. It included special enforcement provisions aimed at areas of the country where Congress viewed the

---

IN CONTEXT   *Black Panther Party's Ten Point Program (Continued)*

7) We Want An Immediate End To Police Brutality And Murder Of Black People. We believe we can end police brutality in our Black community by organizing Black self-defense groups....

8) We Want Freedom For All Black Men Held In Federal, State, County And City Prisons And Jails. We believe that all Black people should be released from the many jails and prisons because they have not received a fair and impartial trial.

9) We Want All Black People When Brought To Trial To Be Tried In Court By A Jury Of Their Peer Group Or People From Their Black Communities, As Defined By The Constitution Of The United States....

10) We Want Land, Bread, Housing, Education, Clothing, Justice And Peace...."
[Source: *War Against the Panthers,* by Huey P. Newton, Writers and Readers Publishing, 1996.]

The full ten point program also included text drawn directly from the preamble to the U.S. Declaration of Independence, suggesting why the party felt compelled to state its grievances and program with such explicit language. Demands or points six through nine represented a striking departure from the more moderate goals of African American civil rights leaders in the Southern Christian Leadership Conference and in organizations like the Urban League and the National Association for the Advancement of Colored People. The tone and nature of the ten point program established the Black Panther Party as a vehicle for expression of black youth dissatisfaction with the moderate goals of the traditional organizations. The more radical demands and their tone of expression captured black youth's discontent over police brutality, over the disproportionate number of blacks serving in the military and in prisons, and over social conditions not addressed by civil rights legislation.

---

potential for racial discrimination to be the greatest. Despite progress, some violent reactions to racial injustice continued. More than thirty people died during riots in the Los Angeles community of Watts. Many American cities also experienced violence in the ensuing months.

There was an increase in election activity as a result of the civil rights movement. More African American candidates were elected to Congress, and the first African American mayors were elected in many cities such as Atlanta, Los Angeles, and Detroit. Educational desegregation continued to be an issue as cases involving school busing wove their way through the courts.

The women's movement continued as well. Several of the ideals of equality, such as the potential of pay equity and promotion, were reflected in legislation and reinforced by organizations such as the National Organization of Women. The group was created in large part to make sure that the Equal Employment Opportunity Commission was taking pay inequity and sexual harassment cases seriously. As time progressed, women were hired in record numbers in industries that had excluded them in the past. Newspapers stopped publishing help-wanted ads segregated by gender. Women became police officers, firefighters, and engineers. They also began going to college in larger numbers. By 1979, female students had surpassed male students in college enrollment figures.

Women expanded their involvement in politics in the 1970s, and the proportion of women in state legislatures nearly tripled. Women entered law schools in large numbers and began to be named as judges. By 1981, the first woman, Sandra Day O'Connor, was named to the Supreme Court. The women's movement also focused on women's reproductive rights. Access to contraception and abortion were ruled legal by the Supreme Court in the 1970s, although issues involving reproductive rights continued to remain controversial.

One political issue that was not successful was passage of the Equal Rights Amendment (ERA). The proposed legislation would have provided equal rights for all citizens regardless of gender. During the 1970s, many men and women lobbied, marched, and picketed on behalf of the new law. The amendment passed both the Senate and the House of Representatives. On March 22, 1972, the proposed Twenty-Seventh Amendment to the Constitution was sent to the states for ratification with a seven-year deadline for the ratification process. The ERA got off to a fast start, gaining twenty-two of the needed thirty-eight state ratifications in its first year. But opposition began to organize, and the pace slowed. ERA opponents such as Phyllis Schlafly and Jerry Falwell argued that the amendment would deny a woman's right to be supported by her husband and that women would be sent into military combat. States' rights advocates and religious groups also fought against the amendment. In 1973, there were eight ratifications but only four more states had ratified by the end of 1976. Illinois, Shlafly's home state, changed its rules to require a three-fifths majority in the legislature to ratify an amendment and thus negated passage in that state. Time ran out. The ERA was reintroduced in Congress in 1982 and has been before almost every session since that year.

Another long-standing reminder of the counterculture movement is Earth Day, which is promoted today through recycling programs in communities and awareness campaigns at elementary schools. The counterculture movement's support of environmentally friendly concepts was supported by some lawmakers. Air pollution in many cities was linked to health problems, and Rachel Carson's 1962 book *Silent Spring* exposed the dangers of pesticides. Congress passed the Clean Air Act and the Water Quality Improvement Act in 1967. By 1970, the Environmental Protection Agency, an independent federal agency, was created to lead the effort to bring air and water pollution under control.

Leading the environmental fight was Wisconsin Senator Gaylord Nelson. He traveled the country and collected information about the numerous volunteer anti-pollution programs. This led to a public awareness campaign about environmental issues: the teach-in program. Nelson's idea was covered by *Time, Newsweek,* and the *New York Times*. He created the nonprofit, nonpartisan organization, the Environmental Teach-In, Inc. Its purpose was to lay a foundation for a nationwide series of conservation teach-ins during 1970. Meanwhile, on April 22, 1970, an estimated 20 million Americans gathered in their communities in one of the country's largest organized demonstrations to celebrate Earth Day. One of the biggest demonstrations was in New York City, led by Mayor John Lindsay. That afternoon, Fifth Avenue was closed to traffic between 14th and 59th Streets, causing midtown Manhattan to come to a virtual standstill. More attention to environmental issues continued throughout the decade.

The widespread drug abuse in the 1960s led to a backlash. In 1970, Nixon announced that drug education was a national issue and should be taught in public schools. By the 1970s, nearly 18,000 school districts had implemented drug abuse education. By the end of the decade, the Cabinet Committee on Drug Abuse Prevention, Treatment and Rehabilitation determined that teenagers would likely continue to experiment with illegal drugs as a natural part of growing up. It recommended that the drug abuse education efforts be altered to focus on the moderation of drug use. The federal government adopted an abstinence only policy, "Just Say No." Future programs, funded by federal and state monies, continued to focus on educating children about the dangers of drug and alcohol abuse with varying results.

The marijuana plant became a symbol for hippies as drug abuse became widespread in 1960s. (Shutterstock)

Some historians say the counterculture movement played a part in the development of the personal computer. The floppy disk first appeared in 1970, and the following year Intel introduced the microprocessor. Some contemporary historians have connected the development of the home computer to Steve Wozniak and Steve Jobs, as well as other pioneers who were at Stanford University and Berkeley while the movement was spreading. According to John Markoff in *What the Dormouse Said: How the Sixties Counterculture Shaped the Personal Computer,* there was a clear connection to the events of the 1960s: "The computer technologies that we take for granted today owe their shape to this unruly period, which was defined by protest, experimentation with drugs, counterculture community, and a general sense of anarchic idealism." This concept was further advanced by Theodore Roszak's 1986 essay "From Satori to Silicon Valley," which connected the birth of computer industry to the values of the counterculture movement. It is perhaps the idealism of the counterculture movement that evolved into the far-thinking entrepreneurship of men like Jobs and Wozniak.

ALTERNATE HISTORY

Had the Summer of Love led to a health epidemic based on a fatal disease that was transmitted through drug needles and irresponsible sexual activities, the historical outcome would have been very different.

In its initial years, the disease would not have had a name and different groups would have referred to it in different ways. The Centers for Disease Control and Prevention would have begun calling it lymphadenopathy, or swollen glands—the first symptom of the disease. It soon would have become clear that the disease was disproportionately impacting those in the counterculture movement, with some calling it the "hippie cancer." Because very little would have been known about transmission, public anxiety would have continued to grow. In addition to the medical responses, there would have been societal reactions of fear, stigma, and discrimination accompanying the epidemic. This stigma would have been used to marginalize and exclude members of the counterculture movement.

Every week a new theory would have proposed how the disease was spreading. As misinformation grew about how the disease was transmitted, landlords would have evicted individuals with lymphadenopathy, and patrol officers would have worn special masks and gloves for use when dealing with hippies. There would have continued to be concern about the public health aspects of the disease. This would have been particularly the case in San Francisco, where communes would have been eliminated and public concerts halted. College campuses would also have become targets of suspicion.

Awareness of the disease would have been brought to the public's consciousness, when popular movement leader Timothy Leary died of it early on, shortly after making public his condition. Many other well-known personalities from the entertainment industry would have added their familiar faces to the cumulative weight of the lymphadenopathy crisis when they also succumbed to the disease.

The onset of lymphadenopathy likely would have led to hundreds of deaths of hippies across the country. The reaction would have been one of fear and anger. With an emphasis on safe sexual practices and personal responsibility, the questioning of authority would have been thwarted. Instead, the government would have been looked to for help. It would not have been the enemy, but instead a partner in fighting the disease.

Rather than rejecting the power structure, the former hippies would likely have joined it. They would have run for governmental office in record numbers. They would have brought their progressive ideas, tempered with the dangers of irresponsible behaviors, to their political careers. With strength in numbers, the groups would have had a unified voice that would have led to underrepresented groups being elected to statewide and national positions. As the voting age would have been lowered from twenty-one to eighteen, more young people would have become politically active.

Using the power structure to their advantage, the former hippies would have made major changes to social structures. They would have taken the ideals of their generation and merged them with the organization structure already in place. The new leaders, with a background in the civil rights and women's movements, would have fought for an institutionalized equality. They would have sought enforcement of policy that encouraged change. For example, government-sponsored day care would have been instituted in workplaces across the country, which would have allowed women to enter the workforce in all fields.

The alarm raised by lymphadenopathy would have meant that issues of sexuality would have been reexamined. Just as there had been an extensive educational campaign about the dangers of drug abuse in actual history, a campaign about safe sexual practices would have been introduced to the school curriculum. This open discussion of sexuality would have led to fewer teenage pregnancies and fewer sexually transmitted diseases.

The political landscape would have been further redefined when Congresswoman Shirley Chisholm, the first woman of color in actual history to make a serious run for the Democratic nomination for president, would have become the vice presidential candidate. In actual history, on January 25, 1972, Chisholm announced her candidacy for president. Chisholm would likely have been the running mate of the anti–Vietnam War candidate, George McGovern. If they had been elected, American soldiers would have quickly left the Asian country. McGovern's plan for a unilateral withdrawal from the Vietnam War in exchange for the return of American prisoners of war and an amnesty program for draft dodgers who had fled the country would have been put into place. Government leaders, particularly those who had been impacted by the Vietnam War, might have vowed not to enter into military conflict again. This would have significantly altered the political future of the United States. The likelihood of future military interventions would have been significantly diminished.

In an alternate history, Shirley Chisholm would have been vice president of the United States. (Library of Congress)

McGovern's and Chisholm's support of the ERA would likely have led to its passage in all states. The ERA would have amended the Constitution to guarantee equal rights under the law regardless of gender. The ERA would have stated (as it did in actual history): 1. Equality of rights under the law shall not be denied or abridged by the United States or by any State on account of sex; 2. The Congress shall have the power to enforce, by appropriate legislation, the provisions of this article; 3. This amendment shall take effect two years after the date of ratification.

The alternative views that would have intersected with the mainstream processes likely would have led to a progressive environmental awareness. The gardens that lined the former hippies' communes would have caused an increase in organic farming. The environmental consciousness that was practiced in the communes would have become part of the political landscape. These hippies-turned-politicians would have advocated numerous environment-friendly causes. They would have fought for governmental funding for hybrid cars, which would have significantly reduced smog and used far less gasoline than conventional cars. Research also would have begun on fuels that were based on ethanol and other energy alternatives. This support for eco-friendly cars would have led to less reliance on foreign oil. And this change would have had dramatic implications for future relationships with Middle Eastern countries.

> The media landscapes also would have been altered. Rather than the corporate structure that eventually took hold in actual history, the importance of independent publications would have been valued. Rather than conglomerations, alternative newspapers and magazines would have thrived and provided numerous viewpoints.

Kimberly Wilmot Voss

Discussion Questions

1. In the alternate history in this chapter, a new disease spreads through the hippie community. How is the impact of this disease different from the spread of the HIV (AIDS) epidemic that in actual history had its initial impact in the gay community?

2. What aspects of the counterculture of the 1960s have become incorporated into the mainstream culture?

3. In what ways could the development of the personal computer reflect the values of the counterculture?

4. What factor do you think was most important in stimulating the rise of the counterculture: war, the generation gap, or the civil rights movement?

5. What elements of the alternate history described in this chapter resemble actual history, and what elements of it represent a departure from what in fact happened?

Bibliography and Further Reading

Braunstein, Peter, and Michael William Doyle, eds. *Imagine Nation: The American Counterculture of the 1960s and 70s.* New York: Taylor and Francis, 2001.

Brown, Joe David. *The Hippies.* New York: Time Inc., 1967.

Friedan, Betty. *The Feminine Mystique.* New York: W.W. Norton: 1963.

Gitlin, Todd. *The Whole World Is Watching.* Berkeley: University of California Press, 1980.

Hoffman, Abbie. *Steal This Book.* New York: Avalon, 2002.

Markoff, John. *What the Dormouse Said: How the Sixties Counterculture Shaped the Personal Computer.* New York: Penguin Books, 2005.

McDarrah, Fred W., Gloria S. McDarrah, and Timothy S. McDarrah. *Anarchy, Protest and Rebellion: And the Counterculture that Changed America.* New York: Avalon, 2004.

Melville, Keith. *Communes in the Counter Culture: Origins, Theories, Styles of Life.* New York: William Morrow, 1972.

Newton, Huey P. *War against the Panthers.* New York: Readers and Writers Publishing, 1996.

Parish, Steve, with Joe Layden. *Home before Daylight: My Life on the Road with the Grateful Dead.* New York: St. Martin's Press, 2003.

Perone, James E. *The Counterculture Era.* Westport, CT: Greenwood, 2004.

Wolfe, Tom. *The Electric Kool-Aid Acid Test.* New York: Bantam Books, 1999.

Mario Savio was a free-speech student leader who protested in 1964. What if Savio had been shot during the violent demonstrations?

INTRODUCTION

Originating at the University of California within the Berkeley campus, the Free Speech Movement had a key role in the development of the 1960s counterculture and the struggle for civil rights. It set up an agenda for students' activism, and by the end of the decade, its spirit had spread to hundreds of other universities, in both the United States and Europe.

The Free Speech Movement cannot be separated from the more general civil rights movement, which, throughout the 1960s, advocated a more inclusive society where African Americans could finally enjoy equal rights with white people. The campaign for civil rights was a dynamic force that shook American society during the whole decade. Although its focus was initially on blacks' rights, the movement soon led to the establishment of a coalition of diverse groups whose concerns included the protest against the Vietnam War, women's liberation, gay and lesbian rights, environmental preservation, and equality for other ethnic minorities. These became the catalysts for the growth of the New Left.

In the beginning, the civil rights movement was encouraged by the policies pursued by the presidencies of John F. Kennedy and Lyndon B. Johnson. Kennedy's program for a New Frontier and Johnson's plan for a Great Society aimed at poverty reduction and equal rights for American citizens. For the number of important political, social, and economic reforms promoted by the Kennedy and Johnson administrations and passed by Congress, the 1960s were years comparable to those of the New Deal. Yet in spite of these reforms, the decade was also marked by social unrest that at times escalated into violence. The Kennedy and Johnson presidencies were characterized by race riots, the murder of President Kennedy and many civil rights activists—including the two national leaders Malcolm X and Martin Luther King, Jr.—and the violence of the Vietnam War.

The presidency of John Kennedy opened with strong optimism. A traditional Democrat, Kennedy believed in the centrality of the social welfare

KEY CONCEPT   Jim Crow Laws, Racial Segregation in the South, and the Poll Tax

The term *Jim Crow* designated the system of institutionalized discrimination against African Americans that southern states began to use in the late 1890s and practiced until the late 1950s. The laws that constituted the backbone of the Jim Crow system were designed to keep whites and blacks as separate as possible in public spaces such as schools, modes of transport, and accommodation facilities and to prevent African Americans from exercising their right to vote. This system of segregation was fully validated in southern states by the 1910s. For white Southerners, Jim Crow was a way to reinstate their supremacy, which had been challenged by their defeat in the Civil War.

The name of *Jim Crow* has its origins in the shows of a white minstrel actor, Thomas "Daddy" Rice. During the 1830s, his face blackened by charcoal, he performed the song "Jump Jim Crow" while dancing a silly jig. Some say that Rice invented this character after seeing a southern crippled slave dancing and singing. Probably a Mr. Crow owned the slave, thus the name in the song. By the 1850s, Jim Crow had become a standard character in minstrel shows. The stereotype became one of the many embodiments of the idea of African American inferiority in American nineteenth-century popular culture along with Sambos and Coons. "Jim Crow" soon developed into a white insult referring to

system in American society. Elected president in 1960 at only forty-three, he provided a stark contrast to the conservative image of his predecessor Dwight Eisenhower. The enthusiasm that followed Kennedy's narrow election, however, soon proved difficult for the president to sustain. During the electoral campaign, his ambitious New Frontier program had promised the end of racial segregation, public funds for education and for health services, and new economic measures to stop the ongoing economic recession. Yet from the very first months, Kennedy faced strong opposition from a conservative Congress, which rejected his bills for federal aid to education only eight months into his administration.

Kennedy's actions against segregation were much more cautious compared with the boldness of his electoral promises. Although he established a presidential committee on Equal Employment Opportunity and issued a tardy executive order to stop segregation in public housing, Kennedy had to compromise with the conservative congressional majority. Civil rights activists were soon disillusioned with his administration and carried on with their nonviolent protests and civil disobedience. King organized the Southern Christian Leadership Conference (SCLC), whose members defied the Jim Crow laws by entering white-only places. The Congress of Racial Equality (CORE) launched its freedom rides in May 1961 when an integrated group of people traveled from Washington, D.C., to southern states, thus desegregating interstate transportation. Many African American students joined the Student Nonviolent Coordinating Committee (SNCC), which was established after the sit-ins to desegregate a lunch counter in Greensboro, North Carolina. The SNCC encouraged southern blacks to fight against segregation and exercise their right to vote. The majority of the SNCC members came from low-income African American families who had firsthand knowledge of the ways racism and poverty combined to shatter their lives. All these organizations would have a key role in the development of the Free Speech Movement at Berkeley.

KEY CONCEPT   *Jim Crow Laws, Racial Segregation in the South, and the Poll Tax (Continued)*

blacks, and by the 1890s, the phrase was used to describe acts of racial discrimination against blacks.

By 1910, every state of the former Confederacy had approved laws that segregated all aspects of public life so that blacks and whites were prevented from mingling. Streetcars had a special area for blacks at their rear. Water fountains, restrooms, waiting rooms, the entrances and exits to courthouses, libraries, theaters, and public buildings started to exhibit "Whites Only" and "Colored" signs. Even hospitals and cemeteries rigidly imposed the division of the color line. Workplaces were segregated too in some states. Jim Crow laws marked the failure of Reconstruction and its hope of creating a more inclusive society.

To keep the races separate, it was instrumental to disenfranchise black voters so that their voices and opinions were not represented on the political scene. As a response to the Fifteenth Amendment (1870), which gave voting rights to all races, many southern states passed poll tax laws that often included a grandfather clause. Only those adult males whose fathers or grandfathers had voted prior to the abolition of slavery could vote without paying the tax. All the others would have to prove the payment of the poll tax to be allowed to vote. These laws effectively led to the disenfranchising of African Americans. Through these new electoral rules, white registrars could legally deny voting rights to blacks.

As the civil rights movement spread throughout the United States, Kennedy pledged himself to more decisive action, but his efforts were cut short by his assassination. The difficult task of completing the civil rights legislation initiated by Kennedy fell to Vice President Lyndon Johnson who stepped in as the new president. Johnson was a skillful southern politician who aimed to unite the country in the legacy of his murdered predecessor. Calling his new legislative agenda the Great Society, Johnson made civil rights his top priority and exploited the national emotion caused by the Kennedy assassination to push through quick approval of the Civil Rights Act of 1964. It officially outlawed discrimination based on race, color, religion, sex, or national origin in public accommodation, employment, and education. In addition, the Twenty-fourth Amendment to the Constitution was ratified, declaring it illegal to deny the vote in federal elections for failure to pay a poll tax.

In spite of these progressive measures, Johnson's record on civil rights was also marked by less noble achievements. In August 1964, at the National Democratic Convention in Atlanta that nominated him the presidential candidate, Johnson supported the openly segregationist delegates from Mississippi against the complaints from the unofficial black delegates of the Mississippi Freedom Democratic Party (MFDP). Although several delegates had been elected to the Democratic Convention by disenfranchised African American voters and white sympathizers, the party refused to accept them. Because of the media uproar that the case was causing, Johnson offered the MFDP a compromise of two seats at the convention, which the unofficial delegates refused. Thus, while the civil rights movement was achieving important successes in the 1960s, some activists felt betrayed. Many African Americans, in both the South and the North, were living in poverty, with unemployment rates twice as high as among whites. In the summer of 1964, race riots erupted in northern cities sparked by violent police behavior in New York and New Jersey.

IN CONTEXT   The 1964 Presidential Election

The 1964 presidential election ended with a lop-sided victory for incumbent Lyndon Johnson, who captured 61 percent of the popular vote, the largest percentage since 1824. Johnson also won in all but six states (South Carolina, Alabama, Georgia, Mississippi, Louisiana, and Arizona, the native state of Republican candidate Barry Goldwater). Thrust forward by the presidential landslide, the Democrats won solid majorities in both the House and the Senate. Johnson succeeded in linking his actions to the legacy of John F. Kennedy and in presenting himself as the most reliable of the two candidates. His opponent, Goldwater, on the contrary, was harmed by his extremist and blunt statements, which strongly appealed to the most conservative wing of the Republican Party but failed to make him a credible candidate for a larger coalition.

The 1964 election signaled an important transition in the Republican Party. Goldwater helped to establish the conservative majority in the party that would lead to Reagan's success sixteen years later. The election also represented a watershed in the southern vote. Since Reconstruction, the South had always been solidly in favor of the Democratic Party. Yet in 1964, for the first time, Mississippi, Alabama, and Georgia voted for a Republican candidate, alienated by Johnson's support of civil rights legislation. Although Johnson managed to win a narrow majority in the popular vote of the former Confederate states, Goldwater's capture of five Deep South states was an important symptom of the process that would turn the South into a Republican stronghold.

Johnson's presidency was also characterized by the escalation of the Vietnam War. In August 1964, the American destroyers *Maddox* and C. *Turner Joy* were allegedly attacked twice in the Gulf of Tonkin by North Vietnamese forces (historians have challenged the reality of the second attack). Johnson announced immediate retaliation and within a few days, an almost unanimous Congress gave him the power to take all necessary measures against the North Vietnamese. The Gulf of Tonkin Resolution, as the document became known, was tantamount to a declaration of war and paved the way for the intensification of American involvement in the fight between the communist-controlled North Vietnam and the capitalist South. Protests against the Vietnam War, although still limited when the Free Speech Movement started in 1964, soon became an essential concern of students' activism.

In the context of America's social and racial unrest and amid debates on the national role in a world dominated by the Cold War, the Berkeley campus, where the Free Speech Movement initially developed, looked like an oasis of order. In his 1963 book *The Uses of the University*, University of California president Clark Kerr described the many separate colleges and research institutes that form the academic institution (a "multiversity," in Kerr's term) as becoming gradually like segments of industry. Universities were to become "factories of knowledge." Consequently, the model of university Kerr proposed was "a mechanism held together by administrative rules and powered by money." With these premises, it is not surprising that many students increasingly felt that Berkeley, the largest campus in the country, was becoming impersonal and managed by bureaucrats. Many students were also conscious that the same power structure that supported the university bureaucratic impersonality favored racial discrimination at home and armed intervention against the communists in North Vietnam.

Student activism had already entered the universities in 1962, when Students for a Democratic Society (SDS) was formed in Port Huron, Michigan. Berkeley, however, had a long history of regulations linked to political movements. For example, as political activity increased during the Depression, President Robert Gordon Sproul prohibited all political and religious meetings on campus in 1934. In 1949, prompted by the hysteria of McCarthyism, the university introduced an anti-communist loyalty oath that was required from faculty members. Kerr, at the time the university chancellor, signed the oath but defended those who did not, speaking against their dismissal. Political activity was partly allowed when the 1934 ban was modified in 1957. Two years later, however, the Sather Gate section of Telegraph Avenue, which was traditionally the heart of off-campus free speech, became part of the campus. Political activities were then restricted to the campus entrance at Bancroft and Telegraph.

During the summer of 1964, many Berkeley students had helped civil rights organizations such as the freedom riders to register African Americans to vote. Some, including the Free Speech Movement's future leader Mario Savio, had also been teaching at the SNCC's Mississippi Freedom Summer Project. Specifically, Savio had taught at a freedom school for black children in McComb, Mississippi. Once back on campus, they set up tables to inform fellow students about the civil rights movement and to solicit donations. In mid-September, university officials, under pressure from conservatives, reminded students that political activity and recruiting for off-campus organizations was prohibited on campus. In spite of the ban, the university administration had allowed students to set up tables to distribute leaflets on the outskirts of campus, on the corner between Bancroft Way and Telegraph Avenue. The new prohibition, however, applied to the whole of the campus.

The growing use and misuse of the area, Dean of Students Katherine A. Towle argued, had made it imperative for the university to take action and strictly enforce university rules. During the last ten days in September, student organization leaders and university administrators entered negotiations. University officials issued contradictory statements. For example, as a result of the picketing triggered by Dean Towle's prohibition, Chancellor Edward Strong allowed the distribution of campaign literature supporting "yes" and "no" votes on motions and candidates, campaign buttons, and bumper strips at Bancroft-Telegraph and at eight other locations on campus. Although Strong justified his position as the result of a reinterpretation of university regulations, this was in clear contrast with Towle's unambiguous ban.

TURNING POINT

The Free Speech Movement began to coalesce when the ban against on-campus political advocacy was extended to the Bancroft and Telegraph area, which had always functioned as a safety valve. It had allowed students to voice their opinions without compromising the university's

A leader of the Free Speech Movement, Mario Savio rallies a crowd at the University of California, Berkeley, on December 4, 1964. (Corbis)

official policy of political neutrality. The turning point in the development of the movement took place between September and October 1964. On September 30, the University Friends of the SNCC, whose spokesperson was Mario Savio, and the CORE set up unauthorized tables. The representatives of both organizations—Mark Bravo, Brian Turner, Donald Hatch, Elizabeth Gardiner Stapleton, and David Goines—were notified that disciplinary action would be taken against them for breach of university rules relating to the soliciting of funds for political causes. This provoked the first of the many Sproul Hall sit-ins that would follow in the next few days.

At 3:00 P.M., 500 students gathered outside the hall where disciplinary action against the SNCC and CORE members was being decided. The protest had reached the heart of the campus. Led by Savio, Arthur Goldberg, and Sandor Fuchs—chairman of SLATE, Berkeley's student party—the 500 students demanded to be considered as guilty as their fellow colleagues. As officials did not give assurances that the students' demands would be accepted, Savio announced that the sit-in would continue through the night. At midnight, an official note from Chancellor Strong announced the indefinite suspension of the five SNCC and CORE activists and the three student leaders from the university. Responding to Strong's note, Savio announced that the demonstrators would not relent, and they would carry on their protests until free speech was ensured throughout the campus. He also directly and polemically referred to President Kerr's notion of "Multiversity Machine" by pointing out that

---

ANOTHER VIEW Clark Kerr's Interpretation of the Events

Clark Kerr is usually depicted as the villain in the story of the Free Speech Movement. Although he was the most reluctant of the university's officials to use force against the students, liberal observers indicted him for his duplicity and for his lack of courage in reforming university regulations in a more democratic direction. Chancellor Strong was really the most hard-line opponent of the students' movement. However, Kerr, as the highest ranking among academic administrators, was the main target of the movement, which denounced him as a puppet in the hands of the regents. Conservatives, however, were equally harsh in their judgment of the university's president, whose actions against the protesters were found largely ineffectual and too hesitant. The Federal Bureau of Investigation (FBI) kept files on him for his liberal credentials and for his inability to repress students more decisively.

In his memoir of his years at Berkeley and in essays on the students' protest that he had to face, Kerr defended his positions in the days of the Free Speech Movement from a liberal standpoint. He depicted himself as a liberal who, ever since his opposition to the anti-communist loyalty oath in the 1950s, had worked to counter the repressive legacy of the Cold War years. The stifling university regulations were a product of Kerr's predecessor, Robert Gordon Sproul, and as a reformer, Kerr was painfully aware of the need to change them. To support his depiction as a liberal, Kerr cited his removal of the ban against communist speakers, which went in the direction of allowing more freedom of speech within the university. The Berkeley president argued that well before the Free Speech Movement was organized, he stood in favor of its main principle, fighting against the university's regents and the legislature to modify the anti-communist clause.

In his reconstruction of the events, Kerr maintained that his reformist efforts were undermined and finally cut short precisely by the development of the Free Speech Movement. Although Kerr admitted that the movement had the support of many faculty members, he charged that the illegal methods it employed, together with its radical demands for quick change, finally alienated the general public from the university and its liberal values. The movement, according to Kerr's view, was responsible for causing the conservative backlash that allowed Ronald Reagan to be elected governor. The Free Speech Movement was not so much the forerunner of the New Left as it was responsible for the rise of the New Right.

Although Kerr's account is a personal one and not entirely consistent with his cautious character and previous choices, his administration was a liberal one. The conflict between the university president and the students is paradigmatic of the 1960s rupture of the progressive front between conventional liberals and more radical leftists. Johnson's refusal to acknowledge the MFDP at the 1964 convention and his defense of American intervention in Vietnam served as national catalysts for the fracture.

---

students had been identified as a faulty part in the mechanism and were, therefore, being expelled. The students named themselves the Free Speech Movement and announced a new sit-in for the next day.

On the morning of October 1, a CORE table soliciting funds was established in the Sproul Plaza. Shortly afterward, university police approached the table and asked the activist who was manning it to identify himself. The man, former student Jack Weinberg, refused to do so and was arrested. As he was taken inside the police car, hundreds of students gathered on the square in his support. They surrounded the police car and prevented it from driving away. The confrontation went on for thirty-two hours. Weinberg stayed inside the car for the whole time while Savio established himself as the demonstrators' leader in several spontaneous speeches from the top of the police car. Mounting the car, he was careful to remove his shoes so as not to scratch the finish.

A philosophy major, Savio was a powerful orator and a talented student. Before enrolling at Berkeley, he had graduated first in his class of 1,200 at Martin Van Buren High School in New York and had been a finalist in the Westinghouse Science Talent Search Scholarship. As negotiations between Savio and the university went nowhere, the students continued their protest, at one point even forcing their way into Sproul Hall.

On October 2, it became clear that the situation was getting dangerously out of control. Violence threatened to explode not only between police and students, but also within students themselves—between those supporting the protest and those against it. The crowd of demonstrators had swelled to several thousand. Hundreds of police officers started to mass around the demonstrators, making the use of police force more likely. Yet Kerr and Strong agreed to meet the student leaders in the afternoon and issued a statement promising no further police action before the end of the meeting. Shortly after 7:00 P.M., the crowd of protesters was informed that an agreement had been reached and signed by Kerr and the student spokespersons. The university agreed not to press charges against Weinberg. A mixed committee, also including the student leaders, would reexamine the suspensions and recommend a new policy to university administrators concerning on-campus political activity. The crowd of students slowly started to disband.

ACTUAL HISTORY

Negotiations between the university and the students, who had appointed an executive committee for the Free Speech Movement, proved difficult from the start. Chancellor Strong chose the members of the Campus Committee on Political Activity (CCPA) without consulting students, although CCPA composition was later modified to accommodate their recommendations. When the CCPA members representing the university administration declared they would stand firm on the prohibition of on-campus political activities, the students invoked the First Amendment, which gave them the right to free speech and to set up tables again. On November 9, the Free Speech Movement announced its members would resume their constitutional right of manning tables on campus. Seventy students were immediately sent letters from the dean's office charging them with violation of university rules. Yet the student movement scored an important victory when, on November 12, the committee appointed by the Academic Senate to investigate the cases of the eight suspensions effectively criticized the administration.

Led by law professor Ira Heyman, the committee proposed the immediate reinstatement of six students with no charges on their records and a six-week suspension for the other two. This meant immediate reinstatement for them too as they had been out of classes for a longer time already. On November 20, the university accepted reinstatement of the six students but did not clear their records. Disappointed, the Free Speech

Movement organized new sit-ins outside Sproul Hall. Faculty members expressed their support of the students.

The Thanksgiving holiday could have offered a respite in the dispute, but during the weekend, student leaders Savio and Goldberg received letters announcing further disciplinary action for illegal acts committed at the beginning of October. This warning of further punishment led the students to organize new protests. Addressing thousands of demonstrators on December 2, Savio once again targeted President Kerr's idea of the university as a factory, giving voice to the estrangement many students felt toward the institution.

The stance against the idea of the university as a machine was a centerpiece of the movement, which placed its central relationships between human beings, not between parts of machines. As an issue of the movement's newsletter put it: "the source of our strength is, very simply, the fact that we are human beings and so cannot forever be treated as raw materials—to be processed. Clark Kerr has declared, in his writings and by his conduct, that a university must be like any other factory—a place where workers who handle raw material are themselves handled like raw material by the administrators above them" (Free Speech Movement Digital Archive at Bancroft Library, University of California, Berkeley).

After the rally of December 2, nearly 800 students occupied Sproul Hall. The young singer Joan Baez performed in support of students' demands.

The following day, December 3, Democratic governor Pat Brown sent a contingent of 600 police officers to the campus to arrest the students involved in the occupation of the university's administrative center. More than 600 students were arrested, the largest mass arrest of students in American history. The entire campus responded with a massive strike, and 900 faculty members gathered to express their support to the students and to their demands for amnesty and complete political freedom. Lawyers and faculty met with a judge and district attorney all day and eventually worked out a bail arrangement. University officials had by then realized that they were facing protests not only from students but also from faculty who were taking part in the Free Speech Movement initiatives in increasingly relevant numbers.

After more days of strikes and deserted classes, on December 8, the Academic Senate voted overwhelmingly (824 to 115) to allow freedom of expression on campus. The university establishment had been defeated. Although the board of regents initially refused to accept the motion approved by the senate, the road to free speech had been opened. On January 2, 1965, the board of regents replaced Chancellor Strong with Martin Meyerson, dean of the College of Environmental Design. In his first speech as chancellor the next day, Meyerson announced the allocation of the Sproul Hall steps for an open discussion forum during certain hours of the day. In addition, he allowed students to set up tables within the campus perimeter.

While originating at a specific time and place, the Free Speech Movement was by no means limited to the Berkeley campus. The mobilization of police against unarmed students came as a shock and a wake-up call for many young people. They felt branded as criminals for protests against racial injustice in their own country. By the end of the 1960s, the student movement had spread to hundreds of other campuses in both the United States and Europe. The Free Speech Movement was a source of inspiration to activists in the diverse coalition of the New Left, which gathered civil rights, anti-war, women's, and gay liberation movements.

The Free Speech Movement contributed in setting the agenda of the New Left, which stressed the importance of genuine human relations as an alternative to the alienation of modern society. Its activists pointed out the increasing alienation of American citizens from institutions, which were built on racism and discrimination. Many also felt their very lives were threatened by the nuclear arms race and the many proxy conflicts of the Cold War, of which Vietnam was becoming an ever more dramatic example. The movement helped shift the United States from the family-oriented society of the 1950s to one that had individual rights at its core. New Left historian Wini Breines has claimed that on-campus freedom of speech was just one point of a larger utopian agenda of movement activists. According to Breines in *Community and Organization in the New Left, 1962–1968,* students wanted to create "communities of equality, direct democracy and solidarity." Such values were "in bold contrast to the values of competition, individualism and efficiency" held by mainstream America.

The student activism born in Berkeley gave rise to the counterculture of the 1960s, which called into question the basic foundations of American society and the notion of authority. Young people started to experiment with drugs and communal living. As violence escalated in Vietnam, the conflict became a specific target of criticism. The outrage was further heightened by the imposition of a compulsory military draft. The Free Speech Movement's critique of the university as a machine resonated with particular significance for those who were drafted. They felt indeed like a mere number, a simple cog in a larger impersonal mechanism.

One of the most popular slogans of the American counterculture became "Make Love, Not War" and university campuses were the site of anti-war marches and demonstrations. Berkeley was again at the forefront of student activism. Many of those who had taken part in the Free Speech Movement helped to establish the Vietnam Day Committee, which campaigned against the war within the campus.

At times, protests on university campuses had tragic endings as in the Kent State shootings of May 1970. Kent State University students had organized a protest against Nixon's decision to invade Cambodia as part of American military strategy in Vietnam. Increasingly tense demonstrations culminated on the fourth day with the National Guard shooting students, killing four and wounding nine. Just a few days after the Kent State shooting, the National Guard opened fire against African American demonstrators at Jackson State College, killing two and wounding twelve. These events led to the formation of the Presidential Commission on Campus Unrest.

Civil rights activists were also energized by the Free Speech Movement. As Johnson's promises of a more inclusive society and better standards of living for African Americans failed to materialize, civil rights causes attracted the sympathies of the student movement. The eruption of the Watts race riots in Los Angeles in the summer of 1965 and riots in many other cities between 1966 and 1968 clearly showed that racism and segregation were still plaguing American society. As the National Advisory Commission on Civil Disorders pointed out in 1968, America was rapidly moving toward two separate nations.

The violence that exploded in black ghettoes confirmed that the movement's support for racial equality needed encouragement rather than banishment. The Free Speech Movement's call for racial cooperation and integration, however, proved a difficult path to follow. As the decade progressed, the civil rights movement took a more radical stance, which challenged King's nonviolent methods. Led by Malcolm X, the Black Muslims espoused African American pride and separatism from white society. After Malcolm X was assassinated in 1965, Stokely Carmichael, the SNCC chairman, took on his legacy, encouraging African Americans to assert their Black Power. In the second half of the 1960s, both the SNCC and CORE, organizations previously committed to racial integration, decided to refuse membership to whites. The Black Panthers Party represented the most radical of African American groups. The Panthers' agenda was a mixture of black nationalism and revolutionary communism, aiming at the subversion of the capitalist system, which was responsible for the oppression of blacks.

To women and homosexuals, the countercultural challenge to established authority meant primarily confronting patriarchy and heterosexism. The student movement engineered a veritable revolution in sexual mores. Feminist thinkers started to ask for comprehensive social change, pointing out that economic structures were at the base of women's subordination. They denounced the organization of women's lives around parenting responsibilities and the double burden they had to bear as domestic and paid workers. They argued for equal access to well-paid employment and for improvement in working conditions. This also entailed a change in the social conditions that led to women's discrimination in the workplace, such as lack of education, shortage of child care facilities, and cultural expectations about what a woman should and should not do.

It was in the 1960s that women started to challenge the cultural expectation that gave them primary responsibility for child rearing. The spread of the birth control pill and the legalization of abortion in 1973 (the Supreme Court ruling in *Roe v. Wade*) were celebrated as important victories in increasing women's social independence from men.

The end of the 1960s also witnessed the organization of gays and lesbians in groups to acquire visibility and to have their identities recognized. In the conformist climate of the 1950s, homosexuals felt that revealing their sexual orientation would lead to unemployment and isolation from their friends and families. Officials regarded homosexuals with the same suspicion reserved for communists. The militancy of the 1960s in favor of free speech encouraged gays and lesbians to speak out for their rights. In June 1969, when the police raided the Stonewall Inn, a gay bar in New York's Greenwich Village, a riot erupted between the patrons and the police. Gays rebelled against the continuous harassment of the police. Stonewall marked a crucial change in the movement for gay rights, from a secret subculture to a larger pressure group, which moved into the open.

In spite of the decade's activism, the 1960s closed on a conservative note. The white middle class started to fear both the excesses of the

Ronald Reagan, elected governor of California in 1966, campaigned to restore law and order on the Berkeley campus. (Library of Congress)

counterculture and the more radical thrust that the civil rights movement was taking. The election year of 1968 was marked by the assassinations of King and of the front-running Democratic presidential candidate, Robert Kennedy. In the 1968 election, American voters turned to conservatism. Republican Richard Nixon defeated the Democrat, Vice President Hubert Humphrey, by a slight margin in the popular vote.

Two developments on the American political scene, partly engendered by the Free Speech Movement, damaged the Democrats' cause. The protests against the Vietnam War highlighted the Democrats' responsibility in a war that, after the North Vietnamese Tet Offensive in January 1968, looked increasingly difficult to win. The Democratic Party was also closely identified with the civil rights struggle. The radicalization of the movement harmed the Democrats' image among the white middle class. Significantly, Humphrey received 97 percent of the votes cast by African Americans, but only 35 percent of those cast by whites.

On a more local level, the decade closed on a conservative note, too. In 1966, Republican candidate Ronald Reagan defeated the two-term incumbent Pat Brown to become governor of California. Reagan had specifically campaigned to restore law and order on the Berkeley campus. The year after his election, Reagan persuaded the university's board of regents to fire Clark Kerr from the position of president for what Reagan perceived as Kerr's lenient behavior during the student protests. Mario Savio, too, did not continue his career to become a national leader. In spite of his charisma, he soon tired of the media attention his leadership had attracted and left Berkeley. He ran for state senate for the Peace and Freedom Party in 1969 and was one of the founders of the Citizens' Party in the 1980s. In 1984, he completed a B.S. degree at San Francisco State University. After earning a master's degree in 1989, he started teaching at Sonoma State University. He taught there until his death in 1996 at the age of fifty-three, caused by heart failure while moving furniture.

Kerr and Savio, sworn enemies during the protests, were paradoxically united in their fate as FBI suspects. The FBI kept files on Kerr for his opposition to the anti-communist loyalty oath and subjected Savio to a massive program of surveillance until 1975.

Since the Free Speech Movement, Sproul Square and Sproul Hall steps (renamed the Mario Savio Steps in 1997) have become the location of many student protests. In the 1960s, they were the site of many sit-ins against the Vietnam War and in favor of the People's Park, the most direct outgrowth of the Free Speech Movement and its spirit. The conflict over the park dramatized, at local level, a polarization between conservatives and radicals that shook America as a nation. The establishment of the People's Park just outside the Berkeley campus (by Telegraph Avenue, which was so central in the 1964 confrontation) took place in April 1969, when hundreds of students and citizens met to clear the rundown area close to the campus and create a free-speech zone with less control than Sproul Square. The park was created as a spot where people could gather and freely express themselves in beautiful surroundings. Yet the establishment of the park coincided with the decision by the university to turn the land into playing fields. Students and citizens were concerned that their efforts would be ruined by the implementation of the university's projects. Berkeley students organized a referendum by which they overwhelmingly voted to keep the park. University officials were conciliatory in tone, reassuring them that nothing would be decided without seeking the consensus of all parties involved. Yet Governor Reagan was eager to show that he could honor his campaign pledge to bring order to Berkeley. He challenged the park as a violation of the university's private property rights and on May 15 ordered the police to occupy and clean the area. The major confrontation that followed resulted in the killing of student James Rector, the blinding of Alan Blanchard, and the wounding of more than 100 people. As the situation was getting out of control, Reagan declared a state of emergency and called in the National Guard with the order to spray tear gas to disperse possible demonstrations. On May 30, an imposing and peaceful march of 30,000 supported the maintenance of the park. Controversies over the area have kept resurfacing throughout the years. More recently Sproul Plaza has hosted demonstrations against apartheid in South Africa and American involvement in the Persian Gulf and in Iraq.

Berkeley linked the pioneering nonviolent protest of the civil rights movement to American campuses, where students learned to challenge the authority and power of academic administrators and, more generally, those in charge of the administration of society.

ALTERNATE HISTORY

The development of the student protest and the rise of the 1960s counterculture might have taken a different course if Mario Savio had been shot by the police during the demonstrations at Berkeley. On October 2, 1964, the policemen who had arrested Jack Weinberg were tired and frustrated after being besieged for more than twenty-four hours by students. Enough policemen had been massed on campus to end the siege with the use of force. The police would have obeyed an order to force their way through the protestors. As they charged against the demonstrators, bullets would have been fired in the air to disperse the crowd. One of them could have fatally injured Savio while he was climbing a police car for one of his many addresses to the demonstrators. The shock of seeing their leader collapse on the roof of the police car, the whistling of bullets just above their heads, and the charge of the police against them would have made the students gathered around the car flee in different directions.

A safety cordon of policemen would have escorted the car outside the campus, while an ambulance with the dying Savio on board would have hurried to the closest hospital, but the run would have been in vain. Out of fear of provoking a revolt throughout American campuses, the news of Savio's death would have been delayed for several hours. Police forces would have occupied the campus, presiding over the administrative centers to prevent the students from occupying them. Governor Pat Brown would have declared a state of emergency and the National Guard troops would have been used to keep the student protesters at bay. A curfew would have also been established and several student leaders would have been arrested.

An emergency meeting at the White House would have informed President Johnson of what had happened. With a month to go before the presidential election, Johnson would not have been willing to have his image damaged by the student revolt. With his strong personality, Johnson would have agreed, together with his secretary of education, Anthony J. Celebrezze, with the need to shut down all the universities for at least a year to prevent large-scale revolts.

With this unprecedented and extreme resolution, the president would have preempted any possible criticism by his opponent, Republican candidate Barry Goldwater, whose most famous sentence in a rather lackluster campaign was that extremism in the defense of liberty was no vice and that, conversely, moderation in the pursuit of justice was no virtue. Johnson would have chosen not to be moderate in the restoration of law and order to avoid being labeled weak in the confrontation with the students. With a challenger such as Goldwater, Johnson would have been sure that his move would not have alienated him from the most liberal of voters. Although they might have resented the use of force to settle the dispute, liberals could not have even contemplated the option of voting for Goldwater, an extreme right-winger, who as Arizona senator had just strongly opposed the Civil Rights Act of 1964.

The decision to close down the universities for a whole year, however, could not have had the desired effect of restoring order and discipline on American campuses. On the contrary, discontent over the death of Savio and the repressive policies against university students might have speeded up the formation of a countercultural movement. With no academic institutions open, students would have sought alternative venues for meeting to discuss the tragic developments of the Vietnam War and the authoritarian decisions of the Johnson administration.

This would have caused experiments in communal living to spread more rapidly and more extensively than they effectively did in actual history. Inspired by the Free Speech Movement and organized by the leaders of SDS, thousands of undergraduates and postgraduates would have founded alternative campuses. Faculty members who did not agree with the extreme measures taken to counter the student revolt could have volunteered to take part in the activities of these substitute institutions. The requests of students for places to congregate without the institutional control of academic administrators would have led to tensions with local communities who might have felt threatened because they perceived the students' behavior as unruly. This would have caused the formation of many citizens' committees to lobby local administrations to deny student access to public spaces and buildings. There would have been a deep fracture within American society between the members of the counterculture and the white middle class.

The counterculture represented in actual history only a minority of American youth, although middle-class parents seemed to spot hippies everywhere and feared that their own children might turn to long hair and drug experimentation. Yet a violent resolution of the free-speech protests at Berkeley could have sparked a strong reaction by a great number of students. Despite the peaceful resolution of the conflict between students and administrators, over the years the activism born in Berkeley in 1964 would have spread to many American campuses. Young people would have been shocked that university administrators and Governor Brown could consider the use of force to solve the dispute. To be treated like criminals only for asking for freedom of speech would have led many students to distrust established authority.

The actual use of force against the students and the killing of their charismatic leader Mario Savio might have had a radicalizing effect on a larger section of American youth. Such an effect would also have been felt more immediately than what happened in actual history. American students would have joined radical organizations in bigger numbers. The class and generation gap, which already constituted an important part of 1960s American history, would have become much wider in much less time.

University campuses were important sites of anti-war demonstrations. The use of force against unarmed students and the repressive measures taken against them would have made immediately apparent to students the link with the escalating violence in the Vietnam conflict. It would have been clear that the university administrators had the full support of the political establishment that was increasing the American presence in Vietnam. With the universities closed, students might not have taken part in on-campus actions against the war, but they would have surely taken part in the national demonstrations against the Vietnam conflicts, and probably in bigger numbers than in actual history.

The April 1965 march on the White House might have mobilized more than the 25,000 people who effectively took part in actual history. The anti-war protests might have developed at a faster pace, challenging the foreign policy of the Johnson administration at an earlier stage and maybe bringing the administration and the Democratic Party sooner to a reconsideration of military involvement. With a larger sector of the American people opposed the war, the dissident voices within the administration might have found the strength to speak up earlier. For example, during the debate among Johnson's advisors about whether to grant more troops to the Joint Chiefs of Staff in July 1965, George Ball might not have been the only one to disagree to dispatch more soldiers to Vietnam. This was a turning point in the war, with the United States taking primary responsibility for fighting the conflict. Ball was the only one to warn that the decision to send in more troops could trigger negative public reactions both at home and abroad. Had the students taken part en masse in the demonstrations against the war, more advisors might have spoken against the decision.

In addition, Secretary of Defense Robert McNamara, who had privately expressed his concerns since 1967 but remained a public supporter of the president until a year later, might have changed his mind more quickly about the military strategies to employ in the war.

The radicalization of students would also have led to a more sustained criticism of Johnson's racial and social policies. More white students might have become members of civil rights organizations. With the universities shut down for a year, even the most conservative of white students would have felt deprived of their most common civil rights. As the failure of the president's Great Society measures to improve the living conditions of blacks in urban ghettoes became apparent, violence would have erupted in American metropolises. Whites as well as black youth might have been side by side in questioning the authority of the administration to deal with social problems. This could have prevented the purging of white membership by influential organizations such as the SNCC and the CORE.

Dismayed by the large protests against U.S. involvement in Vietnam and by the criticism of his social programs, Johnson might have decided to step down earlier from seeking the Democratic Party nomination for the 1968 election. The Democrats might have had more time to organize the campaign for the 1968 primaries of an anti-war candidate who was a real alternative to Lyndon Johnson. The choice of nominating Vice President Hubert Humphrey to run against Republican Richard Nixon was not really a radical departure from Johnson's policies. Humphrey was a loyal supporter of the president, including his decision to escalate the Vietnam War. An alternative candidate might have worked to keep together the New Deal coalition that crumbled in the 1968 election and might have attempted to bridge the gap between the party and the anti-war protesters who besieged the Democratic Convention in Chicago.

The use of force in settling the Free Speech Movement dispute at Berkeley might not have had the desired effect of restoring order on American campuses quickly. On the contrary, it might have led to a much larger student protest movement that would have challenged the fundamental policies of the Johnson administration.

Luca Prono

Discussion Questions

1. What effect do you think a more radicalized youth movement might have had on the course of the Vietnam war?

2. To what extent do you think the policy of the University of California, Berkeley, in treating students as parts of a factory or machine served as a cause of the student protests?

3. Was the university at all justified in banning political expression from the campus?

4. Since CORE and SNCC were not taking a political stand, those student organizations might have been able to get leaflet table permits. Do you think the groups were justified in refusing to seek permits so as to bring the issue to a head?

5. If universities had been closed across the country, do you think faculty and students would have organized "free universities"? If so, what sorts of curricula do you think they would have developed? Would they have survived the reopening of the established universities?

Bibliography and Further Reading

Breines, Wini. *Community and Organization in the New Left, 1962–1968.* New Brunswick, NJ: Rutgers University Press, 1989.

Cohen, Robert, and Reginald Zelnik, eds. *The Free Speech Movement: Reflections on Berkeley in the 1960s.* Berkeley: University of California Press, 2002.

Free Speech Movement Archive. http://www.fsm-a.org/ (accessed September 2006).

Free Speech Movement Digital Archive at Bancroft Library, University of California, Berkeley. http://bancroft.berkeley.edu/FSM/ (accessed September 2006).

Freeman, Jo. *At Berkeley in the Sixties: Education of an Activist, 1961–1965* Bloomington: Indiana University Press, 2004.

Draper, Hal. *Berkeley: The New Student Revolt.* New York: Grove Press, 1965.

Goines, David Lance. *The Free Speech Movement: Coming of Age in the 1960s.* Berkeley: Ten Speed Press, 1993.

Heirich, Max. *The Beginning: Berkeley, 1964.* New York: Columbia University Press, 1971.

Horowitz, David. *Student: What Has Been Happening at a Major University, The Political Activities of the Berkeley Students.* New York: Ballantine Books, 1962.

Kerr, Clark. *The Gold and the Blue: A Personal Memoir of the University of California, 1949–1967.* Berkeley: University of California Press, 2003.

Lipset, Seymour Martin, and Sheldon S. Wolin, eds. *The Berkeley Student Revolt: Facts and Interpretations.* New York: Anchor Books, 1965.

Raskin, A.H. "The Berkeley Affair: Mr. Kerr vs. Mr. Savio & Co." *The New York Times Magazine,* February 14, 1965, pp. 24–25, 88–91.

Rorabaugh, W. J. *Berkeley at War: The 1960s.* New York: Oxford University Press, 1990.

Rossman, Michael. *The Wedding within the War.* Garden City, NY: Doubleday, 1971.

Seaborg, Glenn, with Ray Colvig. *Chancellor at Berkeley.* Berkeley: Institute of Governmental Studies Press, University of California, 1994.

Searle, John. *The Campus War: A Sympathetic Look at the University in Agony.* New York: World Publishing, 1971.

Stadtman, Verne A. *The University of California 1868–1968.* New York: McGraw-Hill, 1970.

Stewart, George R. *The Year of the Oath: The Fight for Academic Freedom at the University of California.* Garden City, NY: Doubleday, 1950.

(G) TURNING POINT

Richard M. Nixon resigned the presidency on August 8, 1974. What if Nixon had not resigned and he had been impeached and convicted?

INTRODUCTION

Richard Milhouse Nixon was born in 1913 in Yorba Linda, California, and raised in the Quaker religion. A 1934 graduate of Whittier College in California and a 1937 graduate of Duke University Law School, Nixon passed the bar exam and practiced law in California from 1937 until 1942. He had been third in his class at Duke. He served in the U.S. Navy in the South Pacific during World War II, achieving the rank of lieutenant commander. In 1940, he married his wife Patricia. They had two daughters, Patricia and Julie.

Nixon began his political career in 1946 when he was elected as a Republican to the U.S. House of Representatives. He had campaigned partly on an anti-communist platform, which was popular during the post–World War II Red Scare. Soon he would become one of the Cold War era's leading political figures. While in the House, he gained national attention for his service to the House Committee on Un-American Activities (HUAC), particularly in the investigation of former government official and accused spy Alger Hiss. In 1950, Nixon was elected to the U.S. Senate. It was during this election campaign that one of Nixon's opponents gave him the enduring nickname "Tricky Dick." Nixon had served only two years of his Senate term when the Republican Party chose him as presidential candidate Dwight Eisenhower's running mate.

The Republicans almost dropped Nixon from the ticket during the campaign after allegations surfaced that he had accepted illegal campaign contributions and gifts. In a famous televised speech, Nixon announced that he had done nothing wrong and that the only gift he had accepted was a black and white Cocker Spaniel his daughters had named Checkers. The sentimental "Checkers speech" was a public relations success and kept him on the ticket, an early example of Nixon's knack for overcoming political defeat. He served as Eisenhower's vice president for eight years. His interest lay in foreign policy, and he traveled extensively, most notably to Moscow in the Soviet Union, where he engaged in the famous July 24,

1959, "kitchen debate" over the merits of capitalism versus communism with Soviet leader Nikita Khrushchev at the American National Exhibition. Although he had little responsibility, his travels gained him recognition, and many historians credit him with establishing the idea of using the vice presidency as a platform from which to launch a later presidential campaign.

Nixon became the Republican Party candidate for the presidency in the 1960 election. The campaign featured a famous series of televised debates with Democratic Party candidate John F. Kennedy. Nixon narrowly lost to Kennedy in one of the closest elections in U.S. history. He then lost the 1962 election for governor of California to Edmund Brown and returned to practicing law. Nixon's retirement from politics would not be permanent, however, as he would win the Republican Party nomination for president in the 1968 election. His campaign platform called for a return to law and order amid the chaotic backdrop of the mid to late 1960s anti–Vietnam War movement, civil rights movement, and other protests. He also promised to end American involvement in Vietnam. Nixon won the election over Democratic candidate Hubert Humphrey and was sworn in as the nation's thirty-seventh president on January 20, 1969.

Nixon felt that his election meant most Americans, whom he termed the "silent majority" who opposed the lawlessness of the counterculture, supported his ideas. Foreign policy remained Nixon's primary interest, with bringing "peace with honor" in Vietnam an immediate priority. His plan called for the gradual withdrawal of U.S. troops, named "Vietnamization." Nixon also initially ordered bombings of Cambodia and later of North Vietnam. The 1971 *New York Times* publication of secret documents known as the Pentagon Papers, which had been leaked by former Pentagon official Daniel Ellsberg, fueled Nixon's determination to stop leaks in his administration. A 1973 cease-fire agreement in Vietnam included the removal of all remaining U.S. troops. North and South Vietnam would later be reunited under communist rule following the 1975 fall of Saigon.

Nixon worked closely with Henry Kissinger, who began as Nixon's national security advisor and became his secretary of state, in other key foreign policy achievements of his presidency. Nixon became the first president to visit both the Soviet Union and the People's Republic of China. He established a thaw in the Cold War politics with the Soviet Union in a policy known as détente, including the negotiation of the Nuclear Nonproliferation Treaty and the first Strategic Arms Limitation Treaty (SALT I). Nixon's opening of diplomatic relations with the communist Chinese government culminated in his 1972 trip and the seating of the People's Republic of China in the United Nations,

President Richard Nixon tossing out a baseball at a Senators' opening game with New York in Washington, D.C., in 1969. (Library of Congress)

replacing the representatives of the former regime who still governed Taiwan.

Nixon's domestic program, entitled the New Federalism, sought to decrease the size of the federal government by transferring some power to the state governments. He sought welfare reform, but most of the programs created under Franklin Roosevelt's New Deal and Lyndon Johnson's Great Society would remain intact. Nixon also created the Environmental Protection Agency (EPA), the National Oceanic and Atmospheric Administration (NOAA), the Drug Enforcement Agency (DEA), the Occupational Health and Safety Administration (OSHA), and the Supplemental Security Income program among others. In order to bolster a sagging economy, he imposed wage and price controls. Nixon also had the opportunity to appoint four justices to the Supreme Court: Warren Burger, Harry Blackmun, Lewis Powell, Jr., and William Rehnquist. His programs proved popular, and he was easily reelected in a landslide against Democratic candidate George McGovern.

During the campaign, a minor story broke regarding an attempted break-in at the Democratic Party's National Committee headquarters in the Watergate building in Washington, D.C., on the night of June 17, 1972. Watergate building security guard Frank Wills discovered the break-in by five burglars: Bernard L. Barker, Virgilio R. Gonzales, James W. McCord, Eugenio R. Martinez, and Frank A. Sturgis. The men had cameras and eavesdropping devices among other things in their possession. Initially, the story drew little interest, and the White House denied

At a meeting of the North Atlantic Treaty Organization (NATO) in 1969, President Richard Nixon proposes the study of environmental problems. (NATO)

any connection to the incident, labeling it a "third-rate burglary." Eventually, however, investigations into the Watergate burglary by *Washington Post* reporters Bob Woodward and Carl Bernstein and their secret source known only as Deep Throat would trace the burglary and subsequent cover-up of White House involvement all the way to the president himself. Soon, the Nixon presidency would be embroiled in a series of scandals that would come to be collectively known as Watergate.

Nixon was known to be secretive and distrustful of all but his closest advisors. After the leak of the Pentagon Papers, an investigative unit of the Committee to Re-elect the President (CREEP) known as the "Plumbers" was created to prevent such leaks in the future. Nixon was also known to keep a list of known or suspected enemies, and the Plumbers also investigated those named so as to discredit them. For example, they had broken into the offices of Pentagon Papers source Daniel Ellsberg's psychiatrist. The Plumbers had also been involved in planning the Watergate burglary.

A federal grand jury indicted the five Watergate burglars, along with G. Gordon Liddy and Howard Hunt, who had helped plan the break-in, on September 15, 1972. Liddy was a former FBI agent and Hunt was a former CIA agent. By 1973, federal District Court Judge John Sirica had convicted the men. Prior to sentencing, convicted burglar James McCord sought a lesser sentence by informing Judge Sirica that President Nixon's close advisors had approved the break-in and tried to cover up White House involvement afterward. On April 30, 1973, Nixon gave a public speech announcing the departures of White House legal counsel John Dean, who had been fired, and Attorney General Richard Kleindienst and White House staff members H. R. Haldeman and John Ehrlichman, who had resigned.

Nixon also directed the new attorney general, Elliot Richardson, to appoint a special prosecutor to investigate the growing Watergate scandal. Richardson appointed Archibald Cox to the position. In the summer of 1973, the U.S. Senate Select Committee on Presidential Campaign Activities, chaired by Sam Ervin (the Ervin Committee), began to hold public hearings on Watergate. The sensationalized hearings featured damaging testimony from former White House legal counsel John Dean among other officials. Dean reiterated the claim that top White House officials had been involved in the cover-up. Also during the hearings, White House aide Alexander Butterfield revealed the existence of a secret White House taping system, sending the investigation to a new level as now the tape recordings would offer definitive proof of the allegations made by Dean and others. The revelation would also spark a legal battle between Congress and the president, as Nixon sought to prevent release of the tapes through his claims of executive privilege.

The committee also heard testimony that the White House paid the burglars cash to maintain their silence on White House involvement and that the White House had pressured the FBI to halt its investigation into the scandal. The Watergate investigation uncovered not just the White House involvement in the burglary and cover-up, but also a wide range of corruption and illegal activities. These included millions of dollars worth of illegal campaign contributions, wiretapping, the use of the Internal Revenue Service (IRS) and other government agencies to harass and spy on the administration's believed enemies, and the use of public funds to make

KEY CONCEPT   The Imperial Presidency

The *imperial presidency* is a term popularized by historian Arthur Schlesinger, Jr., in his 1973 book of the same name. In his work, Schlesinger traced the growth of presidential power over the years, beginning with the first U.S. president, George Washington. The term encompasses not just the president but also his aides and advisors in the executive branch of the federal government. The size of the presidential staff increased significantly in the second half of the twentieth century. The term also refers to times when the president acts without the consultation or approval of the other two branches of the federal government: the legislative branch (most notably Congress) and the judicial branch (most notably the Supreme Court).

Historians frequently use the term imperial presidency when referring to the actions of the Nixon administration, including the attempts of Nixon and his aides in seeking to cover up White House involvement in the Watergate scandal.

Critics of the imperial presidency claim that presidents such as Nixon are attempting to hold the executive branch of government above the legislative and judicial branches, contrary to the balance of power between the three branches built into the U.S. Constitution. Nixon openly sought to use "executive privilege" on a number of occasions to circumvent the wishes of Congress and the Supreme Court. Examples of Nixon's attempts to exercise executive privilege included his attempts to wiretap without first obtaining a judge's approval, his attempts to block the release of the Pentagon Papers in *New York Times Co. v. United States,* and his attempts to resist turning over the secret taped conversations requested by Special Prosecutor Leon Jaworski and the House Judiciary Committee in *United States v. Nixon.* Some scholars feel his losses in these cases and subsequent resignation helped limit presidential powers and place them under more public scrutiny.

improvements on Nixon's private residences. Vice President Spiro Agnew was charged with income tax evasion and taking bribes while serving in his former capacity as governor of Maryland. Agnew was forced to resign on October 10, 1973, and Nixon nominated Gerald Ford as his successor.

Special prosecutor Archibald Cox assumed full responsibility for the continuing investigation when the Ervin Committee finished its hearings. Cox requested several of the tapes from Nixon. Instead, Nixon ordered Attorney General Richardson to fire Cox on October 20, 1973, but Richardson resigned in protest. The resignations of several other officials before Cox was fired led to the events being called the "Saturday Night Massacre." Angry public reaction led Nixon to change his mind and agree to hand over the tapes and appoint Leon Jaworski as the new special prosecutor. One of the surrendered tapes, however, had a noticeable eighteen-minute gap. Nixon claimed the erasure was accidental, but the incident further fueled the public's distrust. In October, an increasingly defensive Nixon declared in a televised press conference that he was not a criminal.

As the list of charges grew and public calls for Nixon's resignation mounted, the House of Representatives began to debate whether there was enough evidence to begin impeachment proceedings. House Resolution 803, passed by a vote of 410 to 4, authorized the House Judiciary Committee to investigate whether there were sufficient grounds for impeachment. Meanwhile, in March 1974, a federal grand jury named Nixon an "unindicted co-conspirator" in an indictment against several former aides over the cover-up of White House involvement of the Watergate burglary.

KEY CONCEPT   Impeachment

Impeachment is an established English governmental process included in the U.S. Constitution. Although to impeach means simply to bring to trial, the term is generally used to refer to the entire process of congressional investigation and trial. Article II, section 4, of the U.S. Constitution states that the president, the vice president, and all civil officers of the United States are subject to impeachment. Impeachable offenses include "treason, bribery, or other high crimes and misdemeanors." The impeachment process is designed to handle serious offenses against the federal government by its high-ranking members and is part of the balance of power among the three branches of government designed to prevent any one branch from dominating the federal government.

Article I, section 2, of the Constitution grants the sole power of impeachment to the United States House of Representatives, with the House serving in a capacity similar to a grand jury. The process begins with the House Judiciary Committee, which debates whether there are sufficient grounds for impeachment, sometimes through public hearings. The committee also draws up specific articles of impeachment for each offense for which they find sufficient evidence. Next, the full House of Representatives debates the articles, with a majority vote necessary to approve an article of impeachment.

Article I, section 3, of the Constitution grants the sole power of trying impeachments to the United States Senate. If the House has voted to impeach, the resident or other official then goes on trial before the full Senate. The chief justice of the Supreme Court presides over the Senate trial. Two-thirds of the Senate must vote guilty in order for a president to be removed from office, at which point the vice president would assume the presidency. A president must be both impeached in the House of Representatives and convicted in the Senate to be removed from office. The Senate may also vote by a simple majority to prevent the president from ever holding another public office. The House of Representatives has impeached two U.S. presidents, Andrew Johnson in 1868 and Bill Clinton in 1998. The Senate found both Jackson and Clinton not guilty so both remained in office.

TURNING POINT

The House Judiciary Committee began its impeachment hearings in May 1974. The Committee consisted of twenty-one Democrats and seventeen Republicans. As the House debated, special prosecutor Leon Jaworski continued his investigation, issuing subpoenas for more of the White House tapes. Publicly released transcripts proved shocking, as they revealed the foul language, racist remarks, and vindictive side of the president. The phrase "expletive deleted" appeared multiple times throughout the pages and became a popular catchphrase. Both the committee and Jaworski were not satisfied with the edited transcripts and demanded that Nixon surrender the tapes. Finally, the 1974 Supreme Court decision in *United States v. Nixon* forced him to release all of the subpoenaed tapes by an unequivocal vote of 8–0 with one judge abstaining. The decision reaffirmed that the president was not above the law, that Nixon could not claim executive privilege to prevent the tapes' release as this would interfere with the administration of justice.

On July 24, 1974, the House Judiciary Committee began six days of televised impeachment hearings against Nixon for high crimes and misdemeanors committed while in office. Ultimately, the committee voted to approve three articles of impeachment. The first article, obstruction of justice, covered Nixon's directed cover-up of the Watergate burglary and investigation. It was adopted on July 27, 1974, by a vote of 27 to 11. The second article, abuse of power, covered Nixon's use of government agencies such as the FBI and IRS to harass suspected enemies and to suppress the Watergate investigation. It was adopted July 19, 1974, by a vote of 28 to 10. The third article, contempt of Congress, covered Nixon's refusal to surrender the tapes subpoenaed by the committee during the course of its investigation. It was adopted on July 30, 1974, by a vote of 21 to 17. The committee-approved articles would next be sent to the full House of Representatives for a vote. If the full House approved any of the three articles, Nixon would become only the second president in American history to be impeached. The first was Andrew Johnson in 1868, later acquitted in his Senate trial.

The White House now faced the question of whether to release the subpoenaed tapes or to defy the Supreme Court. Either way, Nixon was sure to face impeachment and trial in the Senate, so perhaps not releasing the tapes would be to his advantage. The tapes included several of Nixon's conversations with his chief of staff, Bob Haldeman. The content of these conversations, if released, would publicly reveal for the first time that Nixon had learned of the involvement of G. Gordon Liddy and Howard Hunt as well as the CREEP in planning the Watergate burglary and that he had actively participated in the cover-up as early as June 23, 1972. The transcripts would also offer definitive proof that Nixon had ordered the FBI to suppress its investigation and had attempted to use the CIA to block the FBI's investigation. The tapes also would reveal that Nixon had lied to close friends and advisors regarding his knowledge of the break-in and cover-up. Nixon spent the next few days debating the fate of his presidency.

ACTUAL HISTORY

The White House Press Office ultimately released the transcripts of the taped White House conversations on August 5, 1974—the most damaging evidence yet to surface against the president. The June 23 tape, referred to as the "smoking gun," incited a new round of public outcries for Nixon's resignation. After the new revelations, a number of the representatives who had opposed impeachment now stated that their votes would change. Even some of Nixon's staunchest supporters were now leaning toward or openly favoring impeachment. Nixon spent the heated days surrounding the tapes' release at the presidential retreat Camp David in Maryland with family, close friends, and key advisors. On his return to the White House, he continued to waver in his decision about whether to resign the presidency. Meanwhile, crowds surrounded the White House grounds and the House of Representatives prepared for its full House vote on the three articles of impeachment approved by the House Judiciary Committee.

Nixon faced a number of possible decisions, which historian Fred Emery outlined in *Watergate*. He could remain in office and fight the charges against him, a position his family favored, but that could result in a Senate trial that could paralyze the government and threaten foreign policy. Removal from office could also cost him his yearly pension as an ex-president. He could temporarily relinquish the presidency for the length of the Senate trial. He could seek to persuade the House to merely censure, rather than impeach, him. He could resign, which would avoid any constitutional crisis but could subject him to lengthy and expensive civil litigation. He also had the option of pardoning either himself or himself and other Watergate defendants and then resigning. On August 7, 1974, Nixon met with several senior Republican congressmen, Senator Barry Goldwater, Senator Hugh Scott, and House Republican leader Representative John Rhodes. They advised him that he would most likely face full impeachment and conviction if he remained in office.

Amid the swirl of angry accusations, Nixon stepped before the cameras at a televised press conference on the evening of August 8, 1974, to announce that he would resign the following afternoon. Facing the overwhelming odds in favor of his impeachment and conviction, Nixon and his advisors felt that resignation was the best available option. He did not pardon himself or any other Watergate defendants before leaving office. His resignation speech never mentioned impeachment; it merely stated that

Henry Kissinger proved instrumental in President Richard Nixon's foreign policy achievements, including opening relations with China. (Library of Congress)

he no longer had a political base in Congress from which to rule effectively. He also stated that he was not a quitter. Later that evening, he held a formal farewell meeting in the White House, inviting photographers to record the moments with his family. He also spent time alone with trusted advisor Henry Kissinger, during which they reportedly prayed together. On the following morning, Nixon delivered his farewell address to the White House staff and flew out of Washington, D.C., becoming the first American president to resign the office.

Vice President Gerald Ford was sworn in as the nation's new president at noon, declaring that the Watergate scandal was over. Ford nominated Nelson Rockefeller as his vice president. A memorandum from Watergate Special Prosecutor Leon Jaworski recommending Nixon's prosecution arrived at nearly the same time as his resignation, leading to speculation as to whether Nixon would face criminal prosecution once out of office. On August 20, 1974, the full House of Representatives voted 412 to 3 to endorse the House Judiciary Committee's impeachment report. Had Nixon not resigned, he would have been impeached and tried in the Senate. Now the question turned to whether he would face criminal charges in a civil court.

In a televised address on the morning of September 8, 1972, President Ford granted Nixon a full pardon for any crimes committed against the United States of America between his ascension to office on January 20, 1969, and his resignation on August 9, 1974. The pardon protected Nixon from any type of criminal prosecution. There was much speculation that there had been a secret deal in which Ford had promised to pardon Nixon if Nixon resigned the presidency, an allegation that Ford denied. The pardon and its generous terms proved highly controversial among the American public.

Nixon received a full pardon, but many other White House officials were convicted and sentenced to time in prison. Forty government officials were ultimately indicted for their roles in Watergate, including H. R. Haldeman (former White House chief of staff), John Erlichman (Nixon's former domestic policy advisor), John Dean (Nixon's former White House legal counsel), John Mitchell (former attorney general and chairman of CREEP), Howard Hunt and G. Gordon Liddy (planners of the Watergate break-in), Charles Colson (former special counsel to Nixon), and James McCord (Watergate burglar and former security director for CREEP). Some of these key figures wrote accounts of the Watergate scandal from their perspectives. The term *Watergate* became a national synonym for political corruption of any kind, with future scandals being given titles ending with "gate" as the American public became more distrusting of its elected politicians.

President Gerald Ford in 1974 appearing at the House Judiciary Subcommittee hearing on pardoning former President Richard Nixon. (Library of Congress)

Richard Nixon and the Watergate scandal became the subject of numerous books and movies. *Washington Post* reporters Bob Woodward and Carl Bernstein wrote their own accounts of their investigations tracing the scandal and subsequent cover-up all the way to the Nixon White House. Their books included *All the President's Men* (1976), which became a movie starring Robert Redford as Woodward and Dustin Hoffman as Bernstein. Incidentally, former Watergate building security guard Frank Wills, who had discovered the break-in at the Democratic National Committee's headquarters, portrayed himself in the film. Due to the pivotal role played by reporters Woodward and Bernstein in uncovering White House involvement in the Watergate scandal, investigative reporting teams became common features in the American media. Years of public speculation over the possible identities of Woodward and Bernstein's key source, "Deep Throat," ended with a 2005 issue of *Vanity Fair* magazine, which identified him as former deputy director of the FBI W. Mark Felt. Woodward confirmed shortly thereafter that Felt had indeed been their informant.

Nixon's actions in the Watergate cover-up led many historians and political scientists to label his administration an imperial presidency. Nixon's failures in his battles with Congress and the Supreme Court, ultimately resulting in his resignation, served to limit presidential powers in subsequent years. The illegal activities of the CREEP also brought about changes in campaign finance reform in the 1974 amendments to the Federal Election Campaign Act. Changes included the public financing of presidential elections, limits on individual contributions to presidential candidates, and the creation of the Federal Election Commission. Other legislation coming out of the Watergate scandal included the Freedom of Information Act (FOIA). Bob Woodward noted this impact in *Shadow: Five Presidents and the Legacy of Watergate*. He concluded, "As successors to George Washington and Franklin Roosevelt, they expect to rule. But after Vietnam and Watergate, the modern presidency had been limited and diminished. Its inner workings and the behavior of the presidents are fully exposed."

As a result of Watergate, Democrats gained a number of congressional seats in the midterm elections of 1974 and increased their congressional presence even further in the 1976 elections. In the 1976 presidential election, Democratic candidate Jimmy Carter, who ran as a Washington outsider, defeated Ford.

Carter's presidency was highlighted by the brokering of the 1978 Camp David Accords, a framework for peace in the Middle East signed by prime minister of Israel Menachem Begin and president of Egypt Muhammad Anwar al-Sadat. Many historians consider the Accords one of the Carter administration's greatest triumphs.

In 1979 in Iran, the anti-American Ayatollah Ruhollah Khomeini came to power and the deposed pro-American shah (Mohammed Reza Pahlavi) was exiled. After the shah was allowed into the United States to receive medical treatment for cancer, militant Iranian students seized the U.S. embassy in Tehran. Fifty-two hostages were held for 444 days. An April 1980 failed military rescue attempt, which left eight dead, eroded Carter's public support. The fifty-two hostages were finally released on January 20, 1981, when newly elected president Ronald Reagan was sworn into office.

ANOTHER VIEW   What Did Watergate Reveal about U.S. Constitutional Government?

Many historians and political theorists credit Watergate with a dramatic rise in the American public's cynical attitude toward and distrust of politicians, including the president, beginning in the 1970s. These scholars claimed that Watergate highlighted the weaknesses in American constitutional government because Nixon and his aides almost succeeded in their cover-up attempts of illegal activities in the White House. If one of the burglars had not confessed to Judge Sirica before the sentencing phase of their trial, if Woodward and Bernstein had not actively pursued their investigations, if Alexander Butterfield had not revealed the secret White House taping system, White House involvement in the Watergate cover-up could have easily gone unnoticed.

Other scholars have claimed the opposite: the investigation and Nixon's subsequent resignation proved that the constitutional system of checks and balances had worked and that justice had been served. Through the process of the various trials and investigations surrounding Watergate, the truth of White House involvement was slowly uncovered. Proponents of this viewpoint also note the impacts on subsequent presidential administrations. The rise of investigative journalism and the public outcry over the Nixon administration's activities meant that future presidents would govern in a much more open atmosphere where their activities were more closely monitored. Nixon's resignation and the new climate had helped restore balance to the three branches of government.

The so-called Reagan Revolution lasted two terms, from 1981 to 1989. Reagan, a former actor, was known as the Great Communicator and proved to be a popular president. He also benefited from the support of the conservative Christian groups known as the New Right. After his recovery from a 1981 near-fatal assassination attempt, Reagan moved to implement his foreign and domestic policies. Reagan's economic policies, termed "Reaganomics," were based on supply-side economic theory and called for tax cuts and budget cuts to social programs. Although the economy suffered a recession in Reagan's early years, it had rebounded by 1983 and inflation began to drop. On the other hand, the national debt more than doubled.

In his first term, Reagan also renewed the Cold War with the Soviet Union, famously terming it an "evil empire." He oversaw the largest peacetime growth of the U.S. military. In his second term, however, Reagan and new Soviet leader Mikhail Gorbachev implemented a new policy of *glasnost,* or openness, between the two countries. Many historians credit Reagan's earlier tough stance with bringing about the new open policy and the later collapse of communism in the Union of Soviet Socialist Republics (USSR) in the early 1990s.

President Reagan's continuing popularity and high approval ratings during the course of several scandals led to his acquisition of the nickname the "Teflon President." In late 1986, however, a scandal began to emerge that would plague the last years of his second term, the Iran-Contra scandal. Individuals within the Reagan administration had been illegally raising funds through arms-for-hostages sales to Iran and sending these funds to the Contras, a rebel group fighting to overthrow the Sandinista government in Nicaragua.

Revelation of the scandal tarnished the last years of the Reagan administration, although his vice president, George H. W. Bush, won the 1988 presidential election. Bush was in office during the collapse of communism in the Soviet Union as well as the fall of the infamous Berlin Wall and reunification of Germany. Bush proclaimed a New World Order, promoting international cooperation. When Iraqi leader Saddam Hussein invaded neighboring Kuwait, a coalition of international forces fought for its liberation in 1991. Many historians credit Bush's focus on foreign policy versus domestic economic difficulties and his broken campaign pledge of no new taxes with his loss to Democrat Bill Clinton in the 1992 presidential election.

Clinton served two terms as president. During his terms, overseas crises included the break-ups and realignments in formerly Soviet-controlled Eastern European countries. In 1993, NATO forces entered Yugoslavia to help combat ethnic fighting there. Under Clinton, U.S. troops were sent into Somalia and Haiti. The North American Free Trade Agreement (NAFTA) went into effect in 1993. In the 1994 midterm elections, Republicans won majorities in both houses of Congress in what they termed a "Contract with America." President Clinton became only the second American president to be impeached in 1998–1999. The primary charges against Clinton were perjury and obstruction of justice in relation to the Monica Lewinsky scandal, an extramarital affair. The U.S. House of Representatives debated four articles of impeachment, two of which were approved by the full House. The U.S. Senate then held a trial beginning January 7, 1999, to formally try Clinton on the two approved articles of impeachment. Chief Justice of the Supreme Court William Rehnquist presided. The Senate vote on Article I was not guilty (55 to 45), and the vote on Article III was a tie (50 to 50). Neither vote achieved the two-thirds majority required by the Constitution for a guilty verdict, so Clinton was acquitted and remained in office.

Republican candidate George W. Bush won the presidency over Democratic candidate Al Gore in an extremely close, contested, and controversial election in 2000. He was reelected in 2004. Fears of terrorism on domestic soil rose to new heights after the September 11, 2001, terrorist attacks on the World Trade Center buildings in New York City and the Pentagon building near Washington, D.C., leading Bush to implement often controversial new security laws and guidelines. The Department of Homeland Security came into existence. Overseas, U.S. troops fought in Afghanistan against the ruling Taliban regime and in a second Persian Gulf War when the U.S. invaded Iraq and deposed its leader, Saddam Hussein, after Bush claimed Hussein had weapons of mass destruction.

Meanwhile, Richard Nixon remained a controversial figure in his post presidential years. He left a mixed legacy due to his domestic and foreign policy successes, which won praise but were often lost amid the lingering taint of Watergate. He spent his later years traveling and seeking to repair his reputation. He published a number of books, including *RN: The Memoirs of Richard Nixon* (1978). In his last years, Nixon sought U.S. political and financial support for the former Soviet republics after the collapse of communism and the dismantling of the USSR. His writings and activities helped make him a respected voice in foreign affairs. The

Richard Nixon Library and Birthplace was dedicated in Yorba Linda, California, in 1990. In 1991, the National Archives made available over seventy of the tapes acquired by the special prosecutors during their Watergate investigations. Richard Milhouse Nixon died on April 22, 1994, at the age of eighty-one. His April 27 funeral was held on the library's grounds. Then-president Bill Clinton and ex-presidents Gerald Ford, Jimmy Carter, Ronald Reagan, and George H. W. Bush were all in attendance.

ALTERNATE HISTORY

After some debate, the White House ultimately would still have decided to release the final tapes subpoenaed by the special prosecutor as ordered by the Supreme Court, including the "smoking gun" conversations of June 23, 1972. Public outcry over the definitive proof of cover-up and lying found on the transcripts would have led to widespread speculation that Nixon would step before the cameras on August 8 to announce his resignation. It seemed the only logical course of action in the face of such overwhelming evidence against him and almost certain impeachment and conviction.

His family had been encouraging him to stay and fight, however, and Nixon had wavered in his decision a number of times. He would have debated his options again and again, searching for a way to mount an effective defense. His acceptance of the grim outlook for his presidency would have been counterbalanced by his strong antipathy toward quitting without a fight. As the televised press conference began, Nixon would have stepped up to the podium to make his announcement. His family and closest advisors, aware of his doubts and wavering, would have anxiously awaited his decision, which he would most likely have revealed to them in the hours leading up to his nighttime press conference of August 8, 1974.

Instead of announcing his resignation, Nixon could very well have shocked everybody by announcing that he was determined to fight to retain his office despite the bleak warnings of sure conviction earlier offered by senior congressional members of the Republican Party. The American public, along with many congressmen, would have been surprised to hear Nixon vow to fight on, as most would have expected him to resign in the face of the overwhelming evidence against him. In his speech, Nixon would have defiantly noted that he was not a quitter and vowed that while he had made mistakes, he had committed no impeachable offenses and that he wanted a chance to make his case at trial.

He also would have stated that he was not stepping down because of his lack of approval in Congress, because he felt strongly that it would be wrong to allow Congress to pressure a sitting president into leaving office; such an action would have disturbed the balance of power among the three branches of government that was built into the U.S. Constitution. Critics would have later pointed out the irony in those statements, since Nixon had attempted to use executive privilege to protect his taped conversations from the congressional investigations; not until the Supreme Court had declared that the president was not above the law and must surrender them would he release the tapes. Although Nixon would have counseled patience during the surely difficult process to come, his comments would have sparked outrage among many in the public. Angry demonstrations would have been held outside the White House and the Capitol building demanding his impeachment.

Watergate special prosecutor Leon Jaworski's memorandum sent the day after the press conference would have recommended that any question of criminal prosecution be put on hold until after Nixon's congressional impeachment proceedings and any subsequent Senate trial. Congressional impeachment hearings would have begun on April 15, 1974. During several days of testimony, the House would have presented the three articles of impeachment earlier approved by the House Judiciary Committee and the evidence gathered for their acceptance. Nixon and his legal counsel would then have mounted their defense. The vote in the full House of Representatives, like the earlier vote in the House Judiciary Committee, would have featured a coalition of Democrats and Republicans moving to impeach Nixon on all three articles: obstruction of justice, abuse of power, and contempt of Congress. The evidence against him was too overwhelming for the vote to go any other way, raising a new round of speculation that Nixon might now resign and still spare himself and the country the ordeal of a Senate trial. Nixon, however, would have publicly vowed to continue the fight.

Nixon would then have gone on trial in the U.S. Senate beginning in early September, with Chief Justice Warren Burger presiding. People across the nation and across the globe would have anxiously followed each step of the trial. While the actual testimony and deliberations would have been closed to the public, press conferences and news reports would have kept the public aware of new developments. Political experts would have debated the merits of both sides and fostered endless rounds of speculation on the trial's outcome and impact. If the Senate acquitted Nixon, would enough doubt about his innocence exist to prevent him from ruling effectively? Would the public ever find out exactly what was on those tapes Nixon refused to surrender? Had he destroyed them in order to avoid incriminating himself? Would foreign powers seek to exploit the country's vulnerable state as its leader sat on trial awaiting his fate? Would Nixon be the first president forced from office? If so, would the country be thrown into turmoil? Would Nixon willingly surrender his office? If not, what actions would Congress take next?

Tension would have mounted as the public awaited the Senate vote. A two-thirds vote of guilty was needed to remove Nixon from office. The Senate could also vote to ban him from ever holding public office again by a simple majority vote. After hearing all of the testimony and deliberating, the vote would have been held in early October of 1974. The necessary two-thirds majority would have existed to convict Nixon on each of the three articles of impeachment. He would have been found guilty of obstruction of justice, abuse of power, and contempt of Congress. Only a few of his staunchest supporters would have voted not guilty. People would have been anxiously watching live news broadcasts from Washington, D.C., waiting for the news. Despite most people's firm convictions that Nixon would be convicted, it would still come as a shock to hear the official pronouncement that Nixon would be the first sitting American president to be forced from office.

Now the country would wait in anticipation of the next act of this unfolding political drama. As the first American president convicted in the U.S. Senate, would Nixon willingly surrender his power? He would have realized that the fight was lost and that resistance was ultimately futile and dangerous to the country's welfare, and he would have surrendered his office shortly after conviction. Another possibility is that Nixon would have refused to give up the office, invoking his powers as commander in chief and declaring a state of national emergency. However, as he would have called on Secretary of Defense James R. Schlesinger to pass orders to the army to protect the White House from any effort to force him from office, Schlesinger would have resigned, as would his successor in office, Deputy Secretary Bill Clements. The nation would have watched in horror this replay of the earlier "Saturday night massacre" in which Attorney General Elliot Richardson and Deputy Attorney General William Ruckleshaus resigned rather than follow a presidential order to fire special prosecutor Archibald Cox on Saturday, October 20, 1973. However, the effort to invoke military power in defense of his office would amount to an attempted coup d'etat. The tactic would probably have failed, and Nixon ultimately would have accepted removal from office.

Vice President Gerald Ford would then have quickly been sworn in as the new president. If Nixon had resisted removal from office by an attempted resort to the use of military or police power, it is extremely unlikely that Ford would have found it politically possible to include Nixon in a pardon. If he had not been pardoned, Nixon would have been tried and convicted of several crimes and would very likely have served at least a token prison sentence.

Debate regarding the impact and significance of the Watergate scandal would have continued throughout subsequent years, with a slightly different focus. The arguments would have remained over whether the outcome showed that the constitutional process had worked, since Nixon was ultimately caught and convicted, or had almost failed, since Nixon could easily have gotten away with the lying and cover-up if the taping system had not come to light or the Supreme Court decision had gone his way. Presidential powers would still have been limited in light of the new public and media scrutiny that would have followed the scandal. The various campaign finance reform and freedom of information laws enacted in the wake of Watergate would still have come into existence, and the National Archives would have made the subpoenaed tapes and transcripts available to the public. Public resentment against the Republican Party would still have helped the Democrats gain control of Congress in the 1974 midterm elections.

However, if Nixon had resisted removal from office and had later been convicted and sentenced to prison, the presidency would have been even further weakened. As in the decades of the 1870s and 1880s, following the attempt to impeach President Andrew Johnson, presidents in the post-impeachment era of the 1970s and 1980s would have been extremely cautious about exercising presidential powers in the face of any congressional opposition. Thus, even if the same succession of presidents had occurred following Ford's short presidency, Jimmy Carter, Ronald Reagan, and George H. W. Bush would have been in far weaker positions than they were in actual history.

If Ford had not pardoned Nixon, it is possible that after Ford served out the remainder of Nixon's second term in office, he could have been elected to his own four-year term in the 1976 presidential election. Although some still would have viewed him as a caretaker president, his trustworthiness and the absence of his controversial pardon of Nixon would have allowed him to defeat Democratic challenger Jimmy Carter in a close election, despite Carter's popularity as a Washington outsider. Under Ford, the Panama Canal Treaty would most likely not have been negotiated. Ford would have been interested only in a treaty that maintained U.S. military bases in the region to ensure the canal's ongoing neutrality, a position that would have increased Latin American resentment toward the United States.

Ford would have inherited Nixon's cabinet and would have continued pursuing détente with the Soviet Union and China, which had begun under Nixon. He would also have been the one to attempt negotiation of the Camp David Accords, but perhaps without as much success or perseverance as Carter showed in actual history. It would then have been Ford, and not Carter, who faced the 1979 Iranian hostage crisis, as the anti-American Ayatollah Khomeini still would have deposed the shah and risen to power in Iran. Ford would not have attempted the desert rescue that further hurt Carter's popularity. The absence of a Carter presidency also would have meant that aid to Nicaragua would not have been stopped in the late 1970s and that there would have been no Iran-Contra scandal in the following decade.

Ford would have been constitutionally ineligible to run in the 1980 presidential election since he had served more than two years of Nixon's second term. Instead, the Republican Party's nomination would have gone to popular former actor and governor of California Ronald Reagan.

If Nixon had been convicted in the impeachment trial in the Senate, and especially if he had then made some effort to retain his office illegally, Congress could have enacted a series of laws, possibly over the veto of President Ford, that would give Congress far more power over cabinet and subcabinet appointments. It is possible that the struggle between the legislative branch and the executive branch would have transformed the American political system into something rather similar to the parliamentary systems of European democracies, in which the legislature can, by a simple vote of no confidence, remove the whole government. In such a transformation, which could have been accomplished without amending the Constitution, the secretary of state would assume powers similar to those of a prime minister in parliamentary systems. It is even conceivable that with such a move in the direction of a legislatively controlled government, the United States would begin to develop a multiparty system rather than a two-party system. Within parliamentary systems, coalitions of various political parties often form to keep a government in power or to select a new government, and such a system could begin to emerge if Congress acquired the power to remove and replace cabinet and subcabinet officials.

Whether or not the political landscape was so drastically reformed, Nixon's presidential accomplishments would have been almost completely overshadowed by not just the Watergate scandal but by his actions in his final days in office. He still would have attempted to resurrect his reputation after being forced from office, but he would have had a much harder time of it. His decision not to resign, considered either arrogant or an embarrassment that dragged the country through the mess of a presidential trial and conviction, would have alienated many of his potential supporters. Nixon would still have written books, including his memoirs, and would still have sought to offer advice on foreign affairs and to work for projects he believed in. The privately funded Richard Nixon Presidential Library and Birthplace in Yorba Linda, California, still would have opened and offered a record of his accomplishments. Despite his presidential successes, however, presidential historians still would most likely have ranked him much lower among the twentieth-century presidents.

Marcella Bush Trevino

Discussion Questions

1. What factors would make it difficult for an impeached president to retain his office by force of arms? Can you imagine circumstances in which such a presidential coup might be successful?

2. If an officer of Congress had been unable to formally deliver impeachment papers to Nixon because of the presence of armed guards at the White House, would it have been possible for Nixon to continue to administer the government?

3. How would history have been different if Nixon had faced the trial in the Senate but the needed two-thirds vote against him for conviction was not achieved, and he was therefore not impeached? Would Nixon have been able to govern (as did President Andrew Johnson in the last year of his administration)? Or would the scandal and opposition have prevented him from achieving anything further as president?

4. If the scandals surrounding Vice President Spiro Agnew had not been revealed and Agnew instead of Ford had taken over after Nixon's resignation, what sort of president would Agnew have turned out to be?

5. How would history have been different if Watergate building security guard Frank Wills had never accidentally discovered the Watergate burglary? How would Nixon's second term have proceeded without the Watergate scandal?

Bibliography and Further Reading

Ambrose, Stephen E. *Nixon: Ruin and Recovery 1973–1990*. New York: Simon and Schuster, 1991.

Emery, Fred. *Watergate: The Corruption of American Politics and the Fall of Richard Nixon*. New York: Times Books, 1994.

Friedman, Leon, and William F. Levantrosser, eds. *Watergate and Afterward: The Legacy of Richard Milhous Nixon*. Westport, CT: Greenwood Press, 1992.

Genovese, Michael A. *The Nixon Presidency: Power and Politics in Turbulent Times*. Westport, CT: Greenwood Press, 1990.

Greenberg, David. *Nixon's Shadow: The History of an Image*. New York: W. W. Norton, 2003.

Lukas, J. Anthony. *Nightmare: The Underside of the Nixon Years*. New York: Viking Press, 1976.

Nixon, Richard. *RN: The Memoirs of Richard Nixon*. New York: Grosset and Dunlap, 1978.

Reeves, Richard. *President Nixon: Alone in the White House*. New York: Simon and Schuster, 2001.

Small, Melvin. *The Presidency of Richard Nixon*. Lawrence: University Press of Kansas, 2003.

Woodward, Bob. *Shadow: Five Presidents and the Legacy of Watergate*. New York: Simon and Schuster, 1999.

Woodward, Bob, and Carl Bernstein. *The Final Days*. New York: Simon and Schuster, 1976.

Excerpts from the Civil Rights Act of 1964

After a decade of attempts by the National Association for the Advancement of Colored People (NAACP) and other organizations to challenge racial discrimination through the courts, it became clear that unless Congress were to pass legislation overriding state and local "Jim Crow" laws that required private facilities to enforce racial separation, the courts would not be able to eliminate formal and legalized racial discrimination. Under pressure from President Lyndon Johnson, bipartisan support developed for a comprehensive civil rights act that would supersede and outlaw such state and local laws. The Civil Rights Act of 1964, signed into law on July 2, 1964, went into effect one year later. The law had several titles intended to outlaw racial discrimination in public accommodations such as restaurants and hotels, in education, in employment, and in the operation of federally funded activities. The Civil Rights Act of 1964 strengthened the existing Civil Rights Commission, established the Equal Employment Opportunity Commission, and empowered the attorney general to initiate lawsuits to enforce the law. The Civil Rights Act of 1964 explicitly outlawed state and local laws that had been passed requiring racial discrimination or segregation. The law's first title included provisions to outlaw practices that had been used to prevent African Americans from exercising the right to vote. However, within a year it became clear that the voting rights provisions of the law needed to be strengthened, and the Voting Rights Act of 1965 was designed to achieve that goal.

TITLE I—VOTING RIGHTS

Title I outlawed certain discriminatory practices in literacy tests and registration that had been used to prevent African Americans from voting and empowered judges to hear complaints of violations.

TITLE II—INJUNCTIVE RELIEF AGAINST DISCRIMINATION IN PLACES OF PUBLIC ACCOMMODATION

SEC. 201. (a) All persons shall be entitled to the full and equal enjoyment of the goods, services, facilities, and privileges, advantages, and accommodations of any place of public accommodation, as defined in this section, without discrimination or segregation on the ground of race, color, religion, or national origin. . . .

SEC. 202. All persons shall be entitled to be free, at any establishment or place, from discrimination or segregation of any kind on the ground of race, color, religion, or national origin, if such discrimination or segregation is or purports to be required by any law, statute, ordinance, regulation, rule, or order of a State or any agency or political subdivision thereof.

TITLE III—DESEGREGATION OF PUBLIC FACILITIES

SEC. 301. (a) Whenever the Attorney General receives a complaint in writing signed by an individual to the effect that he is being deprived of or threatened with the loss of his right to the equal protection of the laws, on account of his race, color, religion, or national origin, by being denied equal utilization of any public facility which is owned, operated, or managed by or on behalf of any State or subdivision thereof, other than a public school or public college as defined in section 401 of title IV hereof, and the Attorney General believes the complaint is meritorious and certifies that the signer or signers of such complaint are unable, in his judgment, to initiate and maintain appropriate legal proceedings for relief and that the institution of an action will materially further the orderly progress of desegregation in public facilities, the Attorney General is authorized to institute for or in the name of the United States a civil action in any appropriate district court of the United States against such parties and for such relief as may be appropriate, and such court shall have and shall exercise jurisdiction of proceedings instituted pursuant to this section. The Attorney General may implead as defendants such additional parties as are or become necessary to the grant of effective relief hereunder. . . .

TITLE IV—DESEGREGATION OF PUBLIC EDUCATION

Title IV empowered the attorney general to seek relief through the courts in cases of alleged discrimination in admission to public schools.

TITLE V—COMMISSION ON CIVIL RIGHTS

Title V added powers and duties for the Commission on Civil Rights and set procedures for the commission.

TITLE VI—NONDISCRIMINATION IN FEDERALLY ASSISTED PROGRAMS

SEC. 601. No person in the United States shall, on the ground of race, color, or national origin, be excluded from participation in, be denied the benefits of, or be subjected to discrimination under any program or activity receiving Federal financial assistance. . . .

TITLE VII—EQUAL EMPLOYMENT OPPORTUNITY

SEC. 703. (a) It shall be an unlawful employment practice for an employer—

(1) to fail or refuse to hire or to discharge any individual, or otherwise to discriminate against any individual with respect to his compensation, terms, conditions, or privileges of employment, because of such individual's race, color, religion, sex, or national origin; or

(2) to limit, segregate, or classify his employees in any way which would deprive or tend to deprive any individual of employment opportunities or otherwise adversely affect his status as an employee, because of such individual's race, color, religion, sex, or national origin.

(b) It shall be an unlawful employment practice for an employment agency to fail or refuse to refer for employment, or otherwise to discriminate against, any individual because of his race, color, religion, sex, or national origin, or to classify or refer for employment any individual on the basis of his race, color, religion, sex, or national origin.

(c) It shall be an unlawful employment practice for a labor organization—

(1) to exclude or to expel from its membership, or otherwise to discriminate against, any individual because of his race, color, religion, sex, or national origin. . . .

(d) It shall be an unlawful employment practice for any employer, labor organization, or joint labor-management committee controlling apprenticeship or other training or retraining, including on-the-job training programs to discriminate against any individual because of his race, color, religion, sex, or national origin in admission to, or employment in, any program established to provide apprenticeship or other training.

OTHER UNLAWFUL EMPLOYMENT PRACTICES

SEC. 704. (b) It shall be an unlawful employment practice for an employer, labor organization, or employment agency to print or publish or cause to be printed or published any notice or advertisement relating to employment by such an employer or membership in or any classification or referral for employment by such a labor organization, or relating to any classification or referral for employment by such an employment agency, indicating any preference, limitation, specification, or discrimination, based on race, color, religion, sex, or national origin, except that such a notice or advertisement may indicate a preference, limitation, specification, or discrimination based on religion, sex, or national origin when religion, sex, or national origin is a bona fide occupational qualification for employment.

EQUAL EMPLOYMENT OPPORTUNITY COMMISSION

SEC. 705. (a) There is hereby created a Commission to be known as the Equal Employment Opportunity Commission, which shall be composed of five members, not more than three of whom shall be members of the same political party, who shall be appointed by the President by and with the advice and consent of the Senate.

SEC. 707. (a) Whenever the Attorney General has reasonable cause to believe that any person or group of persons is engaged in a pattern or practice of resistance to the full enjoyment of any of the rights secured by this title, and that the pattern or practice is of such a nature and is intended to deny the full exercise of the rights herein described, the Attorney General may bring a civil action in the appropriate district court of the United States by filing with it a complaint (1) signed by him (or in his absence the Acting Attorney General), (2) setting forth facts pertaining to such pattern or practice, and (3) requesting such relief, including an application for a permanent or temporary injunction, restraining order or other order against the person or persons responsible for such pattern or practice, as he deems necessary to insure the full enjoyment of the rights herein described.

Excerpts from the Voting Rights Act of 1965

The Voting Rights Act, adopted initially August 6, 1965, and extended in 1970, 1975, and 1982, was far more successful in guaranteeing the right to vote to African Americans than any prior legislation. The act was designed to enforce the guarantee in the Fifteenth Amendment to the U.S. Constitution that no person shall be denied the right to vote on account of race or color. By spelling out certain practices that had been used to prevent African Americans from voting, such as unfairly administered literacy tests and poll taxes, the act empowered the attorney general to impose stringent requirements in certain jurisdictions throughout the country. As a consequence, Section 4 of the act ended the use of literacy requirements for voting in Alabama, Georgia, Louisiana, Mississippi, South Carolina, and Virginia and in some counties of North Carolina. No voting changes could be enforced in these states and counties until approved either by a three-judge court in the District of Columbia or by the attorney general of the United States. Other sections authorized the attorney general to appoint federal voting examiners who could be sent into the pertinent jurisdictions. The examiners would work to ensure that qualified persons were free to register for elections, or the examiners could assign federal observers to oversee the conduct of elections. After dealing with nearly a century of resistance to the Fifteenth Amendment, Congress had decided to shift the advantage of delay from those preventing the exercise of rights to those attempting to exercise those rights. What this meant was that, if the particular states did not reform, their elections would remain under federal oversight. Within two decades, the percentages of blacks and whites registering and voting in the subject jurisdictions began to even out, and many blacks and Hispanics were elected to local and state offices throughout the region.

AN ACT To enforce the fifteenth amendment to the Constitution of the United States, and for other purposes. Be it enacted by the Senate and House of Representatives of the United States of America in Congress assembled, That this Act shall be known as the "Voting Rights Act of 1965."

SEC. 2. No voting qualification or prerequisite to voting, or standard, practice, or procedure shall be imposed or applied by any State or political subdivision to deny or abridge the right of any citizen of the United States to vote on account of race or color.

SEC. 3. (a) Whenever the Attorney General institutes a proceeding under any statute to enforce the guarantees of the fifteenth amendment in any State or political subdivision the court shall authorize the appointment of Federal examiners by the United States Civil Service Commission in accordance with section 6 to serve for such period of time and for such political subdivisions as the court shall determine is appropriate to enforce the guarantees of the fifteenth amendment. . . .

(c) If in any proceeding instituted by the Attorney General under any statute to enforce the guarantees of the fifteenth amendment in any State or political subdivision the court finds that violations of the fifteenth amendment justifying equitable relief have occurred within the territory of such State or political subdivision, the court, in addition to such relief as it may grant, shall retain jurisdiction for such period as it may deem appropriate and during such period no voting qualification or prerequisite to voting, or standard, practice, or procedure with respect to voting different from that in force or effect at the time the proceeding was commenced shall be enforced unless and until the court finds that such qualification, prerequisite, standard, practice, or procedure does not have the purpose and will not have the effect of denying or abridging the right to vote on account of race or color. . . .

SEC. 4. (a) To assure that the right of citizens of the United States to vote is not denied or abridged on account of race or color, no citizen shall be denied the right to vote in any Federal, State, or local election because of his failure to comply with any test or device in any State with respect to which the determinations have been made under subsection (b) or in any political subdivision with respect to which such determinations have been made as a separate unit, unless the United States District Court for the District of Columbia in an action for a declaratory judgment brought by such State or subdivision against the United States has determined that no such test or device has been used during the five years preceding the filing of the action for the purpose or with the effect of denying or abridging the right to vote on account of race or color: . . .

(b) The provisions of subsection (a) shall apply in any State or in any political subdivision of a state which (1) the Attorney General determines maintained on November 1, 1964, any test or device, and with respect to which (2) the Director of the Census determines that less than 50 percentum of the persons of voting age residing therein were registered on November 1, 1964, or that less than 50 percentum of such persons voted in the presidential election of November 1964.

(c) The phrase "test or device" shall mean any requirement that a person as a prerequisite for voting or registration for voting (1) demonstrate the ability to read, write, understand, or interpret any matter, (2) demonstrate any educational achievement or his knowledge of any particular subject, (3) possess good moral character, or (4) prove his qualifications by the voucher of registered voters or members of any other class.

SEC. 10. (a) The Congress finds that the requirement of the payment of a poll tax as a precondition to voting (i) precludes persons of limited means from voting or imposes unreasonable financial hardship upon such persons as a precondition to their exercise of the franchise, (ii) does not bear a reasonable relationship to any legitimate State interest in the conduct of elections, and (iii) in some areas has the purpose or effect of denying persons the right to vote because of race or color. Upon the basis of these findings, Congress declares that the constitutional right of citizens to vote is denied or abridged in some areas by the requirement of the payment of a poll tax as a precondition to voting.

(b) In the exercise of the powers of Congress under section 5 of the fourteenth amendment and section 2 of the fifteenth amendment, the Attorney General is authorized and directed to institute forthwith in the name of the United States such actions, including actions against States or political subdivisions, for declaratory judgment or injunctive relief against the enforcement of any requirement of the payment of a poll tax as a precondition to voting, or substitute therefor enacted after November 1, 1964, as will be necessary to implement the declaration of subsection (a) and the purposes of this section.

SEC. 12. (a) Whoever shall deprive or attempt to deprive any person of any right secured by section 2, 3, 4, 5, 7, or 10 or shall violate section 11(a) or (b), shall be fined not more than $5,000, or imprisoned not more than five years, or both. (b) Whoever, within a year following an election in a political subdivision in which an examiner has been appointed (1) destroys, defaces, mutilates, or otherwise alters the marking of a paper ballot which has been cast in such election, or (2) alters any official record of voting in such election tabulated from a voting machine or otherwise, shall be fined not more than $5,000, or imprisoned not more than five years, or both.

1960   An American U2 spy plane crashes near the Soviet city of Yekaterinburg while performing a reconnaissance mission on May 1. The United States subsequently claims that the airplane is a weather research aircraft and offers rewards for the whereabouts of the plane's pilot, Gary Powers. Soviet leader Nikita Khrushchev later announces that the pilot is alive and well, and demands an apology. U.S. president Dwight Eisenhower flatly refuses to be conciliatory, and a scheduled summit between the two leaders is cancelled.

Nazi war criminal Adolf Eichmann, who was instrumental in creating the logistical basis for the Holocaust in which approximately 6 million Jews were systematically exterminated, is captured by Israeli intelligence agents in Argentina on May 11. He is later sentenced to death for crimes against humanity.

Inspired by revolutionary movements in Latin America, African nationalists successfully drive out colonial occupiers in Senegal, Ghana, Nigeria, and Madagascar. France and Britain see their colonial holdings significantly reduced.

The United States institutes an embargo on Cuban trade. In response, communist Cuban leader Fidel Castro nationalizes all American-owned property, valued at $770 million.

1961   U.S. President Dwight D. Eisenhower announces the end of diplomatic relations with Cuba, citing the danger of having an ally of the Soviet Union a mere ninety miles from U.S. territory.

Massachusetts senator John F. Kennedy becomes the youngest person to be elected president in U.S. history. At his inauguration, he calls on Americans to "ask not what your country can do for you, but what you can do for your country."

Aboard the Soviet spaceship Vostok 3KA-2, Lt. Yuri Gagarin becomes the first human to travel into space on April 12. While in orbit, Gagarin is alleged to have said, "I don't see any God up here," reflecting the Soviet Union's atheistic policies. He would come to be known in Russian history as "The Columbus of the Cosmos."

Seeking to overthrow Fidel Castro's communist regime, a group of Cuban exiles launches an invasion with the support of the United States. About 1,200 of the exiles are captured by the Cubans and tried for treason when the invasion fails, and U.S. Central Intelligence Agency (CIA) director Allen Dulles is forced to resign.

In the Mercury-Redstone 3 space mission, naval commander Alan Shepard becomes the first American to venture into space, traveling for fifteen minutes at an altitude of 116.5 miles. Soviet leader Nikita Khrushchev calls the mission a "flea hop" in comparison to the earlier flight by Yuri Gagarin.

Soviet cosmonaut Gherman Titov becomes the youngest person in space as he orbits the Earth for a full day for the purpose of studying the effects of weightlessness on the human body. Titov's spaceship makes 17.5 orbits, covering 434,960 miles.

Seeking to prevent a flood of refugees into economically prosperous West Germany, officials in the Soviet-occupied East Germany begin to construct a ninety-six-mile-long wall that physically divides the capital of Berlin between communist and capitalist jurisdictions. The cost of the wall's construction is estimated to be 16,155,000 East German marks.

The Soviet Union successfully tests a fifty-eight-megaton hydrogen bomb known as Tsar Bomba off the coast of the Novaya Zemyla archipelago on October 30. It is the largest man-made explosion ever.

1962   In the space mission Mercury-Atlas 6 on February 20, World War II fighter pilot John Glenn becomes the first American to orbit Earth, circling the globe a total of four times over a span four hours and fifty-five minutes.

On June 25, the Supreme Court rules against prayer in public schools. In the landmark decision of *Engel v. Vitale,* the court rules that it is unconstitutional for a public school to force its students to recite an official school prayer.

For a fearful two weeks in October, the world comes as close as it ever has to nuclear war. Soviet leader Nikita Khrushchev had installed nuclear weapons on the island of Cuba partly in response to the U.S. deployment of weapons in Turkey. When this information becomes public, U.S. president John F. Kennedy resists radical suggestions to launch an invasion of Cuba, which would have provoked the Soviet Union, and instead settles on a naval blockade. Then, in a secret compromise between Kennedy and Khrushchev, nuclear missiles are removed from both Cuba and Turkey. The conclusion of the crisis is seen as a diplomatic victory for the United States, since the removal of missiles from Turkey was not made public.

The Second Vatican Council opens on October 11 with representatives from eighty-six countries present. The council is headed by eighty-year-old Pope John XXIII, and over the next three years, the council would bring about sweeping changes in the Catholic Church.

Great Britain further distances itself from its privileged historical status of being the world's dominant colonial power when it grants independence to the African country of Uganda, the Caribbean nations of Trinidad and Tobago, and Jamaica.

1963   French president Charles de Gaulle and West German president Konrad Adenauer sign the Elysee Treaty. The treaty represents a pledge for the two countries to pursue mutual interests in economic and military matters, in spite of a half-century of waging war against each other in world wars I and II.

At Dr. Michael E. DeBakey implants a plastic heart in a patient in a Houston hospital on April 21. The first recipient of an artificial heart lives four days.

About 250,000 people, four-fifths of them black, descend on Washington, D.C., on August 28 to demand civil rights and employment opportunities for minorities. Southern Christian Leadership Conference (SCLC) leader Martin Luther King, Jr., delivers what is considered to be one of the greatest speeches of all time. His "I Have a Dream" speech encapsulated the hopes of a generation of oppressed peoples. The march puts considerable pressure on the Kennedy administration and Congress to pass civil rights legislation.

A day after Alabama governor George Wallace conducts his own version of the "sit-in" by standing in the doorway of the University of Alabama to prevent African American James Woods from entering, President John F. Kennedy delivers a historic speech in which he promises civil rights legislation and asks white people to give equal treatment to minorities.

The first presidential assassination in the United States in over sixty years occurs as John F. Kennedy is shot and killed while riding in his motorcade through Dallas, Texas, on November 22. The nation's grief over losing a young president who was poised to serve two terms in the turbulent 1960s is compounded by the mysteries surrounding his death.

Betty Friedan, a journalist who once was fired for being pregnant, publishes *The Feminine Mystique,* in which she lambastes the traditional patriarchal society for deceiving women into believing that their highest ambition is to have children and a beautiful house. The book becomes an instant best seller, although it is criticized for addressing only the problems of middle-class white women.

1964   The American destroyer USS *Maddox* is allegedly attacked by three Vietnamese patrol boats while performing a reconnaissance mission in the Gulf of Tonkin. Facing reelection, Lyndon Johnson appeals to anticommunist sentiments and requests congressional approval to escalate U.S. involvement in Vietnam. Congress passes the Gulf of Tonkin Resolution nearly unanimously, 504–2. Within a year, 100,000 American troops are in Vietnam.

Congress passes the Civil Rights Act, outlawing discrimination based on race, color, religion, sex, or national origin. Owners of public accommodations that engaged in interstate commerce were henceforth banned from restricting any person based on prejudicial discrimination. The act also enables the newly created Equal Opportunity Employment Commission to settle disputes between employees alleging discrimination and their employers.

Taking into account the testimony of over 500 witnesses, the Warren Commission, which includes former CIA director Allen Dulles and future president Gerald Ford, drafts a 900-page report concluding that Lee

Harvey Oswald was solely responsible for the assassination of President John F. Kennedy.

1965   Less than a year after converting to orthodox Islam, African American leader Malcolm X (born Malcolm Little) is assassinated while delivering a speech in the Audubon Ballroom in Harlem on February 21. Subsequent investigations conclude that Malcolm X was assassinated by members of the Nation of Islam, the organization to which he had dedicated most of his public life.

Fearing that a revolution in the Dominican Republic will lead to "a second Cuba," U.S. president Lyndon Johnson orders the deployment of 23,000 soldiers, most of them Marines, to the Caribbean island to restore order amid revolutionary chaos.

U.S. president Lyndon Johnson signs into law the Medical Care Act, creating Medicare, which provides all U.S. citizens sixty-five years or older with up to ninety days of hospital care, 100 days of nursing home care, and 100 home health care visits. The act also creates Medicaid, a lesser-funded program for the poor.

By a vote of 407–91, Congress passes the Voting Rights Act, prohibiting states from requiring potential voters to pay a poll tax or pass a literacy test to register to vote. Taxes and tests had earlier been used to make it impossible for impoverished and poorly educated African Americans to be registered. The act grants the federal government the ability to oversee voter registration in state and local elections.

In the Watts neighborhood of Los Angeles, California, race riots occur after a police brutality incident against an African American. The riots cause $35 million in damages; thirty-four people die, 4,000 are arrested, and more than 1,000 suffer injuries.

Consumer advocate Ralph Nader publishes *Unsafe at Any Speed,* in which he addresses the refusal of American automobile manufacturers to introduce life-saving but costly safety features such as seatbelts. The book would propel Nader into running for the U.S. presidency four times.

1966   Migrant laborer Ernesto Miranda is arrested on charges of robbery, kidnapping, and rape in Phoenix, Arizona. During intense police interrogation, Miranda confesses, only to have the Supreme Court later rule that his confession was coerced. The case led to the requirement that all police officers inform suspects of their "Miranda rights."

Robert Weaver becomes the first African American cabinet member in U.S. history when he is selected by President Lyndon Johnson to head the newly created Department of Housing and Urban Development.

On March 1, the Soviet spacecraft Venera 3 crash lands on the surface of the planet Venus, becoming the first spacecraft to land on another planet besides Earth.

Musician John Lennon ignites worldwide controversy when he states during an interview with the London *Evening Standard* that he and his band, the Beatles, are "more popular than Jesus now." Album-burning demonstrations occur all throughout the American Bible Belt.

On April 3, the Soviet Union's Luna 10 becomes the first artificial satellite of the moon.

1967   Starting on June 5, Israel clashes with a multinational force that comprises troops from Egypt, Syria, Jordan, and Iraq. The brief Six-Day War ends with Israel occupying the Sinai Peninsula, Golan Heights, Gaza Strip, and the east bank of the Suez Canal.

Communist China announces to the world that it has detonated its first hydrogen bomb on June 17.

The first African American Supreme Court justice, Thurgood Marshall, is appointed on October 2.

Dr. Christiaan N. Bernard, along with a team of South African surgeons, performs the world's first successful human heart transplant on December 3. The patient dies eighteen days later.

1968   Eighty-three U.S. servicemen are held as spies when North Korea captures the Navy ship *Pueblo* on January 23.

The Vietcong utilizes a force of 85,000 men in a major six-month offensive targeting the U.S. embassy and large South Vietnamese cities. The Tet Offensive results in the deaths of 3,400 American soldiers. While technically a defeat for the Vietcong, the thousands of U.S. casualties convince many Americans that the Vietnam War has been lost. CBS news anchor Walter Cronkite said after touring the battlefields of the offensive that the United States was mired in a stalemate.

On March 31, President Lyndon B. Johnson announces that he will neither seek nor accept his party's renomination in the 1968 presidential race.

Martin Luther King, Jr., one of the most influential leaders of the civil rights movement, is shot and killed on a motel balcony in Memphis, Tennessee, on April 4. James Earl Ray is indicted for the murder.

Massachusetts senator and brother of the former president, Bobby Kennedy, is shot and critically wounded by twenty-three-year-old Palestinian nationalist Sirhan Sirhan in the Ambassador Hotel in Los Angeles after winning the California primary on June 5. When questioned about his motive for killing the presidential candidate, Sirhan admits he was deeply angered by Kennedy's support for Israel in the Six-Day War. Later on, however, he would express suspicion that he was brainwashed by scheming conspirators.

Soviet and Warsaw Pact forces attempt to crush the liberal regime in Czechoslovakia on August 20.

1969   Former vice president Richard Nixon is sworn into office as the thirty-seventh president of the United States on January 20. Marred by corruption and an unpopular war, Nixon's presidency would consistently be ranked as one of the fifteen worst administrations in U.S. history by presidential scholars.

On June 28, in a sudden midnight police raid on the Stonewall Inn, a gay bar in the Greenwich Village section of New York City, angry club goers attempt to violently force the police out of the bar, resulting in a riot. The ensuing chaos helps to unite the gay community, leading to the founding of the Gay Liberation Front (GLF).

Neil A. Armstrong, Edwin E. Aldrin, Jr., and Michael Collins become the first human beings to set foot on another terrestrial body. Man's first step on the moon, made by Neil Armstrong, is on July 20. Armstrong's immortal line, "that's one small step for man, one giant leap for mankind," was considered a redundant error until some experts claimed acoustic analysis revealed that Armstrong actually uttered the grammatical article "a" after the words "small step for."

On May 15, California governor Ronald Reagan dispatches 250 highway patrolmen to the campus of the University of California, Berkeley, where students had created a "People's Park" out of an unused 2.8-acre plot of land. Police officers begin to fence off the park, and angry student demonstrators engage in a hostile protest that results in 128 students being admitted to the local hospital for head trauma. Governor Ronald Reagan then declares a state of emergency, sending in 2,700 National Guard troops to the campus and its surrounding areas.

1970   On May 4, a group of student protestors demonstrating against the U.S. invasion of Cambodia come under fire after throwing rocks at Ohio National Guardsmen on the Kent State University campus. Of the seventy-seven guardsmen present, twenty-nine fire their weapons, resulting in the deaths of four students, two of whom were not at all involved in the demonstrations. President Richard Nixon establishes the Commission on Campus Unrest in response to the disaster.

President Salvador Allende of Chile becomes the first freely elected Marxist head of state in the Western world on November 3. A stock market crash ensues.

King Hussein bin Talal (Jordan) drives Palestinian militants from his country, while President Nasser (Egypt) suffers a fatal heart attack.

After touring a region devastated by a large oil spill, Wisconsin senator and environmental advocate Gaylord Nelson leads the effort to establish Earth Day as a national holiday.

The Environmental Protection Agency (EPA) is established and is given the power to coordinate nature conservation. Congress is inspired to pass legislation creating the agency following alarming incidents such as in 1969 when the heavily polluted Cuyahoga River in Ohio caught fire.

New York City's tallest building at a height of 1,368 feet finishes construction, though the ribbon is not cut until 1973. The World Trade Center would briefly enjoy status as the world's tallest building from 1972 until 1973, when it was surpassed by Chicago's Sears Tower.

On April 24, China launches its first satellite. "Tang Fang Hung" (The East Is Red) is their first cosmic broadcast.

On July 1, President Nixon certifies suffrage to U.S. citizens of eighteen years or older. Many Americans had complained that if a young man could go to Vietnam and die for his country, then he should at least be granted the right to vote.

1971   The foundation of modern electronics and computing is created with the introduction of the microprocessor; patent disputes are filed by Texas Instruments and Intel companies.

Evidence revealing military and intelligence secrets from presidents Dwight Eisenhower, John F. Kennedy, and Lyndon Johnson are released as a series starting July 13 by the *New York Times*. The Pentagon Papers reveal startling contradictions between publicly stated policy and actual policy. The report covers forty-seven volumes and contains 7,000 pages of information; it was released by former State Department official Daniel Ellsberg, whom the Nixon administration would later subject to a smear campaign.

The People's Republic of China is recognized as the legitimate representative of China by the United Nations General Assembly, and the representative from the Republic of China, located in Taiwan, is expelled.

In its ruling for *Swann v. Charlotte-Mecklenburg Board of Education* on April 20, the Supreme Court grants the federal government the right to enforce desegregation.

The United States invades Laos in a failed attempt to cut off North Vietnam's Ho Chi Minh supply line.

Computerized axial tomography (CAT scan), the most influential medical invention since the X-ray, is introduced.

1972   Seeking to gain an ally in the Cold War following a diplomatic split between China and the Soviet Union, U.S. president Richard Nixon travels to communist China accompanied by Secretary of State Henry Kissinger. It is the first time a president has visited China in U.S. history. There, the two statesmen significantly improve relations with their Chinese counterparts. The Soviet Union, fearing a possible Sino-American alliance, eases its hostility against the United States and begins to engage in détente.

Idi Amin, who had anointed himself with the long title, "His Excellency President for Life, Field Marshal Al Hadji Doctor Idi Amin, VC, DSO, MC, Lord of All the Beasts of the Earth and Fishes of the Sea, and Conqueror of the British Empire in Africa in General and Uganda in Particular," seizes the assets of Uganda's 50,000 Asians and gives them ninety days to leave the country. Amin claims that his decision was based on instructions from God. The United States and the United Kingdom would close their embassies in Uganda in response.

Bloody Sunday Riots in Northern Ireland ensue on January 30 when the British Army shoots twenty-six protestors, killing thirteen. The British government subsequently claims that the soldiers reacted to gunshots from members of the Irish Republican Army, but later evidence proves otherwise. The incident leads to the suspension of the Northern Ireland parliament.

During the summer Olympic Games in Munich, West Germany, the Palestinian terrorist group Black September kidnaps nine Israeli athletes and kills two coaches. During failed rescue attempts, all nine athletes would be executed.

Atari, Inc. releases Pong, a table tennis video game featuring two vertical lines (paddles) and a small square (the ball) as its graphics. Despite its primitiveness by twenty-first-century standards, Pong captivated American audiences.

Richard M. Nixon becomes the first U.S. president to visit the Soviet capital of Moscow. There, he and Soviet leader Leonid Brezhnev successfully complete negotiations on the first Strategic Arms Limitation Talks (SALT) treaty, which places limits on the numbers of intercontinental ballistic missiles each side deploys.

On June 17, five men who were later determined to have incriminating ties to the White House are arrested for breaking into the Democratic National Committee headquarters at the Watergate Hotel in Washington, D.C. What followed was a two-year process of investigative journalism by *Washington Post* reporters Bob Woodward and Carl Bernstein that eventually led to the first resignation by a president in U.S. history.

In a 5–4 Supreme Court decision on *Furman v. Georgia* on June 29, the majority opinion concludes that the death penalty is cruel and unusual. The decision requires stringent requirements for the application of the death penalty; thirty-seven states would later update their death penalty laws to meet the Court's ruling.

1973   Egypt and Syria invade Israel over occupied lands; however, in less than a month Israel wins the Yom Kippur War and signs a U.S.-brokered cease-fire.

Organization of Petroleum Exporting Countries (OPEC) doubles oil prices, the first step in soaring oil prices; within a few months oil would rise from $1.50 to $11.56 a barrel. OPEC declares that it would no longer ship petroleum to nations that had supported Israel in its conflict with Syria and Egypt.

With bombs landing around his presidential palace, Salvador Allende Gossens of Chile makes a live radio speech and then commits suicide, reportedly using an AK-47, a gift from Fidel Castro. The number of wounds in his body led independent observers to conclude that he was murdered.

The Supreme Court hears the case of *Roe v. Wade,* declaring first and second trimester abortions constitutional, overturning many state laws.

Congress passes the Endangered Species Act. It is one of the final reactions to the growing environmentalism movement. The act grants protection to endangered species that have been affected by "the consequences of economic growth and development untempered by adequate concern and conservation."

1974   As his involvement in an extensive cover-up of criminal activity is being exposed, U.S. president Richard Nixon resigns on August 9, becoming the first president to voluntarily leave office before the end of his term.

In what would become a great American scandal, Patricia Hearst, the daughter of the wealthy Hearst family, becomes an ally of her captors, the Symbionese Liberation Army, even after her ransom had been paid to the region's poor. She stays to fight with the army, refusing to come home, and a year later she is arrested and convicted to serve seven years in prison.

Atlanta Braves outfielder Henry Aaron becomes the all-time career leader in home runs when he surpasses Babe Ruth's mark of 714 before a record crowd of 53,775 in a game against the Los Angeles Angels on April 8. Aaron, an African American who had played in the Negro League, received numerous death threats as he approached the record.

After failing to respond to a famine that killed over 200,000, Ethiopian leader Haile Selassie is dethroned on September 12. Selassie's reign lasted over forty years, during which he introduced Ethiopia's first written constitution and received *Time's* Man of the Year Award.

Project Smiling Buddha reaches its conclusion on May 18 as India successfully tests its first nuclear weapon in the isolated deserts of Pokhran. India joins an elite nuclear club that includes the United States, the Soviet Union, Great Britain, France, and China.

1975   The Spanish general and fascist leader Francisco Franco, who had come to power during the rise of totalitarianism in Europe in the 1930s and whose reign lasted more thirty-five years, dies on November 20.

The Altair 800 computer first appears as a kit in *Popular Electronics* magazine and is targeted toward computer hobbyists. Its programming language was later purchased by Microsoft, which utilized it to create one of its first products.

Books

Albert, Judith Clavir, and Stewart Edward Albert, eds. *The Sixties Papers: Documents of a Rebellious Decade.* New York: Praeger, 1984.

Albert, Peter J., and Ronald Hoffman, eds. *We Shall Overcome: Martin Luther King, Jr., and the Black Freedom Struggle.* New York: Pantheon Books, 1990.

Allyn, David. *Make Love not War: The Sexual Revolution: An Unfettered History.* Boston: Little, Brown, 2000.

Anderson, David L., ed. *Facing My Lai: Moving beyond the Massacre.* Lawrence: University Press of Kansas, 1998.

Anderson, Terry. *The Sixties.* 2nd ed. New York: Pearson/Longman, 2004.

Andrew, John A., III. *Lyndon Johnson and the Great Society.* Chicago: Ivan R. Dee, 1998.

Andrews, Geoff, et al. *New Left, New Right, and Beyond: Taking the Sixties Seriously.* London: Macmillan, 1999.

Berman, Paul. *A Tale of Two Utopias: The Political Journey of the Generation of 1968.* New York: W. W. Norton, 1996.

Bloom, Alexander, ed. *Long Time Gone: Sixties America Then and Now.* New York: Oxford University Press, 2001.

Bodroghkozy, Aniko. *Groove Tube: Sixties Television and the Youth Rebellion.* Durham, NC: Duke University Press, 2001.

Bradlee, Benjamin C. *Conversations with Kennedy.* New York: W. W. Norton, 1975.

Bradley, Richard. *American Political Mythology from Kennedy to Nixon.* New York: Peter Lang, 2000.

Branch, Taylor. *Pillar of Fire: America in the King Years, 1963–1965.* New York: Simon and Schuster, 1998.

Braunstein, Peter, and Michael William Doyle, eds. *Imagine Nation: The American Counterculture of the 1960s and '70s.* New York: Routledge, 2002.

Brick, Howard. *Age of Contradiction: American Thought and Culture in the 1960s.* New York: Twayne, 1998.

Brinkley, Douglas, and Richard T. Griffiths, eds. *John F. Kennedy and Europe.* Baton Rouge: Louisiana State University Press, 1999.

Brown, Thomas. *JFK, History of an Image.* Bloomington: Indiana University Press, 1988.

Bundy, William. *A Tangled Web: The Making of Foreign Policy in the Nixon Presidency.* New York: Hill and Wang, 1998.

Burner, David. *Making Peace with the Sixties.* Princeton, NJ: Princeton University Press, 1996.

Burns, Stewart. *To the Mountaintop: Martin Luther King Jr.'s Sacred Mission to Save America, 1955–1968.* San Francisco: HarperCollins, 2004.

Busch, Peter. *All the Way with JFK? Britain, the U.S., and the Vietnam War.* New York: Oxford University Press, 2003.

Button, James W. *Black Violence: Political Impact of the 1960s Riots.* Princeton, NJ: Princeton University Press, 1978.

Buzzanco, Robert. *Masters of War: Military Dissent and Politics in the Vietnam Era.* New York: Cambridge University Press, 1996.

Cavallo, Dominick. *A Fiction of the Past: The Sixties in American History.* New York: St. Martin's Press, 1999.

Clymer, Kenton J., ed. *The Vietnam War: Its History, Literature and Music.* El Paso: Texas Western Press, 1998.

Dallek, Robert. *Flawed Giant: Lyndon Johnson and His Times, 1961–1973.* New York: Oxford University Press, 1998.

Davis, James Kirkpatrick. *Assault on the Left: The FBI and the Sixties Antiwar Movement.* Westport, CT: Praeger, 1997.

DeKoven, Marianne. *Utopia Limited: The Sixties and the Emergence of the Postmodern.* Durham, NC: Duke University Press, 2004.

Donaldson, Gary. *Liberalism's Last Hurrah: The Presidential Campaign of 1964.* Armonk, NY: M. E. Sharpe, 2003.

Echols, Alice. *Shaky Ground: The '60s and Its Aftershocks.* New York: Columbia University Press, 2002.

Elbaum, Max. *Revolution in the Air: Sixties Radicals Turn to Lenin, Mao, and Che.* London: Verso, 2002.

Ellsberg, Daniel. *Secrets: A Memoir of Vietnam and the Pentagon Papers.* New York: Viking, 2001.

Evans, Sara. *Personal Politics: The Roots of Women's Liberation in the Movement and the New Left.* New York: Random House, 1979.

Farber, David, and Jeff Roche, eds. *The Conservative Sixties.* New York: Peter Lang, 2003.

Farrell, James J. *The Spirit of the Sixties: Making Postwar Radicalism.* New York: Routledge, 1997.

Franklin, H. Bruce. *Vietnam and Other American Fantasies.* Amherst: University of Massachusetts Press, 2000.

Friedan, Betty. *The Feminine Mystique.* New York: W. W. Norton, 1963.

Gardner, Lloyd C., and Ted Gittinger, eds. *Vietnam: The Early Decisions.* Austin: University of Texas Press, 1997.

Graham, Herman, III. *The Brothers' Vietnam War: Black Power, Manhood, and the Military Experience.* Gainesville: University Press of Florida, 2003.

Green, Jonathon. *All Dressed Up: The Sixties and the Counterculture.* London: Pimlico, 1998.

Gross, Michael. *My Generation: Fifty Years of Sex, Drugs, Rock, Revolution, Glamour, Greed, Valor, Faith, and Silicon Chips.* New York: Cliff Street Books, 2000.

Hall, James C. *Mercy, Mercy Me: African American Culture and the American Sixties.* New York: Oxford University Press, 2001.

Hammond, William M. *Public Affairs: The Military and the Media, 1968–1973.* Washington, DC: Center of Military History, 1996.

Heale, M. J. *The Sixties in America: History, Politics and Protest.* Chicago: Fitzroy Dearborn, 2001.

Hendrickson, Paul. *The Living and the Dead: Robert McNamara and Five Lives of a Lost War.* New York: Alfred A. Knopf, 1996.

Hixson, Walter L, ed. *The Vietnam Antiwar Movement.* New York: Garland, 2000.

Hunt, Andrew E. *The Turning: A History of Vietnam Veterans against the War.* New York: New York University Press, 1999.

Hunt, Michael H. *Lyndon Johnson's War: America's Cold War Crusade in Vietnam, 1945–1968.* New York: Hill and Wang, 1996.

Isaacs, Arnold R. *Vietnam Shadows: The War, Its Ghosts, and Its Legacy.* Baltimore, MD: Johns Hopkins University Press, 1997.

Isserman, Maurice, and Michael Kazin. *America Divided: The Civil War of the 1960s.* New York: Oxford University Press, 2000.

Jacobs, Ron. *The Way the Wind Blew: A History of the Weather Underground.* New York: Verso, 1997.

Jeffreys-Jones, Rhodri. *Peace Now! American Society and the Ending of the Vietnam War.* New Haven, CT: Yale University Press, 1999.

Jones, Howard. *Death of a Generation: How the Assassinations of Diem and JFK Prolonged the Vietnam War.* New York: Oxford University Press, 2003.

Kaiser, David. *American Tragedy: Kennedy, Johnson, and the Origins of the Vietnam War.* Cambridge, MA: Harvard University Press, 2000.

Kimball, Jeffrey. *Nixon's Vietnam War.* Lawrence: University Press of Kansas, 1998.

Kimball, Roger. *The Long March: How the Cultural Revolution of the 1960s Changed America.* San Francisco: Encounter Books, 2000.

Klatch, Rebecca E. *A Generation Divided: The New Left, the New Right, and the 1960s.* Berkeley: University of California Press, 1999.

Knight, Peter. *Conspiracy Culture: From the Kennedy Assassination to the X-Files.* New York: Routledge, 2000.

Laffan, Barry. *Communal Organization and Social Transition: A Case Study from the Counterculture of the Sixties and Seventies.* New York: Peter Lang, 1997.

Lembcke, Jerry. *The Spitting Image: Myth, Memory, and the Legacy of Vietnam.* New York: New York University Press, 1998.

Lind, Michael. *Vietnam, the Necessary War: A Reinterpretation of America's Most Disastrous Conflict.* New York: Free Press, 1999.

Logevall, Fredrik. *Choosing War: The Lost Chance for Peace and the Escalation of War in Vietnam.* Berkeley: University of California Press, 1999.

Lomperis, Timothy J. *From People's War to People's Rule: Insurgency, Intervention, and the Lessons of Vietnam.* Chapel Hill: University of North Carolina Press, 1996.

Lubin, David M. *Shooting Kennedy: JFK and the Culture of Images.* Berkeley: University of California Press, 2003.

Macedo, Stephen, ed. *Reassessing the Sixties: Debating the Political and Cultural Legacy.* New York: W.W. Norton, 1997.

Maga, Timothy. *The 1960s.* New York: Facts on File, 2003.

Mahoney, Richard D. *Sons and Brothers: The Days of Jack and Bobby Kennedy.* New York: Arcade, 1999.

Maraniss, David. *They Marched into Sunlight: War and Peace, Vietnam and America, October 1967.* New York: Simon and Schuster, 2003.

Margolis, Jon. *The Last Innocent Year: America in 1964, the Beginning of the 'Sixties.'* New York: William Morrow, 1999.

Martin, Susan. *Decade of Protest: Political Posters from the United States, Viet Nam, Cuba, 1965–1975.* Santa Monica, CA: Smart Art Press, 1996.

Marwick, Arthur. *The Sixties: Cultural Revolution in Britain, France, Italy, and the United States, c.1958–c.1974.* New York: Oxford University Press, 1998.

McGregor, Peter. *Cultural Battles: The Meaning of the Viet Nam-USA War.* Sydney, Australia: SCAM Publications, 1998.

McMahon, Robert J. *Major Problems in the History of the Vietnam War: Documents and Essays.* 3rd ed. Boston: Houghton Mifflin, 2003.

McMillian, John, and Paul Buhle. *The New Left Revisited.* Philadelphia, PA: Temple University Press, 2003.

McWilliams, John C. *The 1960s Cultural Revolution.* Westport, CT: Greenwood Press, 2000.

Miles, Barry. *In the Sixties.* London: Jonathan Cape, 2002.

Moise, Edwin E. *Tonkin Gulf and the Escalation of the Vietnam War.* Chapel Hill: University of North Carolina Press, 1996.

Moser, Richard R. *The New Winter Soldiers: GI and Veteran Dissent during the Vietnam Era.* New Brunswick, NJ: Rutgers University Press,1996.

Neale, Jonathan. *A People's History of the Vietnam War.* New York: New Press, 2003.

Olson, James S., ed. *Historical Dictionary of the 1960s.* Westport, CT: Greenwood Press, 1999.

Olson, Keith W. *Watergate: The Presidential Scandal that Shook America.* Lawrence: University Press of Kansas, 2003.

Palermo, Joseph A. *In His Own Right: The Political Odyssey of Senator Robert F. Kennedy.* New York: Columbia University Press, 2001.

Rabby, Glenda Alice. *The Pain and the Promise: The Struggle for Civil Rights in Tallahassee, Florida.* Athens: University of Georgia Press, 1999.

Rabe, Stephen G. *The Most Dangerous Area in the World: John F. Kennedy Confronts Communist Revolution in Latin America.* Chapel Hill: University of North Carolina Press, 1999.

Raskin, Jonah. *For the Hell of It: The Life and Times of Abbie Hoffman.* Berkeley: University of California Press, 1996.

Rhodes, Joel P. *The Voice of Violence: Performative Violence as Protest in the Vietnam Era.* Westport, CT: Praeger, 2001.

Riggenbach, Jeff. *In Praise of Decadence.* Amherst, NY: Prometheus Books, 1998.

Robbins, Mary Susannah, ed. *Against the Vietnam War: Writings by Activists.* Syracuse, NY: Syracuse University Press, 1999.

Rorabaugh, W. J. *Kennedy and the Promise of the Sixties.* New York: Cambridge University Press, 2002.

Rubin, Jerry. *Do It! Scenarios of the Revolution.* New York: Simon and Schuster, 1970.

Spann, Edward K. *Democracy's Children: The Young Rebels of the 1960s and the Power of Ideals.* Wilmington, DE: Scholarly Resources, 2003.

Steel, Ronald. *In Love with Night: The American Romance with Robert Kennedy.* New York: Simon and Schuster, 2000.

Stephens, Julie. *Anti-Disciplinary Protest: Sixties Radicalism and Postmodernism.* Cambridge, UK: Cambridge University Press, 1998.

Torgoff, Martin. *Can't Find My Way Home: America in the Great Stoned Age, 1945–2000.* New York: Simon and Schuster, 2004.

Turner, Fred. *Echoes of Combat: The Vietnam War in American Memory.* New York: Anchor/ Doubleday, 1996.

Turner, Karen Gottschang, and Phan Thanh Hao. *Even the Women Must Fight: Memories of War from North Vietnam.* New York: John Wiley, 1998.

Vandiver, Frank E. *Shadows of Vietnam: Lyndon Johnson's Wars.* College Station: Texas A&M University Press, 1997.

Varon, Jeremy. *Bringing the War Home: The Weather Underground, the Red Army Faction, and Revolutionary Violence in the Sixties and Seventies.* Berkeley: University of California Press, 2004.

The Vietnam War Files: Uncovering the Secret History of Nixon-Era Strategy. Lawrence: University Press of Kansas, 2004.

Viorst, Milton. *Fire in the Streets: America in the 1960s.* New York: Simon and Schuster, 1979.

Warlaumont, Hazel G. *Advertising in the 60s: Turncoats, Traditionalists, and Waste Makers in America's Turbulent Decade.* Westport, CT: Praeger, 2001.

Wilson, Sondra Kathryn, ed. *In Search of Democracy: The NAACP Writings of James Weldon Johnson, Walter White, and Roy Wilkins (1920–1977).* New York: Oxford University Press, 1999.

Witcover, Jules. *The Year the Dream Died: Revisiting 1968 in America.* New York: Warner Books, 1997.

Woodward, C. Vann. 1966. *The Strange Career of Jim Crow.* 3rd ed. New York: Oxford University Press.

Young, Marilyn B., and Robert Buzzanco, eds. *A Companion to the Vietnam War.* Malden, MA: Blackwell, 2002.

Journals

American Historical Review

Critical Inquiry

Critical Studies in Mass Communication

Dialectical Anthropology

Ethnic and Racial Consciousness

Historian

Journal of Language and Social Psychology

New Formations

New South

Quarterly Journal of Speech

Questions of Cultural Identity

Southern Communication Journal

Southern Exposure

The Black Scholar

The Nation

Online Resources

http://kclibrary.nhmccd.edu/decade60.html—Kingwood College Library—American Cultural History 1960–1969

www.africanaonline.com/civil_rights.htm—African Online—Civil Rights Movement

www.1960sflashback.com—The 1960s Flashback

www.historyplace.com/unitedstates/vietnam/—History Place—Vietnam War

www.jfklibrary.org—The John F. Kennedy Presidential Library

www.jfklink.com—John F. Kennedy Link

www.legacy98.org—The Women's Rights Movement 1848–1998

www.nixonfoundation.org—The Richard M. Nixon Presidential Library

www.nps.gov/malu—National Historic Site

www.thekingcenter.org—Dr. Martin Luther King, Jr., Official Center

www.vietnampix.com—Vietnam War Timeline

www.lbjlib.utexas.edu—Lyndon B. Johnson Presidential Library